D1566533

—THE—
AZTEC
EAGLES

~THE~
AZTEC
EAGLES

THE FORGOTTEN ALLIES
OF THE SECOND WORLD WAR

WALTER S. ZAPOTOCZNY JR.

FONTHILL

for my Mexican friends

Fonthill Media Language Policy

Fonthill Media publishes in the international English language market. One language edition is published worldwide. As there are minor differences in spelling and presentation, especially with regard to American English and British English, a policy is necessary to define which form of English to use. The Fonthill Policy is to use the form of English native to the author. Walter S. Zapotoczny Jr. was born and educated in the United States; therefore American English has been adopted in this publication.

Fonthill Media Limited
Fonthill Media LLC
www.fonthillmedia.com
office@fonthillmedia.com

First published in the United Kingdom and the United States of America 2019

British Library Cataloguing in Publication Data:
A catalogue record for this book is available from the British Library

Copyright © Walter S. Zapotoczny Jr. 2020

ISBN 978-1-78155-747-1

The right of Walter S. Zapotoczny Jr. to be identified as the author of this work has been asserted by him in accordance with the Copyright, Designs and Patents Act 1988.

All rights reserved. No part of this publication may be reproduced, stored in a retrieval system or transmitted in any form or by any means, electronic, mechanical, photocopying, recording or otherwise, without prior permission in writing from Fonthill Media Limited

Typeset in 10pt on 13pt MinionPro
Printed and bound in England

Preface

Most people are familiar with the major combatant nations of World War II, both Axis and Allied, but many are unfamiliar with the contributions of so-called "Minor Allies." These nations contributed human and material resources to one side or the other, despite, in some cases, intercontinental distances separating them from the main theaters of war. Sadly, Mexico's aid to the United States and the Allies has been largely ignored by historians and is mostly absent from history books. The few works that acknowledge Mexico's contribution of raw materials, fuel, and labor to strengthen the "arsenal of democracies" reflect the perceived overall contribution of the country to the Allied cause in World War II, but, unfortunately, add to the lack of information about Mexico's only unit participating in combat overseas. When the Mexican aviators had the opportunity to show their courage in battle, they did so with valor.

Mexico was not prepared to participate in a modern war when German submarines sank two of its ships in 1942, but her president seized the opportunity to declare war on the Axis powers. It took more than two years for Mexican personnel to enter a combat zone, but the brave pilots and support personnel of the 201st Fighter Squadron of the Mexican Expeditionary Air Force (M.E.A.F.) would make important contributions to the Allied campaign to liberate the Philippine Islands. They overcame persistent problems with a stubbornly monolingual and innately racist U.S. military to become proficient with modern fighter aircraft and operated them at forward airfields under challenging conditions. Their experience is a little-known friendly chapter in the troubled history of Mexico's relationship with its northern neighbor, and its only participation in a war outside its own borders.

The pilots of the 201st Fighter Squadron flew missions supporting ground troops in the Philippines and long-range sorties over Formosa. Allied theater commander General Douglas MacArthur commended the pilots and support personnel. The 201st Squadron earned combat awards from the Philippine, American, and Mexican governments. After the war, the pilots of the 201st Squadron were welcomed home as heroes. This is their story.

CONTENTS

List of Abbreviations

A.A.F.S.A.T.:	Army Air Forces School of Applied Tactics
B.M.W.:	Bavarian Motor Works
B.R.A.A.F.:	Boca Raton Army Air Field
C.O.N.U.S.:	Continental United States
C.I.S.:	Central Instructors School
F.A.M.:	*Fuerza Aérea Mexicana* (Mexican Air Force)
F.E.A.F.:	Far East Air Force
F.A.E.M.:	*Fuerza Aérea Expedicionaria Mexicana* (Mexican Expeditionary Air Force)
G.P.A.:	*Grupo de Perfecaonamiento Aemautico* (Aviation Training Group)
G.E.:	General Electric
H.E.:	High Explosive
H.V.A.R.:	High Velocity Aerial Rockets
J.M.U.S.D.C.:	Joint Mexican–United States Defense Commission
K.I.F.A.:	Killed in Flight Accident
L.S.T.:	Landing Ship Tank
M.E.A.F.:	Mexican Expeditionary Air Force
P.A.:	Pilot Aviator
P.A.C.A.F.:	United States Air Force Pacific Air Forces
P.A.N.:	*Partido Acción Nacional* (National Action Party)
P.B.Y.:	Patrol Bomber and Y = the code assigned to Consolidated Aircraft
P.E.M.E.X.:	Mexican Petroleum
P.N.R.:	*Partido Nacional Revolucionario* (National Revolutionary Party)

R.A.F.:	British Royal Air Force
S.A.P.:	Support Air Party
S.B.D.:	Scout Bomber Douglas
S.W.P.A.:	South West Pacific Area
T.D.Y.:	Temporary Duty
T.N.C.A.:	*Talleres Nacionales de Construcciones Aeronáuticas*
	(National Aviation Workshops)
U.S.A.A.C.:	U.S. Army Air Corps
U.S.A.A.F.:	U.S. Army Air Force
V.F.C.:	Fighter Squadron Composite
W.A.C.S.:	Women Army Corps Service
W.A.S.P.:	Women's Air Service Pilots

Introduction

Squadron 201!
Your planes have taken flight
Joining the clouds
To play their symphony;
With your noble hearts…

Raymundo de la Cruz López, March 1944

Sending men to fight with the United States was an unpopular move among many Mexican politicians and citizens in the early 1940s. The memory of the 1848 Treaty of Guadalupe that ceded 500,000 square miles of Mexican territory to the U.S. was still fresh in many minds. The "Zimmermann Telegram," a 1917 diplomatic proposal from the German Empire during World War I, further acerbated the strained relations between Mexico and the United States. In the telegram, Germany offered Mexico U.S. territory if it would join the German cause against the United States. Mexico declined the German proposal but it angered Americans and led in part to U.S. entry into World War I. As the world moved toward war again in the late 1930s, Mexico reluctantly turned to the United States for help. Mexican President Lázaro Cárdenas had declared his country neutral, but before the 1940 Mexican presidential election campaign, violence between pro-fascist and pro-communist organizations began.

The Republic of Mexico is not a nation that would seem to have had any interest in the war's European origins, nor would the rise of Japanese domination in the Pacific Ocean have been particularly harmful to Mexico. However, the close economic relationship between the United States and Mexico meant that the two were essentially indistinguishable to the enemies of the United States.

Worried by the potential of an unstable government in Mexico, the United States began to provide both open and secret aid to the Mexican government. Some economic cooperation between the U.S. and Mexico resulted when the U.S. purchased silver from Mexico and granted U.S. government-backed loans. In 1941, Ávila Camacho became President of Mexico, resulting in a new market in the United States for Mexican oil.

President Roosevelt had been a constant friend to Mexico. Once elected to a second term, he used both the U.S. Federal Bureau of Investigation and military intelligence to help the Mexican Army in their fight against pro-revolution rebels. Roosevelt gave legitimacy to the Camacho presidency by quickly recognizing him. For years, U.S. and Mexican relations had been plagued with problems. The new relationship with the U.S. put many of the old issues to rest. Once the question of how to handle Mexican citizens who wanted to join the U.S. military was resolved, Mexico became the recipient of "Lend-Lease" assistance. Eventually, Mexican raw materials fueled 40 percent of the U.S. World War II industries.

As attacks on Mexican ships by German submarine began to increase and the United States, England, and France began a massive propaganda campaign against the Axis powers, the tide of public opinion began to change in Mexico. A blunder by Germany provided the momentum to swing public opinion in favor of fighting with the Allies. The German submarine *U-564* torpedoed and sank the Mexican oil tanker S.S. *Potrero del Llano* on May 14, 1942, and *U-106* sank S.S. *Faja de Oro* on May 21, 1942. When Germany refused to compensate Mexico for the losses, Mexico declared war on Germany, Japan, and Italy on May 22, 1942. Leaders of the Mexican military began to clamor for Mexico to enter the war.

Franklin D. Roosevelt tried to persuade Mexico to participate actively in the war when he met Ávila Camacho at Monterrey in April 20, 194. After first being noncommittal, the Mexican president soon decided that Mexico should fight together with the Allies. On November 13, Camacho stated that Mexico was willing to take on an offensive roll as long as its forces served under Mexican leadership in a distinct zone. President Camacho, who was a former army general, also knew the army was unprepared but believed that an air force unit could be made ready with help from the United States.

The *Fuerza Aérea Mexicana* in the 1930s was a small, underfunded part of the army. Its missions were mostly mapmaking, reconnaissance, air support, and airmail. The Mexican Air Force had tactically organized units but no modern pursuit planes. Since Mexico had no indigenous aircraft industry, the United States would have to provide the planes capable of stopping an offshore attack by the Axis. Mexico's citizens began to unify behind the war effort and the government began to receive shipments of U.S. aircraft, including Navy SBD Dauntless dive-bombers, B-25 Mitchell Bombers, and Consolidated PBY Catalina flying boats. Sending troops overseas, however, ran against Mexican tradition, politics, and the more pressing priority of coastal defense. The government began to activate additional Mexican units for service. Coastal patrol and tanker escort missions were increased. Major Luis Noriega Medrano was flying a routine patrol on July 5, 1942, when he spotted a German submarine. Medrano bombed and damaged the German U-boat in the Gulf of Mexico. The war was getting closer to home and President Camacho had to rally support for direct involvement.

In order to help sell the idea of fighting abroad to the public, Camacho directed the air force to stage an air show. More than 100,000 spectators watched on March 5, 1944 as North American AT-6 Texans and Douglas A-24B dive-bombers attacked targets with live ordinance near Mexico City. The show was a spectacular success. Soon after, President Camacho declared that Mexico should fight alongside of the Allies and that the Mexican Air Force would represent the nation in the conflict.

A total 300 enlisted men and officers from all branches of the military joined the new *Fuerza Aérea Expedicionaria Mexicana* or F.A.E.M. They included thirty-eight of Mexico's best pilots. The special group formed in Mexico City. The group comprised specialists chosen in a competitive recruiting process. Colonel Antonio Cárdenas Rodríguez, who had flown goodwill flights throughout Latin America, took command of the group. Having flown combat missions with the U.S. Air Corps' 97th Bomb Group in North Africa, Rodríguez knew senior American officers, including U.S. General Jimmy Doolittle.

Volunteers came from as far north as the Texas border and as far south as the Guatemalan border. They came from large and small towns throughout Mexico. The volunteers were eager to serve with the elite force. On July 20, 1944, President Camacho told the group during a ceremony they would leave for the United States for combat training. He told the group that, if necessary, they would go the Italy to fight alongside their brothers from the Republic of Brazil. After concluding his speech, the president told the volunteers to step forward and ask for whatever they want. The president was probably surprised when Sergeant Angel Bocanegra del Castillo, a former teacher and now squadron crewmember, stepped forward and asked that the president build a school his village. Today, the DeZavala Elementary school still stands in the town of Tepoztlán, Morelos, south of Mexico City.

Families bid farewell to their young pilots and the ground personnel amid tears after the review and ceremonies were over. They waved and sang traditional songs as their loved ones got on the train that would transport them to Nuevo Laredo, on the Texas border. On July 26, 1944, the men arrived, and the entire town cheered and wished success to the first unit in Mexican history to leave the country on a combat mission. Mexican congressional representatives and U.S. military and civilian authorities greeted them as newsreel cameras captured the men crossing the U.S.–Mexican border into Laredo, Texas. They boarded a train to San Antonio, Texas, and began training at Randolph Army Air Field. After being separated by specialty, ground personnel traveled to different bases for additional instruction. The pilots went to Victoria, Texas, for Curtis P-40 Warhawk transition training.

Pilots and ground personnel reunited in October at Pocatello, Idaho, and began training as a unit. At Pocatello, the pilots transitioned to the Republic P-47D Thunderbolt, the largest, heaviest, and most expensive fighter aircraft in history powered by a single reciprocating engine. (See Appendix II for the aircraft information.) The mechanics developed a fondness for the big airplanes. American Captain Paul Miller commanded a special unit designated to train the Mexicans. Fluent in Spanish, Miller had grown up in Peru. Just twenty-four years old, he once served at the U.S. Embassy in Mexico as assistant air *attaché*. Miller believed that tight discipline was necessary to the Mexican pilots' success and safety.

On November 27, 1944, the unit transferred to Greenville, Texas, northeast of Dallas, in order to take advantage of better flying weather. Considered state-of-the-art aircraft, their P-47D Thunderbolts had twin turbochargers that could climb to over 40,000 feet. The aircraft could approach the sound barrier in a dive. It was not only thrilling stuff for new fighter pilots, it was dangerous too. Second Lieutenant Crisóforo Salido Grijalva was attempting a take-off from a muddy taxiway on January 23, 1945 after a rainstorm. He had apparently mistaken it for an active runway. Ignoring warnings from the tower, Salido crashed before getting in the air. His plane ended up overturned, and Grijalva drowned in the mud that blocked in his cockpit before the crash crew could get to him. The men of the 201st Squadron took his death very hard. The men's morale was further lowered when a restaurant in Greenville refused them service. A more serious concern was the refusal of anyone to provide off-base housing. Quick intercession between base officials and local leaders averted an international incident. As authorities found accommodations for the men, they circulated the word that the Mexicans should be treated with courtesy, as they were there as Allies.

Youthful pilots sometimes break the rules, and the Mexican pilots were no different. In one infamous episode, Lieutenant Reynaldo Pérez Gallardo, intent on celebrating his recent marriage, flew his Thunderbolt fast and low over Greenville one evening. The big airplane roared over 300 mph down Main Street—its wingtips barely missed the buildings. Captain Miller and his wife were inside a movie theater, enjoying the show. As Pérez roared over the building, the vibrations shook the people seated in the theater. Miller was furious and immediately grounded Pérez. Captain Miller later restored Pérez to flight status with his unit.

As 1944 ended, Mexico prepared for the deployment of the 201st Squadron as the Mexican Senate gave President Camacho authority to send troops abroad. Ávila Camacho suggested to President Franklin D. Roosevelt that the squadron take part in operations in the Philippines. On February 22, 1945, the 201st Squadron received its battle flag in a formal ceremony. General Francisco L. Uruquizo, Mexican Sub-Secretary of War, presented the Mexican flag to Colonel Cárdenas with a twenty-one-gun salute. Radio stations in Mexico and Latin America broadcast the proceedings live and area newspapers covered it extensively. Theaters across the United States showed the newsreel footage of the event. The squadron eventually came to be nicknamed the Aztec Eagles by the Mexican press after the elite Aztec warriors of Mexico's history. The eagle warriors, or eagle knights as they were sometimes known, were a group of elite infantrymen in the army of the Aztec Empire. Those who belonged in this warrior society were either members of the nobility or commoners who had distinguished themselves on the battlefield.

Brownsville, Texas, and air-to-air gunnery practice was the next stop for the final training event for the pilots. However, tragedy hit the squadron again when Lieutenant Javier Martínez Valle was on the gunnery range on the afternoon of March 10. Martínez was attacking a target trailing from a tow plane when his aircraft went out of control. He died when his airplane crashed. The investigation concluded that his P-47 had struck the target cable or counter weight.

The 201st Squadron boarded the liberty ship S.S. *Fair Isle* in San Francisco Bay on March 27, 1945, joining 1,500 U.S. soldiers headed for the Philippines. The blaring sirens of battle station drills made the men edgy as seasickness and fear of attack by submarines took a toll on them as the voyage wore on. Nonetheless, there were some lighter moments. After arriving at the base at New Guinea, the commander invited the pilots to watch the new color movie *Fighting Lady*. After enjoying too many iced beers, some of the intoxicated flyers fell during the climb up S.S. *Fair Isle*'s cargo net and needed help to get aboard.

After getting underway once again, S.S. *Fair Isle* joined a convoy for the rest of the trip to the Philippines. The spirits of the squadron were high. They sat on their life jackets, playing cards, while some strummed guitars and sang traditional Mexican songs. As the squadron headed toward the South Pacific, General Douglas MacArthur sent a cable to President Ávila Camacho expressing personal gratification that the 201st Squadron was about to join his command. MacArthur told the president he had a long and intimate friendship with his great people.

The S.S. *Fair Isle* entered Manila Bay with the rest of the convoy on May 1, 1945. After a brief ceremony, the men boarded a train that transported them to their airfield at Porac, near Clark Field, about 40 miles northwest of Manila. The Mexican's new airfield was a dirt runway carved out of the jungle. The Mexicans heard small-arms fire at night, and during the day, they could hear the sound of artillery as it pounded the retreating Japanese. A newly liberated prisoner of war camp was near the airfield and the pilots got their first look at undernourished former prisoners. Filipino guerrillas were performing a mopping up operations around the base and Japanese soldiers would occasionally emerge from the jungle to surrender. In the center of the field sat a control tower. The Fifth Air Force's 58th Fighter Group occupied the other end. They consisted of three squadrons and were seasoned veterans of the New Guinea campaign. (See Appendix IV for information about the 5th Air Force and 58th Fighter Group.)

The 201st Squadron answered to the 58th Fighter Group. The 201st formed the fourth squadron of the group and operated in its own area under Mexican command and administration. The 201st pilots flew combat orientation missions on May 17, 1945 with various other squadrons. Within a short time, the Aztec Eagles began flying missions as a unit. About the same time, the U.S. 25th Infantry Division was meeting fierce resistance from the Japanese in the Marikina watershed east of Manila. The 201st's mission was to support them. Their initial targets were Japanese buildings, military vehicles, artillery, and enemy troop concentrations. Four flights of eight pilots each made up the squadron. Senior pilot Captain Radamés Gaziola Andrad was in charge of flight operations. The pilots received briefings every evening on the mission of the next day. Missions were short at first. As the Japanese retreated farther and farther back, the missions became longer. Mechanics and armorers would arm and fuel the aircraft in preparation for the next mission as the pilots studied the next mission details while relaxing in the afternoon sun.

It did not take long for the pilots and ground crew to get into a routine, and it was not long before they began flying missions commanded by their own officers, though their missions were not without costs. On June 1, Second Lieutenant Fausto Vega Santander, the squadron's youngest pilot, died when his P-47 aircraft suddenly rolled and crashed into the sea. Lieutenant José Espinosa Fuentes crashed and died when the P-47 experienced engine failure during a test flight a few days later.

Throughout June 1945, the Japanese Fourteenth Army was holding out in the central highlands. The U.S. Sixth Army troops advanced through rugged mountain passes in pursuit of the enemy. The fighting was a brutal mixture of jungle and mountain warfare. The close air support proved by the 201st was crucial as the U.S. troops pursued the Japanese deeper into the mountains. The Aztec Eagle's missions changed from hitting buildings, military vehicles, artillery, and enemy troop concentrations to attacking hard-to-see Japanese soldiers and fortifications near friendly troops. The targets in the central highlands were usually covered with jungle and nearly invisible. Close air support missions were very risky because of the steep mountains, bad weather, and enemy anti-aircraft fire. Enemy targets would be marked with colored smoke or a rocket by a controller or spotter aircraft. The squadron leader would typically make a pass over the target to confirm. The rest of the squadron would follow, dropping their 1,000-lb. bombs, ripping holes in the jungle canopy. The bombs often threw debris 1,500 feet into the air with black smoke billowing from the jungle floor below. The pilots would dive into the enemy machine-gun and anti-aircraft fire, dropping their ordinance then pulling up so hard they would nearly black out from the *g*-forces.

The Aztec Eagles were quick to act when a Japanese target became visible. Lieutenant Amador Sámano Piña remembered an operation on June 17, 1945 to Payawan, an island province of the Philippines. He described how Flight Leader Lieutenant Héctor Espinosa Galván noticed an enemy convoy and ordered their seven planes to attack it. Piña recalled how they flew directly toward the enemy, attacking with machine guns. Lieutenant Piña lined up his sights on the truck right in front of him, and as he got closer fired two bursts of his machine gun. Piña had to pull up quickly to avoid the flames enveloping the truck and the resultant explosion. The Japanese responded forcefully with small-arms fire, lightly damaging two of the P-47s. This method of engagement was typical of how the Mexican pilots attacked the enemy—diving straight into the enemy fire with no regard for their own safety.

While close air support was hazardous enough, the U.S. Navy was preparing a riskier assignment. The Aztec Eagles were to fly fighter missions across the South China Sea at the limit of the range of the P-47s. The U.S. Navy required control of the sea-lanes south of Japanese island of Kyushu, as it prepared for the invasion of Japan. The area was a heavily occupied Japanese strong point and dominated by the island of Formosa (present-day Taiwan).

Though the Fifth Air Force's bombing campaign had reduced enemy activity, it was still a threat. Straining under a maximum load of bombs and fuel, eight Mexican P-47 Thunderbolts took off from Porac Field early on July 6, 1945, barely clearing the runway. Flying in a cramped cockpit over 600 miles in the vast area of the Pacific, with only basic instruments, was uncomfortable to say the least. As the Mexicans traveled towards their target, with the blistering tropical sun burning through the cockpit glass, the pilots soon became dehydrated. They were well aware that a small problem could force them to ditch in seas patrolled by the Japanese.

The Mexicans encountered no enemy aircraft over Formosa, and the mission concluded successfully. Crew chiefs had to help the pilots from their cockpits. Their legs were numb after wearing their survival gear for over seven hours. The 201st's missions were not without causalities. On July 16, Lieutenant Héctor Espinosa Galván died when he ditched his aircraft just short of Biak, a small island located near the northern coast of Papua, New Guinea, after running out of fuel. Flying into a thunderstorm three days later, Captain Pablo Rivas Martínez and Lieutenant Guillermo García Ramos separated. An Australian Consolidated PBY crew rescued García after he baled out over a Japanese-held island but was unable to find Lieutenant Rivas. On July 21, 1945, Lieutenant Mario López and two American pilots, Second Lieutenant Lee A. Houk and Lieutenant A. Z. Harris, took off from Biak. Encountering bad weather, they descended on instruments, crashing into a mountain range. Both López and Houk died. Lieutenant Harris, who was separated from the formation, survived.

The Aztec Eagles returned to Formosa yet again on August 8, 1945 for their last bombing mission. The Mexican Expeditionary Force 201st Fighter Squadron flew its final mission on August 10, as they escorted a convoy of U.S. Navy ships bound for Okinawa. The Japanese had resorted to the use of *kamikaze* (suicide) attacks and U.S. Navy Intelligence had concerns that Japanese *kamikaze* aircraft would attack the convoy. The 201st Squadron supplied air cover for the convoy until relieved by the U.S. Air Force Northrop P-61 "Black Widows."

The men of the 201st were watching a movie on the night of August 26 when the film stopped. Captain Gaxiola announced that he had received a message from headquarters that Japan had surrendered after the U.S. dropped atomic bombs on two Japanese cities.

The combat experience for the Aztec Eagles was over. The 201st's aircraft had flown ninety-six combat missions, 791 sorties, flown 2,842 total hours, dropped 1,995 bombs, and fired 166,922 rounds of .50-caliber ammunition. The squadron flew fifty-three ground support missions in support of the U.S. 25th Infantry Division and Philippine soldiers.

The squadron lost two pilots in combat action, one missing, and four due to accidents. The Aztec Eagles killed over 30,000 Japanese troops and destroyed countless enemy buildings, armor, vehicles, machine-gun emplacements, anti-aircraft guns, and ammunition.

Upon returning home from the war in the Philippines, the men of the 201st Squadron paraded proudly into Mexico City's national square where they presented their battle flag to the Mexican president. Radio stations broadcast President Camacho speech to the crowd and to the nation:

> General, chiefs, officers and troops of the Expeditionary Air Force, I receive with emotion the Flag that the country has conferred ... as a symbol of her and those ideas of humanity for which we fight in a common cause. You return with glory, having complied brilliantly with your duty and, in these moments, in this historic Plaza, you receive the gratitude of our people.

Many of the young aviators and ground support crews who flew and fought with the Allies became successful in academia, business, and in aviation. The 201st Squadron's Republic P-47 Thunderbolts are long gone, but the battle flag the Aztec Eagles carried rests in the National History Museum in Mexico City. Five of those pilots became *Fuerza Aérea Mexicana* generals.

The Aztec Eagles helped the Allies defeat Japan; they helped end the isolationism of Mexico; they paved the way for important agreements between the United States and Mexico; and they helped modernize the Mexican Air Force and demonstrated that Mexico could mount a successful expeditionary force. Significant as these achievements are, perhaps the unit's most important legacy is that the Aztec Eagles fought for honor and for Mexico as Allies in World War II, creating national pride throughout their homeland. That pride endures and is evident today as the story of the Aztec Eagles can be heard in towns and villages across Mexico.

1

The Mexican Air Force up to World War II

Origins

At the beginning of the twentieth century, visionaries in the management and military use of balloons and airships had the success of sending military personnel to Europe in order to study how to use them in Mexico. Men like Juan Guillermo Villasana López and Eduardo Aldasoro Suárez were already doing tests with automobile engines and wooden and metal structures to try to realize the dream of being able to fly. The need to invent equipment to perform this feat created the need for these inventors to develop the knowledge of design, aerodynamics, weight, balance, and propulsion of some mechanism that would give the necessary support to keep in flight a device heavier than air.

Aviation arrived in Mexico for different purposes than the military. At first, it was considered unique as fun, as a sport, and, above all, a show. On December 9, 1909, the first airplane arrived from France to the country. Its owner was Alberto Braniff, who after putting it together and adjusting the carburetor, made the first motorized, manned, and controlled flight in Mexico and Latin America on January 8, 1910.

The Mexican Air Force (F.A.M.) has its origin in the year 1915, when then-Chief of the Constitutionalist Army Don Venustiano Carranza—convinced of the enormous possibilities of the use of aviation in campaigns—issued on February 5, 1915 the decree by which the Military Aviation Organization was created.[1]

Evolution

After the first flight (carried out in a two-seat Voisin plane) was registered in Mexico by Alberto Braniff on January 8, 1910, and as a result of the flight made by Don Francisco I. Madero, on November 30, 1911, the government confirmed the airplane for military use. In 1912, the government authorized five officers to travel to the United States to study to be pilots.

Aircraft were used for aerial surveys and bombings during the Mexican Revolution. The poor performance obtained with imported engines and propellers, during their employment in the highlands of Mexico, created the need for their own technology that would allow the development and progress of a national aviation program. On November 15, 1915, the National Workshops on Aeronautical Constructions were officially inaugurated for the production of aircraft, engines, and propellers in Mexico, constituting a source of pride for using exclusively Mexican technology. On that same date, the National Aviation School was also inaugurated for the training of aviators in Mexico. Both events had a marked impact on the evolution of the Mexican Air Force.[2]

Airplanes Used by the Mexican Air Force

Moisant-Kenter Monoplano
It was used for reconnaissance, aerial bombardment with hand grenades, and launching of revolutionary propaganda. It was integrated in 1913 into the Air Flotilla of the Constitutionalist Army and in 1915 into the Aviation Weapon of the Constitutionalist Army. It also served as a trainer at the National Aviation School in Llanos de Balbuena.

Martin Pusher Biplane
The Army of the Northwest employed it for aerial reconnaissance and bombing. This airplane carried out the bombing of the gunboat *Guerrero* in Topolobampo, Sinaloa, in 1914. With the remains of this and a Ford motor car, an airplane, which was called *La Guajolota* (The Turkey), was built, which was used to familiarize students with the handling of airplanes in races on land.

Bleriot Series "E"
This type of French aircraft—a similar model to that used by Louis Bleriot during the historic crossing of the English—was initially acquired by the Federal Army of José Victoriano Huerta, after the triumph of the revolution. It was used for the instruction of the first candidates of pilots of the National Aviation School in Balbuena.

TNCA Series "A" Biplane
This was an aircraft of national construction, to which different power plants were adapted. Later, the 80-hp Aztatl engine and the Anáhuac propeller were installed; both were designed by Captain Juan Guillermo Villasana López. They were used for the

instruction of the cadets of the Aviation Military School of Llanos de Balbuena. These aircraft imposed several milestones in the history of national aviation, such as the first airmail in the country, the first aerobatic maneuvers, and the first night flight. Also with a change in its landing gear and the adoption of floats, the first flight of a Hydroplane (as it was called then) took place in the bay of the Port of Veracruz. With this type of plane, the first film was also made for scientific purposes, when flying over the pyramids of Teotihuacán, and the first military airplane in a military parade in 1918.

TNCA Series "C" (Denominated "Microplane Veloz")
A Mexican biplane, designed in 1918 by Juan Guillermo Villasana. It was conceived as the first fighting aircraft in Mexico. It was built in metal structure and equipped with a Hispano-Suiza engine of 150 hp. It achieved a speed of over 130 mph.

TNCA Series "H"
A national airplane type "parasol" (of a single wing, but separated from the fuselage), equipped with Aztatl engine and Anáhuac propeller, it was used for reconnaissance and bombing purposes, when equipped with a side-throw machine gun and a bomb holder under the fuselage.

Farman F-50
The first twin-engined aircraft in Mexico, it was a French biplane bombing aircraft equipped with Lorraine Detreich engines of 250 horsepower and systems of sight for the launch of up to eight bombs of over 800 lb. It had a range of 420 miles and a maximum speed of 93 mph. A three-man crew operated it.

Avro 504k/JY Avro "Anahuac"
These English training biplanes (acquired in Canada) with Rhône 120-hp engines were used for the training of aviator pilots. Later in the National Workshops of Aeronautical Constructions, they were built as national versions called Avro Anahuac. They differed from foreign models by having more resistant landing gear, with which these aircraft were used on unprepared ground for the operation of aircraft. As of 1923, more than thirty were manufactured, which served until 1930. Although they were essentially school airplanes, they were used in tactical tasks such as aerial photography and as bombers in the campaigns of 1924 and 1926.

Bristol Fighter F.2B
The Mexican Air Force acquired ten new airplanes directly from the Bristol factory, equipped with Hispano-Suiza engines of 300 hp. These airplanes carried a synchronized frontal shot machine gun and a pair of flexible machine guns for the observer/gunner of the rear cabin, with which it protected the rear part of the plane. It could also load and launch up to 242 lb. of different types of bombs. It entered into combat in 1929 during the Escobarista Rebellion.

TNCA/Lascurain 3-E-130 "Quetzalcoatl" or "Tololoche"

A plane of national design, it was built in 1923 with special type of plywood. That is the reason why it was called unofficially *La Tololoche* (the musical instrument). It was initially intended as a fighting plane, but because of its large size, it was discarded for this task. It was used to demonstrate the performance and capabilities of the national aircraft of that time, as did Captain Emilio Carranza Rodríguez in September 1927, when with this same plane (modified with a German BMW engine) and renamed *Coahuila* it made the nonstop flight from Mexico City to Ciudad Juárez.

Azcárate O-E-1

It was a reconnaissance-bomber aircraft developed in Mexico in the late 1920s. It was designed by Brigadier General Juan Francisco Azcárate and built at the National Aviation workshops near Mexico City. A trainer version, the Azcárate E-1, was also built. Ten of these copies were made for the Military School of Aeronautical Application. The first was converted into a hydroplane in 1929 and tested in Veracruz.

Douglas 0-2M

An American airplane of advanced training, it was used as a means of observation and attack against the Cristera and Escobarista rebellions. One of these aircraft, the number "17," baptized *Mexican Army*, was modified with a Pratt & Whitney Hornet engine of 525 hp. In this biplane, Colonel Pablo L. Sidar and the Second Lieutenant Arnulfo Cortes made a goodwill flight through Central and South America in 1929, traveling almost 14,000 miles and a total of 265 hours of flight.

Vought/Azcárate Corsario

A U.S. observation biplanes built under license from the *Azcárate* factory, corresponded to the O2U-4A model, but with modifications such as the adaptation of a pair of machine guns for the observer/gunner and bomber carriers. Thirty-one aircraft were built. They were employed from the early 1930s until 1942, when they were still used for patrol flights along Mexican shores during World War II.

Ryan STM-150

Six of these aircraft were the first that the Ryan Aeronautics Company exported. They arrived in Balbuena in 1938. The STM-150 was used as training aircraft. Five were gradually destroyed in plane crashes, and by 1940, there was only one aircraft left.

Ares

Ten of these aircraft were manufactured in Mexico, based on the BW Bird sport aircraft, authorized by the Canadian Car and Foundry—owner of the aircraft rights. Under the name of *Maple Leaf*, the first aircraft was produced in 1941, equipped with a Warner Super Scarab engine of 165 hp. It reached speeds up to 124 mph, and it was used by the Military School of Aviation.

Be Teziutlan

A national monoplane of primary training, it was manufactured by the Antonio Sea factory in Balbuena near Mexico City and financed by General Roberto Fierro. Flight tests were conducted in February 1942. Teziutlan planes were used as aircraft transportation between different units.

Vought/Sikorsky OSU-2U-3 Kingfisher

A U.S. maritime patrol aircraft, it was used by the Mexican Air Force a few months before the start of World War II for the surveillance of the national sealanes. After Mexico declared war, six aircraft were transferred to Squadron 201.

North American AT-6 Texan

An American advanced trainer, it was initially employed as maritime patrol aircraft. A squadron of this type of aircraft was used against the German submarine *U-129* on July 5, 1942, causing minor damage. Approximately 136 copies of this aircraft were acquired, being used also in different air squadrons and in the Aviation Military School. They were retired from the service in 1982, after training pilots for more than forty years in the Mexican Air Force.

Douglas A-24B Banshee

This aircraft had perforated flaps to slow down the speed achieved by these airplanes during the maneuver of aiming and launching bombs. It was designed specifically for the search and destruction of enemy ships. It had a 1,200-hp engine, an armament of two 0.50-caliber machine guns, two 0.30-caliber machine guns, and could carry up to a 2,400-lb. bomb.

Republic P-47D-30 Thunderbolt

An American fighter-bomber airplane, it had a powerful eighteen-cylinder Double Wasp engine and an armament of eight 0.50-caliber machine guns. It had the ability to launch up to 2,500 lb. of bombs and ten 5-inch unguided rockets. The 201st Squadron used them during their participation in World War II. Twenty-five similar aircraft were used in Mexico until the end of the 1950s.

North American B-25J Mitchell

A twin-engined medium bomber aircraft, it had a crew consisting of six (pilot, co-pilot, bombardier, navigator, radio operator, and flight engineer, the latter four also served as machine-gun operators for self-defense on bombing missions). It was acquired during World War II where it was employed for patrol missions of Mexican waters in the Gulf of Mexico and the Caribbean Sea. The front part of the plane (nose) had a transparent Plexiglas cover where the bombardier could aim with the sights on a target on the surface and launch precisely over 3,900 lb. of bombs that this aircraft carried.[3]

Promoters of Mexican Civil and Military Aviation

Alberto Braniff

He was the first to make a powered flight in Mexico. He was born to a wealthy and powerful family during the Porfirio Díaz era. His father was a wealthy industrialist who sent him to study in Europe, where he became interested in aviation. Back in Mexico in 1910, Alberto Braniff made his first short flight in a Voisin Airplane, with a 50-hp ENV Motors Company engine, using the Balbuena Plains in Mexico City as a runway. Not only was this the first flight in Mexico, most believe it was the first flight in Central or South America.

Gustavo Salinas Camiña

Camiña was a true pioneer, being the first person to use an airplane to attack naval vessels in 1914 during the Mexican Revolution. Flying a very early Martin Biplane, Camiña dropped explosives on the gunboats *Guerrero* and *Morelos*. He did no damage but showed the potential for attacking ships from the air. Later, he became the Mexican Air Force's first division general, and was influential in organizing the 201st Squadron during World War II.

Major Alfredo Lezama Álvarez and Lieutenant David J. Borja

They made a nonstop flight from Mexico City to Nuevo Laredo on August 14, 1927 in a national construction biplane with a Hispano-Suizo engine of 300 hp. It was equipped with additional fuel tanks. The flight lasted ten hours and covered a total distance of 776 miles.

Captain Emilio Carranza

In June 1926, Captain Emilio Carranza went to the United States to buy an airplane, which he intended to use for long-distance flights, acquiring a Lincoln Standard airplane in Chicago, which he repaired. He installed a 185-hp BMW engine in the Standard and named it the *Coahuila*. On Friday, September 2, 1927, at 5.50 a.m., the *Coahuila* departed Mexico City for Ciudad Juárez, landing there at 4.48 p.m. The flight lasted ten hours and fifty-eight minutes. Captain Emilio Carranza was received triumphantly. Shortly thereafter, Carranza and Charles Lindbergh became very close friends, and Lindbergh visited Mexico City on a goodwill flight on December 14, 1927. Carranza held the record for the third longest nonstop solo flight, which he established on May 24–25, 1928 by flying 1,875 miles in eighteen hours and thirty minutes from San Diego, California, to Mexico City.

Captain Carranza also made the nonstop flight, with duration of eighteen hours and twenty minutes, from Mexico to Washington, D.C., on June 11, 1928 in *Excelsior*, a special Ryan B-1 Brougham. On the night of July 12, 1928, Captain Carranza died near Mt. Holly, New Jersey, while returning to Mexico after a successful goodwill flight from Mexico City to Washington, D.C. After a short flight, the fuel-laden aircraft went down in a severe thunderstorm, prematurely ending the promising career of this great flier.

Lieutenant Colonel Roberto Fierro Villalobos Avión

Villalobos was one of the most important individuals for the promotion of Mexican civil and military aviation. On August 8, 1913, he joined the revolutionary forces commanded by General Constitutionalists Jesus Maria Rios. In 1920, the government of interim President Adolfo de la Huerta announced the recruitment of pilots for the new Mexican Air Force. Fierro joined as a cadet, graduating in 1922, and was assigned to a bombing squadron. He made a nonstop flight from Mexicali to Mexico City on May 30, 1928 and a goodwill trip to Cuba and Central American countries on August 11, 1928. He subsequently made another flight from Mexico to New York on June 21, 1930. Eventually, he climbed through the ranks and was made Commander of the Mexican Air Force. In this capacity, he was a great proponent of both Mexican civil and military aviation.

Lieutenant Colonel Gustavo G. León González and Second Lieutenant Ricardo González Figueroa

They made the first circumvallation flight through the Mexican Republic in a sesquiplane Azcárate plane manufactured in the National Workshops of Aeronautical Constructions designed by General Brigadier Juan Francisco Azcárate. They started on September 30, 1928 and ended on December 18 of the same year. They flew eighty effective hours and covered 10,900 kilometers.

Colonel Aviator Pablo L. Sidar and Second Lieutenant Arnulfo Cortés

They made successful goodwill flights through Central and South America in August 1929.

Colonel Pablo L. Sidar and Lieutenant Carlos Rovirosa Pérez

At the beginning of May 1930, they flew from Mexico City to Buenos Aires, Argentina. During their flight and due to adverse weather conditions, they crashed into the sea, tragically perishing in a place called Playa Cieneguita in Puerto Limón, Costa Rica, on May 11, 1930.

Colonel Antonio Cárdenas Rodríguez

He participated in the campaign of the Yaqui, in the State of Sonora, and in the campaign during the Cristeros Rebellion in the States of Jalisco and Colima. He was one of the pilots selected to link Mexico City with Nuevo Laredo for the air postal service of the Ministry of Communications and Public Works. He initiated a flight of goodwill to various countries in Latin America. He traveled almost 22,000 miles in 118 hours of flight aboard a Lockheed Model 12 Electra aircraft, returning to the Mexican capital on September 13, 1940. Colonel Cárdenas would eventually be selected to command the Aztec Eagles.[4]

2

The Road to War for Mexico

In the 1930s, Mexico was a devastated land. The Mexican Revolution (1910–1920) had claimed hundreds of thousands of lives. Many more were displaced or saw their homes and cities destroyed.

When the National Revolutionary Party (P.N.R.) nominated Lázaro Cárdenas as presidential candidate in 1934, he already was one of the most important commanders of the army. He also was an expert in politics. He had been the governor of Michoacán and president of the P.N.R. He was not, however, a member of the original group of revolutionary leaders, as he was younger and belonged to the post-revolutionary leadership. He had been a loyal subordinate of President Elías Calles without being his unconditional follower.[1]

On March 18, 1938, President Lázaro Cárdenas announced on all radio stations that Mexico would expropriate the oil companies, since he could not allow foreign corporations to ignore the decision of the highest court of Mexico. He went on to say that if Mexico had not expropriated them, Mexican independence and sovereignty would be at risk. He added that the expropriated properties would be paid for. In one fell swoop, Mexico had done what no other country had ever dared to do, except for the U.S.S.R., and that was to expropriate the holdings of foreign corporations.

On March 19, the nation through news articles and mass demonstrations supported the president's decision. Mexicans were unanimous in their support of expropriations. Diplomatic relations between Mexico and Britain were broken and Mexicans received this with wild enthusiasm. In April, bonds were created to pay for the expropriated land and thousands of Mexicans donated their jewelry, watches, and money to pay foreign creditors. Cárdenas had such widespread support that the U.S. ambassador informed the state department that there was such unquestionable popular support that it was unlikely that Cárdenas could back down now, even if he wanted to.[2]

The official opposition of Britain, whose investment in 1938 was larger than that of the U.S., did not worry Mexico too much. With the U.S., the problem was more delicate. The U.S. did recognize the right of Mexico to nationalize foreign-owned businesses in Mexico if there was fair and just compensation. However, the U.S. and Mexican positions differed. Mexico, from the start, had agreed to pay for what it had taken, not immediately, but in ten years as required by law. For the U.S., this was too long. Ten years was not expropriation, but rather confiscation. The other issue was whether the value of the oil still underground be compensated for by the Mexican government.[3]

It was clear that Mexico could not pay the half billion dollars that the oilmen demanded for the expropriated properties. Cárdenas suggested that they negotiate a fair settlement and that the amount be paid in oil. The companies rejected this and suggested that the only fair solution was for Cárdenas to return the properties back to them. Cárdenas rejected this outright. In 1938, the companies unleashed a tremendous propaganda and public relations campaign against Mexico. They urged people to boycott Mexican goods, to embargo U.S. technology to Mexico, and to close down U.S. markets to Mexican Petroleum (P.E.M.E.X.) so that Mexico could "drown in its own oil." P.E.M.E.X. had a very rough time between 1938 and 1939, but it managed to survive by trading oil for money and machinery to the fascist countries. When World War II began, the European markets disappeared, and Mexico became a minor oil exporter starting in 1940.[4]

The American and British government blocked the export of Mexican oil to their allies and dependencies. However, internal demand was increasing fast. Because Mexico, due to the depression and the global wartime economy, was cut off from imported industrial goods, it began a process of import substitution industrialization (a trade and economic policy which advocates replacing foreign imports with domestic production), which needed much energy.

By 1940, the most dynamic sector of the Mexican economy had ceased to be an enclave owned and controlled by foreigners. However, to put added pressure on Mexico, the U.S. stopped buying Mexican silver for the U.S. treasury, but Mexico would not back down. Meanwhile, the U.S. oil companies relentlessly lobbied the U.S. government to use military force and invade Mexico. However, President Franklin D. Roosevelt was trying to implement what he called "The Good Neighbor Policy" to solidify an inter-American alliance against fascism. In addition, when World War II started, the U.S. desperately needed Mexican cooperation. It would be the tensions of the international context of World War II that probably saved Mexico from being invaded by the U.S to protect a handful of U.S. oil companies and their profits.[5]

In 1940, Cárdenas finally reached an agreement with the Sinclair Oil Company and continued to negotiate with Standard Oil. The deal with Sinclair was a diplomatic coup, for it showed that if Mexico could not reach an agreement with Standard Oil, it was not because of Mexico, but rather because of the greed of Standard Oil. By the end of the Cárdenas regime, settlements still had not been reached with most of the foreign companies. It was clear that these companies would not return to Mexico. Mexican oil would be controlled by, and to the benefit of, Mexicans.

The high point of the Cárdenas policy was the nationalization of the oil fields in March 1938. From that point on, the Cárdenas regime would be wracked by problems. A decrease in land distribution, the boycott decreed by oil corporations, international pressure due to the oil problem, and attacks by the right wing of the revolutionary family on the Cárdenas regime all occurred between 1938 and 1940. Veteran politicians within the revolutionary family after 1938 started to fight for their own interests. Within the official party and other government organizations, anti-Cárdenas factions were developing. In fact, from 1937 onward, inside the Party of the Mexican Revolution (P.R.M.), there was an explosion of futurism where sector leaders began to decide who would be the next president three years before Cárdenas' term would expire.[6]

After 1938, a civilian, but equally conservative party was created called the National Action Party (P.A.N.). Late in 1938, two years before Cárdenas' term was to expire, two of his main secretaries resigned so that they could work for their respective candidates. One was Manuel Ávila Camacho.

In November 1939, the P.R.M. announced that its candidate for the 1940–1946 term would be the ex-Secretary of War Manuel Ávila Camacho. This did not prevent numerous groups of workers, army officers, and peasants from supporting Juan Andrew Almazán, who was very much an opponent of Cárdenas' reforms. Political passions were unleashed across the whole country. Of all the groups opposing Cárdenas and the official candidate Camacho, the most effective and dangerous was that of General Almazán. Almazán was right of the official candidate. Almazán started his campaign in mid-1939 with a very vague political slogan that had widespread appeal: "Work, cooperation and respect for the law."[7]

Ávila Camacho started his campaign in April stating that he would advance the march of revolution. Both candidates searched for a middle ground. This was a clear indication that the Cárdenas' reforms would not be continued. In spite of this search for moderation on issues, the presidential campaign of 1939–40 was anything but orderly and calm. There were frequent and violent clashes between the followers of Ávila Camacho and Almazán. More and more people were killed in clashes. On July 7, Election Day, there were gun battles in the street and bottle throwing clashes and assaults on voting booths. Both the police and the army were called out to suppress the chaos. In spite of allegations of voting fraud and irregularities, Ávila Camacho was declared the winner. Almazán left Mexico after the election. Many of his followers felt betrayed, but they could do nothing to stop the political withdrawal. This marked an end to the revolutionary regimes and to the most violent and disputed election of revolutionary Mexico.

The expropriations of the oil fields cost Mexico investment money, access to markets, oil technology, and loans. The reform program of Cárdenas could not be fully implemented because of these costs. When Cárdenas handed the presidency over to Ávila Camacho, the P.R.M. continued the party line that class struggle was the engine of historical development, and that the ultimate goal of the revolution was to build a society controlled and in the interests of the workers.

The *ejidos* (a piece of land farmed communally under a system supported by the state), the cooperatives, and state property had to be the economic and social cores of the new Mexico. Opposing forces were on the rise inside and outside the country, and by the end of 1940, the Cárdenistas plan was all but over.

Cárdenas nationalized Mexico's vast oil reserves and the property of foreign oil companies over the protests of the United States, but the Americans, seeing war on the horizon, were forced to accept it. When General Ávila Camacho assumed the presidency in 1940, it was clear to many people that the construction of a Mexican socialism had ended. In addition, the idea that with the end of the Cárdenas administration, the revolution itself had finally ended became more and more common.

As war looked inevitable, many Mexicans wanted to join on one side or the other. Mexico's loud communist community first supported Germany while Germany and Russia had a pact. They then supported the Allied cause once the Germans invaded Russia in 1941. There was a sizeable community of Italian immigrants who supported entry in the war as an Axis power as well. Other Mexicans, disdainful of Fascism, supported joining the Allied cause. The attitude of many Mexicans was influenced by historical grievances with the United States. The loss of Texas and the American west, intervention during the revolution and repeated incursions into Mexican territory caused a lot of resentment.

Some Mexicans felt that the United States was not to be trusted. Many Mexicans did not know what to think. Some felt that they should join the Axis cause against their old antagonist, while others did not want to give the Americans an excuse to invade again and counseled strict neutrality.

The road to war for the Mexican Air Force was not an easy one. Sending men to fight with the United States was an unpopular move among many Mexican politicians and citizens in the early 1940s. The memory of the 1848 Treaty of Guadalupe, which ceded 500,000 square miles of Mexican territory to the U.S., was still fresh in many minds. The Zimmermann Telegram, a diplomatic proposal from the German Empire during World War I, further exacerbated the strained relations between Mexico and the United States. In the telegram, Germany offered Mexico U.S. territory if it would join the German cause against the United States. Mexico declined the German proposal but it angered Americans and led in part to U.S. entry into World War I.

As the world moved toward war again in the late 1930s, Mexico reluctantly turned to the United States for help. Mexican President Lázaro Cárdenas had declared his country neutral, but before the 1940 presidential campaign, violence between pro-fascist and pro-communist organizations began. Worried by the potential of an unstable government in Mexico, the United States began to provide both open and secret aid to the Mexican government. Some economic cooperation between the U.S. and Mexico resulted when the U.S. again purchased silver from Mexico and granted U.S. government-backed loans.

In 1941, Ávila Camacho became President of Mexico, resulting in a new market in the United States for Mexican oil. President Roosevelt had been a constant friend to Mexico. Once elected to a second term, he used both the F.B.I. and military intelligence to help the Mexican Army in their fight against pro-revolution rebels. Roosevelt gave legitimacy to the Camacho presidency by quickly recognizing him.

The Mexican government wanted to do everything possible to insure that Mexico did not become a battleground if Germany or Japan invaded the continent. They secretly permitted agents of the U.S. to enter the country to train Mexican counterintelligence forces. Mexico's contribution to the American and Allied war effort was significant, but a strong alliance with the United States did not come easy. Attacks on Mexican ships by German submarines began to increase and the U.S., England, and France began a massive propaganda campaign against the Axis powers. These factors began to turn the tide of public opinion in Mexico.[8]

When the German Navy began concentrated attacks against shipping leaving American ports, it was inevitable that ships from neutral countries would come under attack as well. On May 14, 1942, *U-564* sank the small oil tanker S.S. *Potrero de Llano* off the east coast of Florida. The ship was operated by P.E.M.E.X., and was bound for New York out of the port of Tampico. Twelve of her crew of thirty-five were lost. The survivors were picked up by an American patrol boat. The U-boat's commander, Reinhold Suhren, had observed a large illuminated tricolor flag on the side of the ship, but because only Mexican naval vessels were allowed to display the full national ensign with the eagle emblem, Suhren concluded the vessel was masquerading as Italian. While Mexico's government was still debating its response to this incident, another Mexican oil tanker was attacked on May 21. The S.S. *Faja de Oro* was returning empty from Marcus Hook, Pennsylvania, to Tampico, when she was spotted off Key West by *U-106*, commanded by Captain Lieutenant Hermann Rasch. It ultimately took four torpedoes for the German submarine to sink the small tanker, which was set afire by the final hit. Ten of her crew of thirty-seven were lost when the ship sank just after 4.30 a.m. S.S. *Faja de Oro* was operated by P.E.M.E.X., with its homeport in Tampico.

This second sinking, so soon after the first, made it clear that the German Navy had not attacked Mexican shipping by accident or mistake. Any ship bound for or sailing out of Allied ports were liable to be sunk without warning, whether their nation of registry was at war or not. President Manuel Ávila Camacho had pursued a long military career prior to entering politics, so it was predictable that he would offer an aggressive response to the provocation. His speech asking the country to declare war was broadcast on national radio, and for many Mexicans, it was as memorable as North Americans found Roosevelt's address to Congress after Pearl Harbor. The Mexican government agreed to declare war on Germany, Italy, and Japan on June 1, 1942. A number of patriotic or adventurous Mexicans enlisted and began training and working to modernize Mexico's armed forces. President Ávila was soon in Washington, negotiating his country's larger contribution to a continental war effort.

In the aftermath of its declaration of war against the Axis powers, the Mexican government recognized that it did not have the necessary financial resources to enter into the fighting. Therefore, Camacho looked to the United States for support to send troops into combat. Seven months after Mexico declared war on the Axis powers, he offered to join with the United States in its war effort. He told U.S. Undersecretary of State Sumner Wells in November 1942 that he wanted to have troops ready for overseas combat by the spring of 1943. He again extended a proposal to form an army at an April 1943 meeting in Monterrey with Roosevelt. Ávila Camacho qualified both proposals upon the United States supplying the necessary equipment, material, and finances for the Mexican force.[9]

The United States did not respond to Mexico's offer of troops. Consequently, Ávila Camacho tried other means to enlist U.S. support. He invited U.S. Army Chief of Staff General George Marshall to be his guest as Mexico commemorated 133 years of independence on September 16, 1943. The Mexican president honored his visitor by sitting next to him at every ceremony, and on the day of observance, they stood together at a military review of 25,000 ground troops. Camacho intended to influence Marshall and the United States with this show of military strength. Later, he told the American general that Mexican forces were available, if required by the Allies.[10]

After returning from Mexico, Marshall wrote President Roosevelt about Ávila Camacho's offer of troops. The tone of the letter reflected his chagrin for a possible breach of protocol, because he had accepted and scheduled the trip without consulting either the president or the secretary of war. He apologized for becoming involved in an affair without due and formal reference of the matter.[11]

In reply to Marshall, Roosevelt expressed no concern for the general's perceived impropriety. Instead, he congratulated him for a successful trip and then revealed a surprisingly supportive attitude concerning the offer of troops. Remorsefully, he ended his letter with the philosophical comment: "I wish that we could think up some method of using even a token force of Mexicans at some point outside of Mexico."[12]

Although Roosevelt did not necessarily want to disregard the Mexican offer, several reasons prevented his possible acceptance of the offer. His military advisors cautioned about the difficulty of incorporating a unit with a different language, customs, diet, and training into the framework of an American army. Mexico's fiscal inability to put an army in the field remained another obstacle. Moreover, Mexico had yet to make a formal request to participate in combat.[13]

The intensity of Ávila Camacho's desire for Mexico to be a part of the war tapered off after his first offer to participate in October 1942. Mexico's failure to request a battle assignment did not rest solely on financial inability. Prior to September 1943, the Mexican army did not have the competency for combat. In addition, the Mexican president had not satisfied himself with regard to the public attitude for sending an expeditionary force overseas. Late in 1942, Foreign Minister Ezequiel Padilla Peñaloza tested the national sentiment to send troops into combat. He announced: "… if circumstances demand the sending of a Mexican expeditionary force abroad, the government would place before the people the necessity of doing so, and I am sure that they would respond affirmatively without the slightest vacillation."

Newspapers in Mexico City placed his address on the front pages, under modest headlines, as if to comply with the government's objective to propagandize as gently as possible. Although the Ávila Camacho government continued to treat the possibility of sending troops into battle with caution, the matter soon became a national issue. Active participation of Mexican troops would obviously enhance Mexico's position among nations after the war. Camacho continued to express a desire to furnish Mexican troops for the Allied cause, although both he and General Lázaro Cárdenas, now the Secretary of National Defense, displayed a certain hesitancy to act on the matter. This attitude became even more restrained after the debriefing of Mexican officers who had been in North Africa to study U.S. Army command and support systems at the fighting fronts in April 1943. For reasons not known, the Mexican government hurriedly called them back to Mexico three months later.[14]

Mexico's reluctance changed in mid-September 1943. General Lázaro Cárdenas told visiting American Joint Mexican–United States Defense Commission officers that the Mexican army had overcome its problems with training and equipment. He hoped that Mexican troops would be allowed the opportunity to undergo "the sacrifice of blood and the stress of combat so that after the war Mexico would hold its head up." The chief of the North American section suggested that Mexico submit a concrete proposal and state what it expected from the United States.[15]

Ávila Camacho, now confident that he could supply troops to the Allied cause, lobbied for military and public support. In a speech to the graduating class of the Mexican national military academy, given at a luncheon in his honor on November 17, 1943, he stressed Mexico's readiness to send an army abroad to fight, if asked by the Allies. One day later, *The New York Times* printed an extract of his speech. In bold type, the headline read "Mexicans to fight abroad if needed." The article named three former presidents of Mexico, two of them political rivals, who attended the luncheon. Commenting editorially, *The New York Times* suggested that the meeting reflected Mexico's desire to show that their country was united politically behind the nation and its war effort.[16]

Ávila Camacho's continuing efforts to gain support from the United States eventually led Roosevelt to look for ways to use a Mexican military force. After meditating over Mexico's desire to participate for more than a year, the president decided to find a way for Mexican troops to join the fight. Late in January 1944, he summoned Ambassador to Mexico George Messersmith to Washington for talks. At this meeting on January 31, the ambassador advised the president of the increasing desire of the Mexican military to fight against the Axis nations. While reminding the president of Mexican loyalty and collaboration, he surmised that it would strengthen Mexico directly and the United States politically if they took part in actual combat. Many in Mexico opposed the use of land forces, he said, including General Lázaro Cárdenas, Secretary of National Defense, because they believed the Mexican nation could make only a small contribution in that way. Messersmith then proposed the idea of using an air squadron.[17]

The president liked Messersmith's idea and asked General E. M. Watson, his military aide, to make a note that he wished to see General H. H. Arnold the following day. Roosevelt then said that after he had seen General Arnold that Arnold would get in touch with Messersmith regarding any arrangements. The president stated further that if General Arnold also approved of the plan, then the ambassador, upon his return to Mexico, could indicate to the president of Mexico that participation of one or two Mexican air squadrons would be acceptable.[18]

A series of meetings followed that set the Messersmith proposal in motion. On February 3, 1944, Arnold contacted the ambassador in New York, saying that he wanted to meet and talk with him concerning a vital matter. That same day, Messersmith returned to Washington, D.C., and met with Army Chief General George Marshall, who acknowledged his understanding and ratification of the proposal made to the president. The next day, the ambassador met with Arnold, who supported the plan and said that the president gave him the authority and responsibility to develop a Mexican Air Force squadron. Both men agreed that the joint Mexican–United States military mission should not know of this matter until all arrangements were finalized.[19]

Before Messersmith returned to Mexico, General Arnold instructed him regarding exploratory talks with President Camacho. If the Mexican government agreed to develop an air force squadron, United States commanders in the battle zones were then to determine how best to use it. After the feasibility study was completed, the ambassador would so inform the Mexican president.[20]

Early in February 1944, one top-ranking U.S. Army officer pressed for acceptance of Camacho's offer to join with the United States in the war effort. On February 9, 1944, Brigadier General A. R. Harris, Military *Attaché* in Mexico City, wrote Washington concerning meetings with two Mexican generals and gave his opinion on the possible benefits derived from accepting Mexico's offer to fight. Air Force Chief General Gustavo Salinas told Hams that he wanted to take the lead in the formation of a Latin American expeditionary air force. Later, a considerably annoyed Army Chief General Guzmán Cárdenas reminded General Hams that none of the Allies had responded to Mexico's offered to furnish army troops for combat service. The mood for war in Mexico was strong, Hams related, and the summons to send a Mexican expeditionary force to the fighting front was gaining momentum. In a supportive final comment, he said: "… it would be a magnificent thing to aid in the development of such a force, because it would further friendly relations between our governments for the next one hundred years."[21]

On February 10, 1944, Messersmith returned to Mexico to discuss Roosevelt's proposal with Ávila Camacho. The Mexican president, although obviously pleased when told of Roosevelt's decision, said that he did not want to give an answer until he had conferred with his advisors. In an attempt to explain the reason, Messersmith speculated that Ávila Camacho probably wanted to discuss the matter with General Cárdenas, the Secretary of National Defense. Still, he judged that the president would overrule any objections because the developing sentiments for action were so strong.[22]

General Harris, unaware of the ongoing talks for the development of a Mexican air squadron, continued to report his opinions on Mexico's impatience to participate actively in the war. On February 14, in a confidential memo to the chief of Military Intelligence Service, Harris cautioned that the Mexicans were becoming impatient as well as dismayed at the coolness to which their patriotic offer had been received. He advised that the great national enthusiasm, generated by Camacho's strong stand against Nazi aggression, diminished when none of the Allies solicited their participation in combat. "These are very sensitive and proud people," he wrote, "and they take offense very easily." He closed by saying: "… there is a real danger that the war spirit will perceptibly cool unless some consideration—however small—is given to the country's offer of troops."[23]

Despite his concern, General Harris oddly enough recommended against accepting the Mexican offer. He raised the question regarding problems involved with a foreign language, customs, and diet. As a gesture of military good will, he advanced the idea of inviting five or six Mexican generals to visit the Southwestern Pacific theater of operations.[24]

Several days after Ambassador Messersmith advised State Department officials why Ávila Camacho failed immediately to adopt the plan to use a Mexican air force squadron, these officials became anxious to know with certainty when he intended to accept. Messersmith responded to their inquiry on February 17, 1944, and two days later again replied, saying that he previously gave them all the information available to him and asked them to be patient. He did not understand the haste after all these months, because the initiates of the program all knew that there were certain definite steps to accomplish first. "I have seen the president several times since our original conversation," he reported, "and he is still uncommitted." The president, Minister of Foreign Affairs Padilla, and all of the generals wanted to go ahead, but he cautioned that Ávila Camacho must move carefully. "No answer will come forth," he related, "until the Secretary of National Defense, General Cárdenas returns from an inspection tour."[25]

Although resolute in his desire to send an armed force into combat, Camacho wanted to measure the extent of support for sending an Air Force squadron before making a final commitment. He staged two events that later served to justify his decision to enter the war officially. First, the Mexican Air Force held a major air show in Mexico City on March 5. Ávila Camacho intended the demonstration to strengthen public opinion for support of his position to send an air force unit to fight with the American forces. The exercise went exceedingly well, and the flying skills displayed by the pilots confirmed the quality of their discipline and training. Because of the extraordinary publicity given by the press and the hundreds of thousands of spectators who witnessed the event, the president judged the interest shown by the public supported his position.[26]

The second event occurred three days later. Ávila Camacho decided to accept Roosevelt's offer after receiving full Mexican Air Force support for his proposal at a luncheon banquet honoring him at Campo Marte in Mexico City. Camacho told those attending that Mexico stood ready to defend the Allied cause. He said that although the army exhibited a wish to be of service in the war, the air force would carry the Mexican flag to the battlefield.[27]

The manner in which Camacho developed backing from the public and the air force support did not go unnoticed. In a letter to Larry Duggan, Messersmith speculated that the president carefully arranged the air maneuvers and the dinner to lay the basis for agreeing to develop an air force group. Their participation, therefore, would come as a direct manifestation of the desire of the people and the armed forces, and not of the initiative of the president. Ambassador Messersmith supported the prudent fashion in which the Mexican president handled this situation.[28]

From the outset, the Mexican Army vigorously opposed the use of any other military service. This long-established organization (and a former president) reacted negatively when Ávila Camacho told the Air Force that he intended to use only the air force for combat. He received several petitions from Mexican generals for the army's direct participation in the war. The army's protest did not end with petitions. Major General Guy V. Henry, a member of the Joint Mexican–United States Defense Commission, discovered an attempt by the Mexican army to sabotage the Mexican air force. An individual, considered as reliable, showed him a copy of a letter written to General Lázaro Cárdenas by the Mexican military *attaché* in Washington, Brigadier General Luis Alamillo Flores. The note contended that the Mexican Air Force pilots were undisciplined and untrained and that the service had no knowledge at all of supply. Furthermore, it stated that only six pilots had qualified to fly combat-type aircraft. Alamillo declared that high-ranking American officers had advised him that the United States army preferred Mexican ground forces to help in the Pacific Theater against the Japanese. He therefore recommended using cavalry and mechanized forces numbering approximately 50,000 men. In his opinion, Mexicans and especially Yaqui Indians could do well in the Pacific, as they had been subject to most of the diseases prevalent in that area. The Yaquis, he noted, were natural guerrilla warriors.[29]

General Henry attempted to defuse the significance of the Alamillo letter. He wrote that although some influential Mexican Army generals wanted only their ground troops to participate in the war, the United States War Department was not in accord with the Alamillo statement. He stated: "… the Mexican Air Force had many recent pilot graduates from the American Army and Navy and that several were presently engaged in advance combat training and reported to be excellent."[30]

Ávila Camacho committed Mexico to accept the Roosevelt plan on March 14, 1944. Messersmith received a formal request from the Mexican government to establish and train an air force squadron in the United States. Ávila Camacho also asked that no publicity be given to his acceptance until Arnold or his designate came to Mexico. Messersmith sent word to Roosevelt and commented that the Mexican aviators would give a good account of themselves.[31]

Less than two weeks after Ávila Camacho made his decision, the United States began the developmental stages of the Mexican Air Force squadron. General Arnold sent an American Air Force delegation to Mexico City for organizational discussions with

President Ávila Camacho and his advisors. On March 26, 1944, General William E. Hall, U.S. Deputy Chief of Air Staff, along with several other staff members, came to Mexico City. To screen the nature of their visit, the Mexican government announced that Hall came to fulfill a previous commitment to decorate General Salinas, Chief of the Mexican Air Force.[32]

Because protocol required that he meet first with Mexico's Foreign Minister Hall, his advisory team, and Ambassador Messersmith paid Doctor Esquiel Padilla a visit on the afternoon of March 27. They briefed him for a later conference with the president on the composition requirements of an air squadron. He also received a secret memorandum containing data on the specialty requirement for a fighter squadron.[33]

The following day, General Hall paid a courtesy call at the home of Air Force Chief General Salinas. The real purpose of his visit was to present General Arnold's invitation to visit a theater of war. Salinas seemed pleased to receive the invitation and said that he would confirm a date to go after securing the necessary authority. As they talked afterward, Salinas wanted to know more about Mexico's possible participation in the war. The manner of his inquiry revealed to Hall that the general did not know of the commitment to send a Mexican Air Force squadron to the combat front. For unknown reasons, Ávila Camacho had failed to confide in his top air force general. Because of this, Hall was careful to relate only the general blueprint of their plan for the development of the squadron, emphasizing that for the system to formulate, Mexico must make a commitment to participate. Salinas, excited about the possibility of developing a special air force fighter squadron, did not ask if Hall had discussed the matter with others in the Mexican government.[34]

Later that same day, President Camacho met with the American military delegation at Los Piños, the presidential residence. They discussed and concurred on all elements concerning the development and use of the air force squadron. From the outset, Ávila Camacho wanted to know the degree to which Hall had discussed the matter with General Salinas. In order to maintain absolute secrecy concerning this project, he asked all concerned not to notify Salinas until after approval of the plan. Ávila Camacho, after examining an air squadron composition memorandum, learned that the squadron would train for a minimum of five months at a United States air base and that the P-47 Thunderbolt was designated as the combat aircraft. After completing their training, the unit would be assigned to the Mediterranean theater. All parties agreed that a Mexican officer must command the squadron. In addition, they discussed the desirability of English proficiency in order to absorb textual material, regulations, and flight instruction. Finally, Ávila Camacho agreed to the conditions presented to him and gave a firm commitment to have a Mexican Air Force squadron participate at a combat front.[35]

President Ávila Camacho then addressed several other matters of special interest. He asked for information about squadron operating costs, including pay for a comparable American unit. Conference observers surmised that he was thinking in terms of paying his flyers on the same basis as the U.S. Ávila Camacho requested details concerning the welfare and religious duties of a chaplain in the U.S. Army. Although Mexican military law prohibited the use of a priest, he concluded that a minister should accompany his squadron to the front; in closing, Ávila Camacho asked when he would receive this information, and Hall assured him that it could be easily and quickly furnished. They set the organizational date of the squadron for no later than the middle of June. The president decided to appoint the Mexican squadron commander and pick the squadron personnel. The officer selected, he said, would be in a grade similar to that of an American squadron commander. The last item on the agenda involved an admonition by Ávila Camacho for all to maintain absolute secrecy about the matter.[36]

Near the end of their meeting and as an afterthought, Ávila Camacho mentioned a possible delay in sending the squadron into combat. As president, he said: "I do not have the unilateral authority to send troops out of the hemisphere, only congress could give this authorization." This disclosure was vexatious to the Mexican president, but he anticipated no difficulty. He related that it was his intention to ask both Mexican legislative houses for authority to send a Mexican Air squadron abroad after the ratification of a U.S.–Mexican water treaty then before the United States Senate. The Mexican public, he believed, was prepared for that step.[37]

Many believed that General Cárdenas wielded great influence over President Camacho's decisions and particularly in the development of the Mexican air force squadron. Cárdenas biographer, William Cameron Townsend, did not believe that Cárdenas tried to influence Camacho unduly. He wrote:

Some of the cooperation requests explained ... by General Hall did not particularly appeal to General Cárdenas, but no one ever knew it. He simply referred such details to President Ávila Camacho and if the president agreed, Cárdenas carried out his wishes. As Minister of Defense, Cárdenas was just as silent as ever on politics and affairs of state, but his being near the center of things revived talk about him being the power behind the throne.[38]

Ambassador Messersmith concurred with Townsend. In his memoirs, he wrote: "When General Cárdenas was Minister of War ... he did nothing to interfere with the sound basis on which the military collaboration had been established and was going forward." After three weeks, the information that General Hall promised failed to reach Ávila Camacho, and he asked Messersmith to find out why. The ambassador wrote to Larry Duggan at the state department, asking that he contact either General Arnold or Hall about the matter. In his opinion, the U.S. might take a delay as an indication of lack of interest.[39]

When Hall discovered that Ávila Camacho had not received the information promised, he sent it and additional data by special messenger and Messersmith received it on April 16. He apologized for the delay without explaining the reason. Under instructions, the ambassador gave the material directly to the foreign minister who in turn handed it directly to the president. Among the items of information received included an approximate budget for a single-engined fighter squadron, a statement of pay and allowances of personnel for such a squadron, and the duties of a chaplain.[40]

After receiving the necessary data that he needed to make a decision, President Camacho issued orders to begin the squadron recruitment process. For the next three months, brisk recruitment activity surrounded the selection of officers and men. Enlistment response was enthusiastic. Everyone in Mexico knew that Mexico was going to war. Enlistment inquiries came from all branches of the services as well as from civilians, and the government basked in the patriotism of its people and their sense of responsibility. Including the Air Force, conscription came from all branches of the armed services, the general intendancy of the army, the general command of communications, administration of artillery, administration of military sanitation, infantry, and military transports. Outside the military, the war material administration contributed gunsmiths, munitioners, and chemical engineers. President Camacho directed the selection of squadron personnel with great care, choosing those he believed had a genuine desire to do combat duty abroad.[41]

Toward the end of May 1944, a circumstance beyond Camacho's control delayed his plan to obtain authorization to send the squadron overseas. The president intended to ask for approval to send Mexican forces to war at a special session of the Mexican congress that was called to ratify the U.S.–Mexican water treaty. However, the United States Senate Committee on Foreign Affairs found it advisable to postpone consideration of the treaty for the present and it stalled in the United States Senate. Now the disappointed Mexican president was reluctant to call his congress into session for other than the water treaty. He believed that a called special session created certain risks in obtaining authority. Reluctantly, he would wait until September, when the congress met in regular session. Because of the president's desire for secrecy, Doctor Padilla made this known to Messersmith and no one else in Mexico.[42]

During the latter part of May 1944, Ávila Camacho questioned why it was necessary for his Air Force to train in the United States. He asked his Minister of Foreign Affairs to inquire concerning the reasons for not training in Mexico. Doctor Padilla told the president that he believed it was impractical, but to be certain, he asked Messersmith to raise the question with General Hall.

On May 31, 1944, the ambassador received an answer in a State Department secret memorandum. The memo carefully explained the logic for training in the United States. Normally, the already existing operational training system absorbed such training. Training in Mexico would require transferring to Mexico an aerodrome squadron— some 262 men and 290 officers and men of a fighter squadron. An additional requirement concerned the need for a considerable amount of critical maintenance equipment. The U.S. viewed it inadvisable to deplete training facilities already used to the maximum, making it inappropriate to send so many men to Mexico. Operating costs and system of training were also considered. Under the current system, it was easy to absorb additional trainees, and at a reasonable added cost. It would be a sacrifice, the memorandum stated, to train pilots outside the United States.[43]

Needing to know the status of the Mexican air squadron, General Hall returned to Mexico City on June 10, 1944 to talk with Ávila Camacho about this matter. The president told him that the selection of officers and men was almost complete. Camacho believed that the unit could schedule to leave, by rail, for the United States early in July. The information given him by Ávila Camacho allowed Hall ample time to make arrangement to receive the Mexican air squadron when they came into the U.S. He asked the president to notify air command, through Ambassador Messersmith, of the exact date of departure of the squadron. If the squadron started early in July, it would require four months of training before they could ship overseas. Again, Ávila Camacho requested that there be no publicity until the Mexican congress gave him the authority.[44]

On July 10, 1944, with the Mexican air squadron complete and ready to begin training, both governments formulated a treaty providing for the training of the Mexican Air Force personnel in the United States. The treaty consisted of two components. Annex A established the number of troops participating in training, all qualification prerequisites, dates for training and site locations, and replacement procedures. It stated that all training was to be done in the United States and in the same manner as an American fighter squadron, using U.S. Army Air Force organizational manuals. Proficiency standards were to be the same as that of any American fighter squadron. The total squadron personnel were to be forty-four officers and 249 enlisted men. The treaty established squadron standards at twenty-five aircraft for operational flying, with seventeen kept in reserve. To comply with the Mexican Law of Loans and Rents, Annex B specified the procedure to charge Mexico for financial arrangements and costs. Reimbursable charges included costs for transportation, food and lodging, clothing and equipment, fuel, supplies, munitions, and burial costs.[45]

Six days later, after completing organizational procedures, the Mexican Secretary of National Defense issued orders for the formation of a special Air Force Unit. This unit, known as the *Grupo de Perfecaonamiento Aemautico* (aviation training group), later became the Mexican Expeditionary Air Force. The original squadron consisted of 300 men, including thirty-six pilots. Ávila Camacho selected Colonel Antonio Cárdenas, a veteran pilot, to command the group. He had flown with a United States Air Force unit commanded by Lieutenant General Jimmy Doolittle, as an observer, on bombing missions in 1943 over Sicily and Italy. His official recognition as squadron commander came on July 21.[46]

In 1943, President Roosevelt met with Mexican President Manuel Ávila Camacho at the historic Monterrey Summit. President Roosevelt called for even more collaboration between the countries. President Ávila Camacho responded with his famous broadcasted speech "Good Neighbors—Good Friends: Mexico the Bridge between Latin and Saxon Cultures." President Camacho pointed out: "We deserve to live together free of the perpetual threats which derive from those who seek supremacy." He concluded:

I repeat to you, Mr. President, together with the sentiments of solidarity of my country and our wish for success of our common cause, the desire that the relations between Mexico and the United States of America may develop—always—along the channels of mutual esteem and unceasing devotion to liberty.[47]

The presidents kept collaborating. Mexico sent one Mexican Air Force squadron to fight the Axis powers. It was the first time in Mexico's history that Mexico sent troops to fight overseas. In exchange, President Roosevelt allowed the Mexican Air Force squadron to train in the United States.

The Joint Mexican–
United States Defense Commission

The Joint Mexican–United States Defense Commission (J.M.U.S.D.C.) was the primary mechanism for coordination of the U.S. and Mexican military. In order to coordinate actions related to the common defense of both countries, the J.M.U.S.D.C. was constituted on February 1942. Most of the initial coordination took place in Washington, D.C., and the head of the Mexican part was Mexico's military *attaché*, Brigadier General Luis Alamillo Flores. The agenda of the J.M.U.S.D.C. included a program to coordinate activities of the Mexican Pacific Military Region and the U.S. Western Defense Command and Western Sea Frontier Command.[1]

It also contemplated advance training in U.S. schools.[2] The J.M.U.S.D.C. also handled the military part of Lend-Lease to Mexico. According to Howard F. Cline, the Mexican Army received equipment, including tanks and airplanes, for about $18 million. The arrangement allowed them to pay for it at a discount price of $6 million. By 1949, Mexico had paid the price set on the equipment.[3] The Lend-Lease agreement covered the cost of the program related to the training and equipment of the Mexican Expeditionary Air Force, whose organization was discussed in the J.M.U.S.D.C.[4]

The organization of an aerial unit to be employed in combat overseas, representing the Mexican military, offered many advantages for both countries. Operational and tactical considerations favored such an organization. An aerial unit would be able to concentrate the military power of a small unit against different objectives in the theater of operations, in contrast with the requirement for a larger ground force deployed in the front. Strategic considerations also supported this type of organization. An aerial unit could better seek combat with a retreating adversary force, which was the overall war situation since 1942.

Many other aspects indicated that the best option for a military force overseas was an air force unit. One important consideration was that there would be a lower number of people participating in training in the U.S. and in the operations overseas. This reduced the chances of incidents that could affect the program, and contributed to reduce the expected amount of casualties, which, combat experience showed, were higher for ground forces. In addition, there was the experience in the U.S. of the organization and training of a Brazilian aerial unit that fought in the Mediterranean Theater of Operations.

The coordination resulted in the organization of a Mexican squadron, which later became the operational unit of the Mexican Expeditionary Air Force. Because of this coordination, on July 1944, Mexico organized a group to receive advanced training in the U.S. The group developed around the Mexican Air Force's existing 201st Air Squadron, augmented with personnel selected from different army and air force organizations.[5]

Organization and proficiency were key considerations during the organization of the squadron. The unit's organization was to be the same as a P-47 squadron in the United States Army Air Forces, in accordance to the corresponding tables of organization. The required standards of proficiency were identical to those of the same type of unit in the American Air Force.[6] These considerations guided the planning of the training and the requirements of the trainees for the ground and flight echelons. Coordination in the J.M.U.S.D.C. allowed agreement on a training plan for the fighter squadron, presented on July 10, 1944.[7] The plan considered approximately forty-two officers and 249 enlisted men, most of them fluent in English, if possible to arrive to Randolph Field, Texas, not later than July 25, 1944. Training included three broad areas:

1. Individual training: During five weeks on different bases, starting August 1, 1944.
2. Unit training: For two months on Pocatello Air Base, Idaho, from September 10 to November 10, 1944. In P-47 aircraft under supervision of Commanding General 2nd Air Force, and according to Standard 10-1-1.
3. Replacement training: If necessary, to start four months prior to the date required.

After January 1945, when the governments of Mexico and the U.S. reached an agreement regarding the participation of the Mexican squadron overseas, the J.M.U.S.D.C. also coordinated details for the employment of the force. The agreement established the participation of the Mexican squadron, accompanied by a senior officer and a small staff group. The squadron and adjutant personnel were to be handled as an integral part of the U.S. Army, with exceptions in the command, administration, expenses, and equipment and supply.[8]

The command and control coordination are particularly important due to the terms of the agreement. The commander of the squadron had been a Mexican colonel, and it did not represent any problem during training. However, the Mexican Congress approval for the participation of a force overseas and the terms of the agreement with the U.S. government for such participation required changes.

The regular command line for an American P-47 Squadron, normally commanded by a major or a captain, was a fighter group headed usually by a colonel or lieutenant colonel. The rank of the commander of the 201st Fighter Squadron was higher than usual, a normal designation for independent forces, but unnecessary for the agreed structure. Since the squadron would be operating under tactical tasking from a U.S. fighter group, it was necessary to appoint a new commander. A Mexican officer, qualified to command in accordance with the standards applied for selection of a commander for a fighter squadron in the U.S. Army, was to be in command of the Squadron. As a result, Captain Radamés Gaxiola Andrade was appointed for this position after the creation of the Mexican Expeditionary Air Force.[9]

The Mexican government, given the importance that this force represented for Mexico and in accordance to the nature of its mission, created the Mexican Expeditionary Air Force. This organization was the squadron's superior unit overseas, except in tactical tasking. The commander of the M.E.A.F. was the senior Mexican officer accompanying the squadron, and he represented the Mexican Army in matters pertaining to the squadron. The Mexican government appointed for this position Colonel Antonio Cárdenas Rodríguez, the previous commander of the 201st Fighter Squadron. His responsibility included to further the administrative efficiency of the Mexican Expeditionary Air Force and foster good relations with other United Nations troops. He organized a small staff group to assist the training and operations of the 201st Squadron.

Colonel Cárdenas received instructions from Mexico's Secretary of Defense on March 1945, regarding the Mexican Expeditionary Air Force mission performance overseas. They contemplated a variety of details, including organization, command, legal and disciplinary aspects, administration, logistics, payment, and communications. These instructions established the organization of the Mexican Expeditionary Air Force, which included command and staff, the 201st Fighter Squadron, and replacements.

The J.M.U.S.D.C. also coordinated the Mexican Expeditionary Air Force deployment to the South West Pacific Area (S.W.P.A.). The Mexican government preferred to participate in the liberation of the Philippines, due to the historical and cultural connections between both nations. This decision proved beneficial beyond the combat aspect, since the Mexican Expeditionary Air Force personnel also became a valuable social contact with the Spanish-speaking Filipinos.[10]

See Appendix I for Executive Order 9080 and a transcription of the agreement.

Creation of
the 201st Fighter Squadron

Members selected to serve with the new *Grupo de Perfecdonamiento Aemautico* that later became the Mexican Expeditionary Air Force came from all occupations and all regions of the nation. The candidates came from towns from the Rio Grande to the Guatemalan border. Corporal Ramiro Bastarrochia Gamboa was an administrative clerk came from the state of Yucatan. Sergeant First Class Pedro Martínez de la Concha was a mechanic who came from La Paz, Baja California. They came from the ancient city of Durango, from Cuidad Juárez across the Rio Grande, from Matamoros, and from tiny Colima on the Pacific coast.[1]

Mexico City contributed most of the ground crewmembers. Armament clerk Rubén Silva Richards studied at the Republic of Paraguay University before enlisting in the army. Second Sergeant Daniel Grajeda Gómez worked as a reporter for the *Mexico City Herald*, an English-language newspaper, and Corporal Guillermo García González, a squadron cook, formerly worked in a downtown Mexico City bakery. The professional cadre included men like Sergeant First Class Luis Mondragón Hoyos, an eleven-year veteran of military service. Manuel Alcantar Torres, a U.S. paratrooper with combat drops in Casablanca, Bizerte, and Sicily, asked for and received an honorable discharge from the U.S. Army in order to join the Mexican air squadron. Others left civilian jobs to join the group.[2]

Under the watchful eye of President Ávila Camacho, Mexico selected 300 to serve in the squadron. The group included thirty-six pilots and the remainder were the ground personnel—both officers and enlisted. Approximately two-thirds of the pilots had previously received flying instruction in the United States before joining the squadron. Scholarships offered by the United States allowed many Mexican pilots to receive valuable training in the U.S. Army and Navy Air Corps. Other pilot members received primary, basic, and advanced flight training in Mexico. Several were senior-rated pilots, with many having logged from 800 to 3,000 hours of flying time.[3]

Mexico City native Captain Radamés Gaxiola Andrade, whose father was a Mexican Army general and his uncle a former Minister of National Economics, was one of the first pilots selected. He attended primary and secondary schools in Los Angeles. Besides Spanish, he spoke fluent English, Portuguese, and Italian. In 1936, he graduated from the *Colegio Militar* (Mexican Military Academy). After serving a year as an officer in an infantry battalion, he transferred to a Mexican flight training school and graduated in 1939. That same year, he came to the United States for graduate flight training at Randolph and Kelly fields where he completed the U.S. Air Force courses. He returned to Mexico to serve as a flight instructor and test pilot. Mexican Air Force Chief General Salinas selected Captain Gaxiola to fly him to England and the European fronts after accepting General Arnold's invitation to visit a theater of war. At the time he became a member of the group, his cumulative flying time exceeded 3,000 hours, mostly in United States Army and Navy aircraft.[4]

The assignment of Mexico City-native Carlos Garduño Núñez as a member of the Grupo came late in the pilot selection. In 1936, at the age of fourteen, he entered the *Colegio Militar*, graduating three and a half years later as a second lieutenant. The army assigned Garduño to the infantry. Although at that time army regulations stipulated that an officer could not transfer to another service branch, this young officer soon secured an appointment to the Military School of Aviation.[5] Garduño never attended the Military School of Aviation. Within a few weeks after this appointment, his fluency in the English language earned him a flight training scholarship at Randolph Field, San Antonio, Texas. He learned English at an early age. Later as a nine-year-old exchange student in Los Angeles, California, Garduño added to his proficiency in English. He was one of the first among the very few Mexican citizens who came to the United States to train to fly with the U.S. Army Air Corps. Previously other Mexican pilots came to train in the United States, but only to complete specialization courses.[6] After successfully completing a rigorous three-week examination, nineteen-year-old Second Lieutenant Carlos Garduño came to Texas for nine months of flight training. For final and advanced training, Garduño and this class moved across town to Kelly Air Force base.[7]

Graduating August 6, 1942, Carlos Garduño received his silver wings and diploma. His dream of being a pilot became a reality. During the graduation ceremony, Mexican Air Force Colonel Eliseo Matin Del Campo removed the silver Air Corps' wings from his tunic, replacing them with wings of the Mexican Air Force. He then informed Garduño of his promotion to a first lieutenant flying pilot in the Mexican Air Force.[8] A short time later, to upgrade his flying skills, the Air Corps transferred Garduño to Kelly Field for training in twin-engined aircraft.[9]

After Garduño completed his flight instructor school at Randolph and twin-engined training at Kelly, he asked Colonel Fierro to transfer him to March Field, Riverside, California, for combat aircraft training. Because he had qualified to fly twin-engined aircraft, the Army Air Corps assigned him to a squadron flying twin-engined P-38 fighters.[10]

Two weeks after arriving at March Field, Riverside, California, Garduño created a fuss in Washington. Colonel Fierro had authorized him to remain in the United States despite orders to the contrary from Washington. Then the Mexican Army got involved. The U.S. Army Air Corps had never approved the training of Mexican tactical pilots in the United States and the Mexican Army insisted that he return to Mexico. Soon Washington and the Mexican Army prevailed and First Lieutenant Carlos Garduño went home.[11]

Back in Mexico City in November 1942, Garduño reported to Balbuena Air Base, his new duty station. He trained pilots to fly the thirty-six AT-6 aircraft that Mexico had obtained from the United States. He directed a training program of only six flying hours. Later his superiors reduced the training time that to only three hours and thirty minutes. From November 1942 to January 1943, he trained over thirty pilots.[12]

In January 1943, the Air Force transferred Garduño to patrol duty, flying out of Veracruz, Mexico. The Mexican Air Force patrolled the Gulf up to a distance of 10 miles from the coast and sometimes it escorted ships. When on submarine patrol, the pilots flew as far as 50 miles from the coast. The patrol's flightpath followed a line from Tampico south to the middle of the Yucatan channel, Point Y, off the coast of the island of Cozumel, where the Cuban Air Force took over. Mexican pilots flew every day. Garduño served as the instrument instructor for his squadron during his duty in Veracruz through October 1943.[13]

In November, Garduño returned to the United States for an undisclosed special assignment. Six other pilots accompanied him: Julio Cal y Mayor Sauz, Graco Ramirez Garrido, Carlos Cervantes, Fernando Hernández Vega, Crisóforo Salido Grijalva, and Jacobo Estrada Luna. Except for Carlos Cervantes, these pilots later became members of the 201st Squadron. From Mexico City, they went first to Ensenada, Baja, California, where they stayed for five weeks without knowing their final destination. Finally, they received orders transferring them to the North Island Naval Base at San Diego, California.[14]

After the seven Mexican pilots arrived at the naval air base in San Diego, no one knew exactly what to do with them. The commander of the 11th Naval District at San Diego, Marine pilot Major Mike Sampas, a Boston native, was the coordinator between the Mexican pilots and the Naval District. Sampas took an instant liking of the seven pilots and accepted the responsibility for their training. Major Sampas placed them in a U.S. Naval SBD dive-bombing squadron, making them go through the entire dive-bombing syllabus. They remained in training at San Diego for eight months under his strict disciplinary routine. Although a stern taskmaster, Sampas provided them with special living quarters on North Island and many of social activities, making their stay pleasant and enjoyable.[15]

After the Mexican pilots finished the combat dive-bombing training course, Sampas notified the commander of the Naval Air Force, U.S. Pacific Fleet, that they were ready for deployment to combat. To his surprise, all were incorporated into the Mexican 201st Fighter Squadron and sent to Texas for retraining.[16]

After finishing their dive-bombing training, the pilot group remained in California and joined a U.S. squadron undergoing the same training. At a San Diego air show, an announcer informed the audience that the seven pilots would be the first representatives of Mexico to go to war in the Pacific. Eventually, Colonel Antonio Cárdenas arrived to take charge of the squadron. They later returned to Mexico City to join the 201st Squadron.[17]

Mexico maintained several flight training schools. One was located in Monterrey, where Presidents Roosevelt and Ávila Camacho met in April 1943. During the visit, President Roosevelt granted scholarships for seventeen Mexican citizens to go to the United States for flight training at the Corpus Christi, Texas Naval Flight School. The Aviation School in Monterrey sent eleven students to study under this program. After eleven months' training at Corpus Christi, they graduated as United States Navy pilots. Six of these, Joaquín Ramírez Vilchis, Amadeo Castro Almanza, Pablo Rivas Martínez, Javier Martínez Valle, José Espinoza Fuentes, and Héctor Espinoza Galván, subsequently became pilots in the 201st Squadron.[18]

While in Corpus Christi learning to fly, one student pilot, Héctor Espinoza Galván, wanted to get married. First, he had to obtain permission from Washington, D.C.—an easy problem to overcome. His next and more formidable obstacle concerned bringing his bride-to-be to Corpus Christi or obtaining a leave of absence and going to Monterrey, Nuevo Leen, where his intended wife lived. However, she could not come to Corpus Christi and he could not go to Monterrey. The never-ending ingenuity of the military mind to accomplish something personal, especially during a time of war, came into full focus here. Héctor Espinoza Galván and Oralia García were married over the telephone by proxy on June 15, 1943. He was twenty-six years old and she was twenty. Oralia, who spoke no English, was an American citizen. She was born in Laredo, Texas, during a visit by her Mexican mother.[19]

Another Corpus Christi-trained pilot, Joaquín Ramirez Vilchis, a Mexico City native, came from a distinguished family. His father, Colonel José Maria de la Torre, served in the forces of General Venustiano Carranza during the revolution in 1914. In 1932, at the age of nineteen, Joaquín received an appointment to the Mexican Military College. Graduating four years later as second lieutenant of cavalry, the army stationed him in Guadalajara where he remained four years. During his last year there, he taught school at the college. He then made a Mexican goodwill mission to South America in March 1940. Returning from the mission, Vilchis decided that he wanted to learn to fly airplanes and enrolled in the Aviation School in Monterrey, Nuevo Leon.[20]

Amadeo Castro Almanza was born in Veracruz. His father was Spanish and his mother Irish. An alumnus of Mexico's *Colegio Militar*, he was one of the six to graduate as United States Navy pilots.[21]

Justino Reyes Retana came from Cuidad Juárez. After finishing his training at the Military Aviation School and receiving his wings, the army assigned him as a second lieutenant. Reyes served as pilot for Russian Ambassador Constantine Oumansky for six months. Just before a scheduled trip to South America with the ambassador, he received notice of his induction into the new Mexican Air Force unit, later known as the 201st Squadron.[22] The background of the enlisted men selected is no less worthy. Sergeant Pedro Martínez Pérez, born in Nuevo Laredo, Tamaulipas, had military family ties. Two of his uncles had served as generals under Venustiano Carranza during the revolution. Another uncle served as a captain of cavalry. Early in May 1942, Martínez joined the cavalry, and six months later, he transferred into the air force. One and a half years of training in the Air Force Mechanic School gave him the knowledge and ability to be a select member of the new *Grupo de Perfecdonamiento Aemautico*.[23] Martínez epitomized the ideal soldier, disciplined and skilled in his field; he wore his uniform with pride and loved his country, his flag, and the Air Force.[24]

Cervantes volunteered for service, anticipating that with his educational qualifications, the army would place him in the pilot training program. Instead, the army inducted him as a second sergeant of administration and placed him in the office of national defense. He never entered the pilot training program. However, the army did transfer him to the newly formed air force squadron and he became secretary to the commanding officer, serving in this capacity until the 201st Squadron disbanded. Cervantes remained in the air force after the war ended, later received a commission, and retired as a captain.[25]

Other civilians and army personnel, without formal flight training, enlisted in the newly formed air force unit, thinking that they would be trained to become pilots. None of their expectations came true. The new organization only considered those previously qualified to fly became pilots in the *Grupo de Perfecdonamiento*. By July 20, 1944, the squadron was complete and ready to depart for training in the U.S. However, before leaving, they passed in review for President Camacho. In his farewell speech, Camacho said that he came to greet them, not to tell them goodbye. He announced that they were to attend flight-training courses in the United States to perfect their skills. If the expedition went to a theater of war, he hoped to come see them personally. If he could not visit them, he said the Secretary of Defense would do so. "We are the allies of other nations," he reminded them, "who are fighting to the death for liberty in a war that has not touched Mexican land." "You must remember," he said, "that you are the depositories of the dignity of this nation and its army. Carry the flag of the Mexican people very high."[26]

Early in the morning of July 24, six special first-class railroad cars stood by at Buena Vista station, ready to transport 300 Mexican squadron personal to Laredo, Texas. Publicity about the departure drew a large crowd. People massed on the station platforms to witness this unique and historic event. Ministers of the national defense, commanders and officers of the army, many ordinary civilians, as well as many relatives of the men, came to see them off. Captain Manuel Cervantes wrote in his memoirs:

> There was sadness amongst all this enthusiasm, tears from the mothers, sisters, sons, acquaintances and friends.... There was the ever-present advice from the mothers,

"we're praying for you, be as good a soldier as your fathers were in the Revolution, remember everywhere you go that you're a Mexican."[27]

The train departed Buena Vista station at 8:30 a.m., headed north toward Laredo, Texas. The trip, which normally required ten hours, took thirty-six, as the train stopped in important towns along the route to allow the populace to see the squadron. The torch of patriotism burned brightly as large, emotional crowds met and displayed their admiration and respect for the troops. In Monterrey, although in failing health, Division General Eulogio Ortiz met the train—much to the delight of the airmen.[28] Another display of public emotion greeted the men as they arrived in Nuevo Laredo early in the evening of July 25. Well-wishers lined the route as the squadron members marched from the train station to the international bridge.[29] A commission of Mexican senators and deputies of congress had flown to this border city to honor them. The demonstrations of support pleased the airmen. A sacred role in the nation's history awaited them in the future.[30] Their next destination was San Antonio, Texas.[31]

Organization and Personnel of the 201st Fighter Squadron

Squadron Organization

	Flight Echelon		Ground Echelon	
	Officers	Enlisted	Officers	Enlisted
Command	3	2	1	6
Medical Service	1	1	0	3
Subsistence (Food)	1	17	0	0
Administrative Supply	1	1	0	3
Transportation	0	0	1	9
Ordnance	1	9	1	19
Communications	1	8	1	24
Engineering/Maintenance	3	8	0	28
Technical Supply	1	1	0	3
Intelligence	2	2	1	1
Operations	3	2	0	3
Flight "A"	7	13	0	12
Flight "B"	7	11	9	11
Flight "C"	7	11	0	11
Flight "D"	7	12	0	11
Replacement Pilots	15	0	0	0
TOTAL:	60	98	5	144

Total Squadron members: 307[1]

Squadron Pilots (Command Section)

Colonel P. A. Antonio Cárdenas Rodríguez, Commander; First Captain P. A. Radamés Gaxiola Andrade; Second Captain Pablo L. Rivas Martínez

The squadron was divided into four flights, which were lettered, "A" to "D."

Flight "A" Pilots
Captain Roberto Legorreta Sicilia was the flight commander. The pilots were Lieutenants P. A. Fernando Hernández Vega, Carlos Varela Landini, and Graco Ramirez Garrido Alvarado and Second Lieutenants P. A. José Luis Pratt Ramos, José Miguel Uriarte Aguilar, and David Cerón Bedolla.

Flight "B" Pilots
Lieutenant P. A. Carlos Garduño Núñez was the flight commander. The pilots were Lieutenants Julio Cal Y Mayor Sauz, and Reynaldo Perez Gallardo and Second Lieutenants P. A. Miguel Moreno Arreola, Práxedis López Ramos, Fausto Vega Santander, and Angel Sanchez Rebollo.

Flight "C" Pilots
Lieutenant P. A. Héctor Espinosa Galván was the flight commander. The pilots were Joaquín Ramírez Vilchis, Carlos Rodríguez Corona, and Amador Sámano Piña and Second Lieutenants P.A. Raúl García Mercado, Guillermo García Ramos, and Gabriel Torres Gonzáles.

Flight "D" Pilots
Lieutenant P. A. Amadeo Castro Almanza was the flight commander. The pilots were Jacobo Estrada Luna and José Luis Barbosa Cerda and Second Lieutenants P. A. Mario López Portillo, Roberto Urías Avelleyra, Jaime Zenizo Rojas, and Justino Reyes Retana.

Replacement Pilots
The replacement pilots comprised Second Lieutenant P. A. Manuel Farías Rodríguez, Emilio Enríquez Ruiz, David Cerón Bedolla, Javier Martínez Valle, Raúl Maciel Peña, David Mendoza Márquez, Rafael Lizardi Formento, Reynaldo Pérez Gallardo, Carlos Garduño Núñez, José Miguel Uriarte Aguilar, Miguel Moreno Arreola, Julio Cal y Mayor Sauz, José Espinosa Fuentes, José Luis Pratt Ramos, and Crisóforo Salido Grijalva.[2]

Other Personnel in the 201st Squadron
Technical Officer: Lieutenant P. A. Jesús Carranza Herández.
   Armament Officer: Second Lieutenant Francisco Viveros García.
   Meteorology Officer: Second Lieutenant Luis López Molina.
   Communications Officer: Lieutenant Raúl Rodríguez Carreón.

Intelligence Officers: Second Captain Jesús Blanco Ledezma and Lieutenant César Velazco Cerón.

Statistics Officer: Lieutenant Armando Rodríguez Contreras.

Administrative Officers: Second Captain Edmundo Santamaría Velasco, Lieutenant Joaquín Alvarez de la O., and Second Lieutenant Samuel Cueto Ramírez.

Radar Officer: Second Lieutenant Luis Hurtado Tinajero.

Draftsman: Sergeant Second Class Armando González Guzmán.[3]

Office Clerks: Sergeants Second Class Armando Ramírez Campillo, Jesús Guerrero Uribe, Javier Armenta Sánchez, Heriberto Cañete López, Salvador Rangel Urrutia, Salvador Soto Uribe, Carlos Garay García, José Luis Trejo Patiño, Ramiro Bastarrachea Gamboa, José Ponce Olmos, Hugo Seaman Jiménez, José Torres Vara, Jorge Vázquez Vega, Ignacio Gómez Estrada, Ernesto Martínez Trujillo, Rafael Martínez Vivanco, Mario Luis Higuera Rábago, Manuel Cervantes Ramos, Othon Gutiérrez Medina, Ismael Pérez Becerra Ernesto Hernández May, Rafael Acuña Aguilar, and Enrique Domínguez Rendón; Corporal Ricardo Tinoco Lima; and Privates Martínez Sánchez, Antonio Henríquez Guerrero, Baudelio Rodríguez Martínez, Rubén Silva Richards, and Juan Villafaña Avila.[4]

Armorers: Sergeant First Class Robertó Wellhes Guerrero; Sergeants Second Class Alfredo Boybin Sánchez, Enrique Arenas Noreña, Julio Solórzano López, Juan López Vilchis, Pedro Guerra García, Juan Bautista Báez, Ramón García Vega, Guillermo Reyna Sánchez, Carlos Ortiz Moreno, David Lozano Hernández, Genaro Jacinto Orduña, Mario Salcedo Cruces, José Hernández Bailón, Jesús Arrona Calderón, Andrés Ramírez Maines, José Uriza López, Fortino González Gudiño, José Luis Rubio del Riego, Angel Muñoz Nicolás, Manuel Estrada Sosa, Alfonso Cuéllar Ponce de León, Rubén Ledezma Yáñez, Silvestre San Vincente Ovando, Rogelio Salcedo Saldaña, Raúl Alvarez Ortega, José Alvarez Morales, Alfonso Real Martínez, Adolfo Ortiz Jiménez, Eduardo Aguiluz Rosas, Fernando Juárez, Jiménez, Gilberto Escalante Arias, Salvador Flores Sandoval, Juan Vázquez Guarneros, and Ignacio Espinoza Contreras; and Corporals Carlos Torres Vallejo, Jorge Estrada Ochoa, Justo Becerril Sosa, Sergio Morales Bernal, José Muñoz Alvear, Ignacio Fragosa Selilla, Jesús Pérez Chávez, Fernando Miranda Gómez, Urbano Díaz Treviño, Alfredo Vega Fernández.

Radio Mechanics: Sergeants First Class Guadalupe González Herández, Felipe Yépez Martínez, Pedro Ramírez Corona, Gregorio Ramírez Lawre, Salvador Rueda Gallardo, Daniel Ramos Méndez, Fidel Correa Valenzuela, and Leonardo Soto Rodríguez.

Air Force Radio Operator: Sergeant Second Class Gilberto de la Rosa Alvarez.

Mexican Air Force Radio Operator/Mechanics: Sergeants Second Class Maximiliano Gutiérrez Marín, Horacio Castilleja Albarrán, Héctor G. Gómez Oaxaca, Enrique C. Ortiz Jiménez, and Carlos Graillet Colorado.

Radio Operator/Mechanics: Sergeants Second Class Elías Francisco Díaz Aguayo, Raúl Gamas Quevedo, José de J. Solís Tapia, Juan A. Gonzáles Báez, Humberto García Vázquez, Agustín F. Martínez Cortés, Joaquín Jonás Silva, Zamora, Francisco Rodríquez Castañeda, and Carlos Centeno Medina and Corporals Gerardo Díaz Bolaños, Recendil

Vázquez Magaña, Luis Mandujano Gallegos, Héctor Tello Pineda, Luis Jorge Alfonso López, and Luis Jorge Oviedo Villa Alfredo García Orocio.[5]

Telegraph Machine Mechanic: Sergeant Second Class Luis Gallegos Mendoza

Telephone Lines/Telegraph Repairman: Corporal Raúl Vargas Gómez

Airplane Engine Mechanics: Sergeants First Class Luis Soro Servín, Manuel Espinoza Gonzáles, Filemón Vargas Jiménez, Luis Gonzáles Sánchez, José A. Galindo Alfonseca, León Mondragón Hoyos, Luciano Vázquez Santibáñez, José Gutierrez Gallegos, Miguel A. Chávez Delgado, Luis Mondragón Hoyos, Agustín Vallejo Montiel, Jesús Herrera Zayas, Rubén Celis Peña, Aurelio Becerra Suárez, Salvador Vázquez Morales, Alfonso Carbajal Aransolo, Alberto Camacho García, Armando Grejeda Gómez, Carlos Gálvez Pérez, Pedro Martínez de la Concha, Teodoro Carrillo García, Leonardo Beltrán Gutiérrez, Luis Martínez Miranda, Francisco de la Vega Guzmán, Fernando Vergara García, Agustín Velasco Alegría, Juvenal Delgado Meza, Miguel Martínez Márquez, Rosendo Alarcón Santana, Onésimo Miranda Spíndola, José Blanco Talavera, Carlos Beltrán Gutiérrez, Javier Córdoba Ruiz, Jesús Silva Ruelas, Eduardo Moreno Brillas, Luis Pérez Lara, Francisco Esquivel Reyes; Corporals Bernardo Mendoza Hernández, Felipe Gonzáles Labastida, Eduardo Sánchez Ortiz, Oscar Hermosillo Ficachi, Julio Spíndola Miranda, Adolfo Ireta Martínez, Jesús Gutiérrez Figueroa, Carlos Colín Portilla, Genaro Romero Parra, Sergio Carrillo Díaz, Ramiro Pérez Calvillo, Pedro Martínez Pérez, Gustavo Toledo Belmont, Erasmo Meza Rivera, Gilberto Tovar García, Juan de Asco Betegui, Jesús Salas Olivas, Samuel Garrido Mendoza, and Wenceslao Martínez Vázquez.[6]

Airplane Sheet Metal Mechanics: Sergeants Second Class Joaquín Rodríguez Aldana, and Benito Rivera Aguilar.

Warehouse Helpers: Sergeants Second Class Daniel Grajeda Gómez, Luis Guzmán Reveles, José Rayón Varela; Corporals Carlos Mendoza Jáuregui, Javier Ibáñez Carrillo, and Agustín Resendis Mireles.

Airplane Electrical Specialist: Sergeants Second Class Andrés Gonzáles Herrera, Eduardo G. Peredo Muñoz, and Gustavo Díaz Campomanes.

Airplane Instrument Specialists: Sergeants Second Class Joaquín Sáncnez Montes, and Héctor Zapeda Vázquez and Corporal José Bonilla Domínguez

Airplane Propeller Specialists: Sergeant First Class Gonzalo Retana Guevara; Sergeant Second Class Abel Martínez Hernández; and Corporal Enrique Molina Pérez.

Structure and Coating Specialist: Sergeant First Class Angel García Martínez.

General Mechanic: Sergeant First Class Miguel Castillo Torres.

Parachute Rigger and Repairer: Corporal Manuel Alcantar Torres.

Welder: Sergeant First Class Eusebio Alvarez Huerta.[7]

Bakers/Cooks: Sergeant First Class Frederico Arreola Romero; Sergeants Second Class Dionisio Ledezma Espinoza, Franciso Bautista González, Leandro Avila Sánchez, Eugenio Pérez Herández, and José Roque Huerta; and Corporals Luis Ramírez Pérez, Guillermo García González, and Franciso Díaz Merás.

Photo Lab Technicians: Second Lieutenant Ramón Caracas Enríquez and Sergeant First Class César Gonzáles Mata.

Motorized Equipment Mechanics: Sergeants Second Class Jorge García Herrera, and José León Gómez Domínguez and Corporal Juan López Murillo.

Motorized Equipment Operators: Corporal Manuel Guerrero Muñoz; Privates Felipe Soto Martínez, and Angel Bocanegra del Castillo.

Heavy Motorized Equipment Operators: Corporals Félix Zaragoza González, Jesús Segura Ríos, Jorge Serralde Ganot, Arnulfo Bonilla García, Privates Gibberto Correa Juárez, and Manuel Pérez Jaques.

Carpenters: Sergeants First Class Felipe Manterola Cruz and Pedro Cárdenas Pérez.

Painter: Sergeant Second Class José Sánchez García.[8]

Ordinance Assistants: Sergeant First Class Aristeo Díaz Flores; Corporal Fidel Borunga Salcedo, Privates First Class Miguel Toledo López, and Bernardo Gómez de los Santos; and Privates Isauro Esparza Hinojosa, Leoncio Pérez Juárez, Raúl Esteva Aquino, Diego López Félix, Herminio Sánchez Luis, Mario Zamora Aguilar, Enrigqu Moedano Gómez Ugarte, and Domingo Sarmiento Herrera.

Surgical Technicians: Second Lieutenant Pablo E. Herrasti Dondé; Corporal (Medicine) Manuel Rico Badillo and Corporal (Surgery) Higinio Monroy Alvarado; and Private (Medicine) Alfonso Vega Gómez and Private (Surgery) David Méndez Aburto.

Artillery Weapons Mechanics: Sergeant First Class Carlos Obregón Martínez, Neftalí González Corona, Enrique Barragán Aguila, and Jesús Jurado Pulido.

Ammunition Handlers: Corporals Jesús Rivera Arce, Luis Jiménez Sánchez, David Santana García, Rafael Valdez Valleza, Alfredo Mendoza Mendoza, Eligio Barajas Espinosa, Antonio Esclante Flotes, Rodolfo Ambriz Martínez, Hilario Avila Curiel, Manuel Munguía Moreno, and Lino Morales Guadarrama.

Chemical Decontamination Technicians: Corporals Raymundo Acosta Ordaz and Juan Reynoso Fuentes.[9]

Personnel of the Staff of the M.E.A.F. assigned to the "V" Fighter Command, June–July 1945

Lieutenant Colonel E. M. Alfonso Gurza Farfan, Secret Section; Major Enrique Sandoval Castarrica, A2 section; Major P. Guillermo Linage Olguin, A4 section; and Chaplain Roberto Salido Beltran, A3 section.

Pilot Replacement Group: Major Rafael J. Suarez Peralta.

American U.S.A.A.F. Personnel assigned to the 201st Mexican Fighter Squadron in the Philippines

Officers
Lieutenant Colonel Arthur W. Kellong, assigned to the command and staff of the M.E.A.F.; Lieutenant Sheridan Kenny, Jr., assigned engineering officer 201st Fighter

Squadron; Lieutenant William L. Kester, operations officer 201st Fighter Squadron; Lieutenant Peter Economy, communications officer 201st Fighter Squadron, *aide-de-camp* and interpreter to Colonel Cárdenas; Lieutenant Howard B. Riggs, pilot 201st Fighter Squadron; Lieutenant John J. Haley, pilot 201st Fighter Squadron, 310th Fighter Squadron/58th Fighter Group, and later 201st Fighter Squadron.

Enlisted Personnel

Technical Sergeant John S. Tsaguris; Staff Sergeant Conrad C. L. Cuellar; Staff Sergeant Grant J. Knechtel; Staff Sergeant Cornelius Orzatti; and Sergeant William E. Miller.[10]

6

Overcoming Discrimination

Before the War

Mexicans were a minority in the United States since before the Mexican–American War (1846–48). Their numbers greatly increased between 1900 and 1930 when about 1 million Mexicans moved north of the border due to a range of push and pull factors.[1] Mexicans were pushed north by the situation in their home country, including grinding poverty, attributable to regressive wages and the lackluster education system, and the tumultuous Mexican Revolution (1910–20). Mexicans were also pulled by shortages of inexpensive and unskilled labor required for the growth of agribusiness, mining, and the railroad construction.[2] Life was difficult for the new immigrants who often had the lowest-paid and most-difficult manual-labor jobs. Although Mexican-Americans were largely spared the worst of official racism directed towards African-Americans in the Jim Crow era, they were not fully accepted as white, and consequently experienced extensive discrimination. Mexican-Americans faced segregation enforced by local ordinances in real estate and the practices of local businessmen, unionization was restricted, and low quality and levels of education due to segregated schools. About 42 percent of children received no education at all.[3]

The Great Depression magnified and strengthened their sense of isolation and separation.[4] "Times were hard," Mexican-American Joe Henry Lazarine said when describing the difficulty of family life during the depression years.[5] Mexicans were blamed for unemployment, leading to favoritism towards white workers and fewer job opportunities. In one case, Kansas Governor Clyde Reed sent a letter to railways urging for all Mexican workers to be fired.[6] Mexicans were also targeted as "illegals" in a new spate of anti-immigrant sentiment.[7] This led to the forced and voluntary repatriation of an estimated 400,000 Mexicans in the 1930s.[8]

The Wartime Experience

As proud loyalists, Mexican-Americans enthusiastically supported the war effort. "We are children of the United States. We will defend her," the Spanish-speaking Congress declared in their official communication.[9] This extensive support came both on the home front and in military action.

The war effort necessitated rapid mass mobilization and production, creating substantial new job opportunities in industry and agriculture that dramatically reduced unemployment.[10] Initially, jobs were exclusively offered to whites; however, soon, demand for labor outstripped supply and hundreds of thousands of Mexican-Americans were hired.[11] Mexican-Americans had the opportunity, especially in the case of urban factory workers, to earn wages equal to those of white workers for the first time.[12] In the shipyards alone, Mexican labor increased from zero in 1941 to over 17,000 by 1944. The demand for labor also provided the first opportunities for women to get higher-paying jobs outside of limited domestic work.[13] The necessity for labor also led to the importation of additional temporary agricultural workers from Mexico under the Bracero Program (see Appendix IX for a brief description of the program), totaling over 168,000 people between 1942 and 1945.[14] Mexican-American groups, including the Spanish-speaking members of Congress, opposed this program on the basis that it often exploited Mexican workers, pushed down wages for already existent Mexican-American labor, and made the challenge of assimilation more difficult.[15]

Mexican-American groups supported the war effort in other ways, including collecting gift packages for soldiers and holding rallies to encourage the purchase of War Bonds, effectively loaning money to the government.[16] This led to positive publicity, including a front-page article in the *Los Angeles Times* under the headline "Racial Groups to Buy Bonds."[17] The necessities of the war provided substantial opportunities for economic advancement and mobility, and for the many able to take advantage of them, their lives improved.[18] Moreover, despite the negatives of the Bracero Program, it did provide the Mexican government leverage to petition for better treatment of Mexican-Americans.[19] Mexican-Americans were also able to use their contribution to the war to lobby for recognition of rights. American local, state, and federal governments and public service agencies responded more positively than ever before, albeit partly from the necessity to improve morale and strengthen diplomatic relations with Mexico.[20] In a massive step, the Texas legislature unanimously passed a resolution that said Mexican-Americans were "entitled to the full and equal accommodations, advantages, facilities, and privileges of all public places of business or amusement." However, there were significant limits to the provision of help. The Texas resolution did not have the enforcement of law, and much of the reason for poverty was seen as self-imposed, not the fault of discrimination.[21]

Anti-Mexican sentiment is a negative attitude to people of Mexican descent, Mexican culture, and/or accents of Mexican-Spanish most commonly found in the United States. In general, it is closely associated with Mexican and American independence wars and the struggle over the dispute in the southwestern territories that once belonged to Spain through the establishment of building Catholic missions. This eventually would lead to war between the two nations and the defeat of Mexico, which came with a great loss of territory. In the twentieth century, anti-Mexican sentiment continued to grow after the Zimmermann Telegram incident between the Mexican government during the Mexican Revolution and the German Empire during World War I.[22]

Mexican citizens had been traveling north for economic opportunity since the Spanish Conquest, but during the Great Depression, the United States adopted a series of policies directed at restricting Mexican access to its soil. There was also an official policy of repatriation directed at families who had come to the United States during the Mexican revolution of the early twentieth century. The U.S. deported over 500,000 people to Mexico during the 1930s. With the advent of World War II, the United States was suddenly confronted with the need to replace millions of laborers who were now to be inducted into the armed forces or, at the least, retrained and relocated to work on defense-related industry.[23]

The deported Mexican laborers were now urgently needed back in the United States, and Mexico agreed to allow its citizens to travel to America to work in nearly every state of the Union. One notable exception was Texas, which declined to participate in the program, preferring to institute something it called an "Open Border Policy." For its part, Mexico declined to send any laborers to Texas, citing abuse of its citizens in that state. As many as 75,000 Mexican farmworkers and 50,000 railway workers were present in the United States at any time between 1942 and 1947. Each one of them arguably replaced a pair of boots now free to approach German or Japanese soil. The program was also of sufficient economic value that it continued well after the war was over and was not formally suspended until 1964.

Military Experience

Mexican-Americans were conscripted and volunteered to be part of the American military even before the declaration of war. As Richard Steele states: "… military service offered an honorable, even adventurous, alternative to a hardscrabble existence." Over half a million Mexican-Americans enlisted, almost a fifth of their population of 2,690,000. Proportionally, more Mexican-Americans served in combat divisions than any other ethnic group.[24] Military service suited Mexican-Americans well because of its emphasis on performance rather than race, and recognition for achievement not found in civilian life. Moreover, unlike African-Americans, they were not placed in segregated units, giving many the first opportunities for interaction on an equal footing with the white population. "There was no discrimination in the service," veteran Angel Zavala recalled, "because we were all the same and there was no difference."[25]

Proportionally, Mexican-Americans achieved the distinction of gaining more decorations for bravery in the battlefield than any other group. Marcario Garcia from

Texas became the first Mexican-American to receive a Congressional Medal of Honor for single-handedly disabling two enemy machine guns with complete disregard for his personal safety. Company "E" of the 141st Regiment of the 36th Texas Infantry Division, a largely Mexican-American company, was awarded three Medals of Honor, thirty-one Distinguished Service Crosses, twelve Legions of Merit, 492 Silver Stars, eleven Soldier's Medals, and 1,685 Bronze Stars. Spanish-American newspapers proudly celebrated Mexican-Americans being honored as Americans for the first time. For survivors, the military experience provided the various skills and access to allow for better engagement with American society.[26]

World War II had an enormous impact on Latinos in the United States, including Mexican- Americans. Mexican-Americans were drafted into or volunteered for the U.S. armed services, where they had the highest percentage of Congressional Medal of Honor winners of any minority in the United States.[27]

Hispanics not only served in ground and sea-bound combat units, they also distinguished themselves as fighter pilots and as bombardiers. In 1944, Puerto Rican aviators were sent to the Tuskegee Army Air Field in Tuskegee, Alabama, to train the famed 99th Fighter Squadron of the Tuskegee Airmen. The Tuskegee Airmen were the first African-American military aviators in the United States' armed forces. Puerto Ricans were also involved in clerical positions with the Tuskegee unit.[28]

During the 1930s, dance halls were popular venues for socializing, swing dancing, and easing the economic stress of the Great Depression. Nowhere was this truer than in the uptown Manhattan neighborhood of Harlem, home of the intellectual, social, and artistic explosion called the Harlem Renaissance. Style-conscious Harlem dancers began wearing loose-fitting clothes that accentuated their movements. Men donned baggy trousers with cuffs carefully tapered to prevent tripping; long jackets with heavily padded shoulders and wide lapels; long, glittering watch chains; and hats ranging from porkpies and fedoras to broad-brimmed sombreros. The image of these so-called "zoot suits" spread quickly and was popularized by performers such as Cab Calloway, who, in his *Hepster's Dictionary,* called the zoot suit, "the ultimate in clothes—the only totally and truly American civilian suit."[29]

As the zoot suit became more popular among young men in African-American, Mexican-American, and other minority communities, the clothes garnered a racist reputation. Affluent whites increasingly viewed Latino youths in California as *Pachucas* (a teenage youth who belongs to a street gang).

After the bombing of Pearl Harbor and the U.S. entry into World War II, wool and other textiles were subject to strict rationing. The U.S. War Production Board regulated the production of civilian clothing containing silk, wool, and other essential fabrics. Despite these wartime restrictions, many bootleg tailors in Los Angeles, New York, and elsewhere continued to make the popular zoot suits, which used large amounts of fabric. Service members and many other people, however, saw the oversized suits a flagrant and unpatriotic waste of resources. The local media was very happy to fan the flames of racism and moral outrage. On June 2, 1943, the *Los Angeles Times* reported:

Fresh in the memory of Los Angeles is last year's surge of gang violence that made the "zoot suit" a badge of delinquency. Public indignation bubbled up as warfare among organized bands of marauders, prowling the streets at night, brought a wave of assaults and finally murders.[30]

In 1943, with the United States was involved in World War II, the country was rocked on the home front. Thousands of Mexicans had migrated to the city of Los Angeles, California, in order to bolster the defensive effort of the United States. However, what followed instead was chaos as the Marines and sailors of United States attacked young Mexican-Americans wearing broad-shouldered drape jackets, balloon-leg trousers, and flamboyant hats.

The riots were mainly caused by the hostilities and fears that gripped Americans after the murder trial of "Sleepy Lagoon," where a young Latino man was killed in a *barrio*. This triggered several attacks in various cities of the United States.[31]

What exacerbated the problem was that most of the white Americans and service members had little to no knowledge of Mexican-American culture. The tension between Mexican-Americans and white Americans had been around for a long time, as Mexicans were generally classed as migrant workers and were discriminated against when it came to jobs in the country. [32]

The "Sleepy Lagoon Murder Case" dominated all the national news in 1942. Some Mexican-American teenagers who were from the 38th Street Gang were alleged to have murdered José Gallardo Díaz, who was discovered unconscious and dying on a road near a swimming hole (known as the Sleepy Lagoon) in Commerce, California, on the morning of August 2, 1942. Díaz was taken by ambulance to Los Angeles County General Hospital, where he died shortly afterwards, without regaining consciousness. The hospital's autopsy showed that he was inebriated from a party the previous night and had a fracture at the base of his skull. This might have been caused by repeated falls or an automobile accident. The cause of his death remains a mystery to this day. However, Los Angeles Police were quick to arrest seventeen Mexican-American youths as suspects. Despite insufficient evidence, the young men were held in prison, without bail, on charges of murder. The trial ended on January 13, 1943, under the supervision of Judge Charles W. Fricke. Nine of the defendants were convicted of second-degree murder and sentenced to serve time in San Quentin Prison. The rest of the suspects were charged with lesser offenses and incarcerated in the Los Angeles County Jail. The convictions were reversed on appeal in 1944 and this created further animosity between the white American community and Mexican-Americans. The police and the media presented all Mexican-American youth as gangsters, thugs, and hoodlums, which did not help matters at all.[33]

Tensions were reaching fever pitch levels between Mexican-American youth in the country. The zoot-suiters paraded around Los Angeles and were instantly recognizable by their clothes. This did not please the white military service members in the U.S. Army who believed that the Mexican youth were deliberately not following the rationing regulations. Due to the media sensationalizing the Mexican youth, there was mass hysteria and paranoia among the white Americans who frequently got into fights with Latinos in all the major cities across the United States.[34]

On June 4, 1943, around 200 U.S. Navy service members got into taxicabs and headed to the center of the Mexican settlement. The sailors confronted the zoot-suiters and actually assaulted them with clubs, then stripped them of their clothes and burned them in a pile. This kick-started the "Zoot-suit Riots" and all hell broke loose in Los Angeles.

The ensuing violence was some of the worst that has been seen in the United States in history, and the riots lasted for several days. There were thousands of servicemen marching down the streets, entering movie theatres and bars, and openly assaulting every young Latino or Mexican male. Police accompanied the servicemen but were ordered not to arrest any of them, and after several days of this madness, around 150 people were injured, and the police had arrested nearly 500 Latinos on charges related to vagrancy and rioting.[35]

The local press hailed the attacks by the servicemen, and described them as an act of cleansing, where Los Angeles was being cleared of hoodlums, thugs, and miscreants. The City Council of Los Angeles banned the wearing of zoot suits within the city, and the dress was turned into a badge of thuggery and hoodlumism. All sense of law and order in Los Angeles was lost as servicemen started viciously attacking everyone they met in zoot suits—even African-Americans were targeted. The situation got so bad that the Marine and Navy Corps had to intervene in order to stop the attacks, and actually declared Los Angeles to be off limits for military personnel. They declared that the sailors and servicemen had acted in self-defense, but it did little to curb the race riots that had started springing up all across America.[36]

Once the zoot-suit riots had been stopped, the entire nation publicly condemned the attacks by the military officials. The relations with Mexico had also seriously deteriorated at a time when the United States was embroiled in war and needed help in different industrial sectors. Many declared that the riots were caused due to racism and blamed the media for aggravating the situation by labeling zoot suits as the badges of thuggery and hoodlumism. This was the atmosphere in America when the Mexican squadron arrived in Texas for training.

The decision to begin the Mexican pilots' training at Randolph Field in San Antonio, Texas, was presumably motivated by geographical proximity to Mexico and the possible presence of Spanish-speaking personnel. However, it also immediately exposed them to the institutional racism of American society. In Texas, Mexicans were subjected to the same bigotry and segregation as black Americans. When a detachment of the 201st rolled into Majors Army Airfield in Greenville, Texas, one of the first tasks undertaken by American liaison officers was to convince the local storeowners to take down the signs reading "No Mexicans. No Dogs." Not that prejudice ended at the base perimeter. Very few instructors were interested in training the Mexican pilots, and those who were allegedly bilingual proved to have only rudimentary skills in Spanish. In practice, the pilots received much of their instruction from Women's Air Service Pilots or W.A.S.P.[37]

From August to October of 1944, the 201st Squadron was dispersed to training fields at San Antonio and Victoria, Texas, and Pocatello, Idaho. Weather conditions in Idaho proved too difficult, even in summer, and there was further delay as those pilots and instructors were transferred back to Texas. They were collected back together under the command of F.A.E.M. Colonel Antonio Cárdenas Rodriguez in Greenville on November 30. Here the pilots would receive their first fighter planes, and use them to learn air combat tactics, gunnery, and formation flying. Captain First Class Radamés Gaxiola Andrade was appointed squadron commander.[38]

The pilots were enthralled by their experiences in the air, but on the ground, they were isolated and generally ostracized by Anglo officers and personnel. They responded to the discrimination by emphasizing their Mexican patriotism, adding Mexican insignia to their aircraft and adopting the name coined by the Mexican press after the elite Aztec warriors of Mexico's history—*Las Aguilas Aztecas*, or "The Aztec Eagles." Throughout their experience, officers thought to be bilingual had to be taught Spanish in order to communicate technical issues related to aviation. The situation was sufficiently frustrating that a special section of bilingual instructors, known as Section "I," was formed under the direction of U.S. Army Captain Paul Miller.

When Captain Miller was relieved by Lieutenant Colonel Arthur Kellogg in January 1945, Section "I" would become the liaison between the 201st and the Army's 58th Fighter Group. American observers apparently formed the impression that Kellogg was the *de facto* commander of the squadron, and his section clearly had considerable responsibility for the flow of information in and out of it. However, the commanders of the 58th Fighter Group, which the Aztec Eagles would eventually join, always acted with respect for Captain Andrade's authority. It may have been helpful to allow more racially prejudiced elements of the American chain of command to believe that the Mexicans were under white supervision.

One pilot who was particularly conscious of Anglo prejudice was Angel Sánchez Rebollo, whose dimpled face inspired the nickname of "*Sapo*" ("Frog"). Discouraged from contact with local girls during his assignment in Victoria, he still found himself dating a Texan teen named Nancy Hudson. Her father forbade the relationship, but they could not be discouraged and eventually eloped to Brownsville in March 1945. A Justice of the Peace married them for $2, and their marriage lasted until Nancy's death in 1986.[39]

Panchito Pistoles

Sapo Sánchez was billeted with three other pilots with equally colorful nicknames. Amadeo Castro Amarillo was so small he was called "*El Camaron*" ("The Shrimp"); a big pilot with wide-set eyes was known to the others as "*El Pescado*" ("The Fish"); and the diminutive Jaime Zenizo Rojas, who probably had to jump to reach his listed height of 5 feet 1 inch, was known as "*El Pato*" ("The Duck")—this was because when Sánchez first saw him, his arms were filled with three seat cushions and his flying helmet, and the load obscured everything except Zenizo's spindly, birdlike legs (he needed the three cushions to be able to see over the instrument panel). Zenizo made a sign for the door of their tent that read "Welcome to the Aquarium," and this became an informal lounge for pilots in their off hours. The residents were among the first in the squadron to adopt the cartoon character Pancho Pistoles, one of Disney's *Three Caballeros*, as an unofficial squadron mascot.[40]

Panchito Pistoles is a cartoon character drawn as an anthropomorphized rooster. He appeared in the film *The Three Caballeros*, later he appeared in several Disney comics, including *Don Rosas, The Three Caballeros Ride Again*, and *The Magnificent Seven Caballeros*. Panchito was a friend of Donald Duck and José Carioca and he lives in Mexico and rides on a horse called Señor Martínez.

The word Pistoles does not exist in Spanish, although Pistolas would mean guns, probably the "E" in Pistolas was a phonetical adaptation to ease pronunciation for non-Spanish speakers in the United States. During World War II, the 201st Squadron used Panchito Pistoles as its mascot.[41]

Training in the United States

The Mexican group of approximately 300 men entered the U.S. at Laredo, Texas, on July 25, 1944. They would become part of the first Mexican military organization to leave the country with a war mission. The group arrived at Randolph Field, Texas, for initial processing. All personnel took a medical exam and the pilots took a flight examination.[1]

Individual training started on August 1, 1944. The squadron divided according to specialties and went to different training centers. The largest groups went to Pocatello, Idaho, and the Republic Aviation Corporation in Farmingdale, Long Island, New York. Others went to Boca Raton, Florida, and Scot Field, Illinois. (See Appendix III for U.S. training facilities used by the 201st Fighter Squadron.)

Training for the ground echelon consisted of instruction in English, basic military subjects, and on-the-job training in different specialties. Instructors and trainees worked hard to accomplish the mission. In the opinion of their instructors, the Mexican maintenance men were demonstrating a commendable seriousness of purpose, initiative, and comprehension.[2]

Personal Five-Week Training in Pocatello, August 1, 1944

Personnel from Randolph Field were sent here and directed to the Commander of the Army Air Base.

Armament and Artillery, Statistics, Supply, Dining Rooms, and Transportation Officers

Training included preparation of daily distribution statistics, procedures for following U.S. publications, Army regulations, preparing memoranda, Army circulars, the decimal system, maintenance forms, property records, flight operations, parachute maintenance, chemical warfare, personnel management, statement of charges, terminology and phrases, management of chemical substances, medical documentation, fuel and lubricant management, technical orders, waste and garbage disposal, ration and nutrition planning, meal lists, use of canned foods, protection of food against gasses, administration of clothing, reception and delivery of laundry, change and repair of footwear, and Morse Code and use of signals and pilot pre-flight assistance.

Specialized Five-Week Training in Pocatello

The remaining 169 troops were sent from Randolph Field for individual training in their specialties.

Armament Personnel

Training included the description and nomenclature of the .45-caliber pistol, .30-caliber machine gun, and .50-caliber machine gun, description of the electric aiming devices, description of the camera for machine guns, camera and target devices, knowledge of ammunition and machine-gun ammunition on the wings of aircraft, use of instruments for regimentation, regimenting machine guns on airplanes, live firing with the weapons indicated above, maintenance of material, academies against aggressive chemicals, regulations of the Mexican Army and the Army of the United States, and infantry instruction and English academies.

Munitions Personnel

Training covered knowledge of the different types of bombs and ammunition, munitions management, description and nomenclature of the bombs, fuses and ammunition, pyrotechnics, handling, maintenance and transport of pumps, and ammunition cautions.

Chemical Personnel

Training included knowledge, nomenclature, and maintenance of the mask, placement of fumigant tanks on aircraft, knowledge of the different aggressive chemicals, operation of the gas chamber, repairing oxygen and argon equipment, and decontamination of aircraft, engines, personal, equipment, barracks, and ground. The personnel practiced with their respective masks in the gas chamber and made combat practices in the field demonstrating their correct employment.

Medical Services Personnel

The flight surgeon and other personnel assigned to the medical service also received valuable lessons in the dispensary of the flight line of the base itself. They included both the function of the medical department and the work of the flight surgeon, airplane accident reports, monthly sanitary inspections, registration of the sick and injured, food handler reports, pharmacy procedures, and bakery procedures. They were trained for seven weeks until September 30.

Five-Week Training at Farmingdale, Long Island

A further sixty-three individuals were sent from Randolph Field for training at the Republic Aviation Corporation.

Electricity Specialist, Flight Crew Chiefs, Assistant Crew Chiefs, Propeller Specialists, and Instrument Specialists

They received twenty hours' training in the hydraulic system of airplanes; twenty-eight hours on the structure of airplanes; thirty-two hours on the Pratt & Whitney R-2800 engine and its lubrication system; sixteen hours on the system of gasoline and induction; twenty-eight hours on the electrical system; twelve hours on propellers; eight hours on instruments of airplanes and their facilities and accessories; 240 hours on hangar and line study; and ninety-six hours on the operations in hangars and on the line.

Communications staff

The group that was sent to Scott Field, Illinois, took a ten-week course, including two weeks of theory in circuits of radio devices, usually used in bombing planes and some of fight; four weeks on the circuits of the same equipment and working in the laboratories of the base; one week studying the theory of the radio equipment with which the P-47 fight planes are equipped; and three weeks in the laboratories of the base, practicing on the circuits and the handling, transport, and maintenance of the equipment.

In the opinion of their instructors, the Mexican maintenance men were demonstrating a commendable seriousness of purpose, initiative, and comprehension. The pilots commenced refresher training in Foster Field, Texas, which was completed in October 1944. Twenty-seven pilots were needed to fill the tables of organization, and the original training plan included eleven replacements. They flew transition, formation, instruments, navigation, night flying, and strafing mission in the AT-6 and P-40 aircraft. Two pilots were considered not apt for the training and returned to Mexico in August 1944, together with six enlisted men eliminated in the medical exam.

After individual training finished, the squadron concentrated in Pocatello, Idaho, for unit training. The purpose of unit training was to create a force able to operate independently. On October 20, 1944, the only absences were the intelligence officer and six radar men. The squadron received eighteen P-47 aircraft.[3]

The Second Air Force, to assist in the unit's training, organized Section "I" in Pocatello, Idaho, in August 1944. This organization, commanded by Captain Paul B. Miller, included instructors and interpreters selected for their technical knowledge and ability to speak Spanish. Lieutenant Colonel Arthur W. Kellond replaced Captain Miller in February 1945. Ten members of this unit, including Lieutenant Colonel Kellond, remained on temporary duty with the 201st Squadron, and accompanied the M.E.A.F. overseas.

Flying training in the new aircraft started on October 22, 1944 with good results, attributed to the pilots' flying experience. They proved to be well above average as a whole. The pilots flew a minimum of three sorties in the Vultee BT-13 aircraft before flying the P-47 Thunderbolt. The complete training program was the standard for U.S. pilots, and it included 120 flight hours in five phases.

The communications personnel of transmissions travelled to the base of Boca Raton, Florida, for a course of ten weeks, studying the operation, repair, and maintenance of radar equipment. The group of pilots left Randolph Field to the Foster Army Air Field, Victoria, Texas, on August 6. On the basis of a flight test made to the staff on July 31, a transition course was taken that ended on October 14 without registering any issues. The commander of the squadron also carried out training in the P-40 fighter plane. In the first days of November, the personnel were signed off in the P-40 airplane.

Inclement weather in the winter of 1944 prevented flying activities in Pocatello. To solve this problem and continue training, the M.E.A.F. relocated to Majors Field, Texas, on November 30, 1944.

The Planned Flight-Training Program in the P-47 Thunderbolt

Phase 1: Transition (Twenty-One Hours)
Flight transition (engineering); flight transition (engineering—high altitude); elementary training; tactical training; tactical training (high altitude); navigation (average altitude); and supervised acrobatics.

Phase 2: Pre-Gunnery (Thirty-Six Hours
Camera shots; shot with camera (white towed) 3,000-foot take-off and landing; shot with camera (great altitude) 3,000-foot take-off and landing; grounding, two machine guns; grounding, four machine guns; high-altitude navigation; low-altitude navigation; night navigation; combat as an individual; combat in unit (500-foot altitude); and combining training.

Phase 3: Aerial Gunnery (Twenty Hours)
Aerial Gunnery, two machine guns; aerial Gunnery, two machine guns (high altitude); aerial gunnery, four machine guns; aerial gunnery, four machine guns (high altitude); earth attack with rockets; bombing; and chemical spraying.

Phase 4: Post-Gunnery (Twenty Hours)
Acrobatics (high altitude) 3,000-foot take-off and landing; individual combat, 3,000-foot take-off and landing; chemical assault launch, 3,000-foot take-off and landing; tactical formation (high altitude); combat as a unit (high altitude); shot with camera

(high altitude), 3,000-foot take-off and landing; shot, two machine guns; shot, two machine guns (high altitude); night training; earth attack (six rockets); and combined training.

Phase 5 (Twenty Hours)

Instrument fight flight, 3,000-foot take-off and landing; instrument fight flight, 3,000-foot take-off and landing (cloudy); individual combat (high altitude); earth attack, four machine guns; tactical formation (high altitude); combat as a unit (operational ceiling); night training; combined training; combined training (high altitude); and theater tactics.

The pilots soon demonstrated their flying ability, and during the first week, all except one had been checked out in the P-47. The commander of Section "I" proclaimed the Mexican pilots to be considerably above average in judgment, technique, take-off, landings, and in general performance. He also reported on December 16, 1944 that "their formation flying ranged from excellent to superior."[4] On December 29, 1944, the Mexican Senate authorized President Camacho to send Mexican troops overseas.

On January 2, 1945, Squadron "C" left for Abilene Army Airfield, Texas, to perform the tasks they were not able to accomplish at Majors Field. On February 2, 1945, the pilots were ready to start gunnery training, the final phase of the 201st Squadron training program. The unit moved to Brownsville Army Air Field, Texas, for this training, but, unfortunately, weather continued to be a delaying factor. The highest score for air-to-air impacts was almost 25 percent, and the best result for air-to-ground strafing was over 30 percent. The unit completed gunnery training at Matagorda Peninsula Army Airfield (sub-base of Foster Field) and returned to Majors Field, Texas, on March 14, 1945.[5]

On January 16, "C" Major M. C. Ricardo Blanco Cancino departed from Majors Field to Randolph Field in order to take a course in aviation medicine, which was completed on January 19, 1945, the date in which he joined the unit. During his stay in Majors Field, the squadron continued in its training, functioning at the same time as an organized unit. The medical service attended to the personnel, as well as to food. The administrative and technical suppliers and the transports worked by providing their ordinary services to the dependencies of their unit. The technical division of the squadron, in its branch of mechanics and maintenance, maintained the unit aircraft for flight conditions. During this period, the flight training program continued as follows: pilots in training (thirty-two); flying hours at Majors Field, P-47 (291, forty-five minutes); hours flown in Abilene (178, ten minutes); flying hours on BT-13, night flight (thirty-eight hours, fifteen minutes); total flight hours (508, ten minutes); and average flight hours per pilot (sixteen hours). This report does not give the result of the machine-gun missions because Squadron "C" was transferred to Abilene, Texas, and did not complete these missions.

Ground Training Results

Intelligence and recognition: 226 hours—7 hours per pilot.
Tactics and combat technique: 148 hours—4.6 hours per pilot.
Navigation: 22 hours—0.7 hours per pilot.
Armament: 148 hours—4.6 hours per pilot.
Machine gunning: 21 hours—0.7 hours per pilot.
Aircraft and engine maintenance: 43 hours—1.3 hours per pilot.
Destruction of equipment: 21 hours—0.7 hours per pilot.
Precision shooting: 84 hours—2.6 hours per pilot.
English: 176 hours—5.5 hours per pilot.

The training of replacement pilots and ground personnel started on February 1945. In March, sixteen pilots were flying the refresher course; ten were almost ready to fly the P-47 and six were about a month behind. The replacement training plan considered forty-eight more pilots for refresher and P-47 training. The training, initially conducted at Foster Field, Texas, was changed to Napier Field, Alabama, near Maxwell Field. Maxwell Field was the home of the Air Corps Tactical School, the U.S. center for development of air power tactics and strategy.

After finishing the unit training, the M.E.A.F., which received the Mexican flag on February 22, 1945, was ready to go overseas. The pilots went to Topeka, Kansas, for final processing by the 21st Bombardment Wing, and the ground personnel left Majors Field by train on March 18.

Language difficulties were inevitable during their training, but the Eagles overcame that hurdle with help from U.S. Army Air Corps combat veterans chosen for their bilingual ability. These flight instructors were most effective when practicing aerial combat maneuvers as there were no two-seat Thunderbolt trainers in 1944.[6]

Including personnel processing, refresher and technical courses, several relocations, and inclement weather, the Aztec Eagles completed the 120-hour training program in eight months, guided by the standard U.S. Army Air Corps pilot curriculum. The training schedule was comprehensive and emphasized the two levels at which these pilots would most likely operate: low-altitude gunnery (strafing) and air combat tactics at 35,000 feet.[7]

Several factors affected the training. The time necessary for preparation and the language barrier were critical. Weather in the U.S. and in the S.W.P.A. was a factor that caused delays and imposed restrictions. The equipment of the unit as a whole also required a great amount of effort. After the 201st Squadron program started, time for training was critical if the unit was to be sent to combat. The original training plan contemplated that the squadron would be ready in November 1944; however, more realistic estimates indicated five months of training. It took over seven months before the unit was ready to leave the U.S., and the training was not completed as established in the program, due mainly to weather.[8]

Language was probably the biggest barrier for pilots and ground personnel, and English classes were added to the training program. The instructors of Section "I" agreed that the chief difficulty in the training of Mexican personnel was the language difference. This was a particular handicap in the on-the-job training program. Results were not completely satisfactory when the Mexican mechanics were put to work with the base mechanics.[9] The interpreters of Section "I" at Pocatello and Majors Field were a great help. Some considered that training at the Republic Aviation Corporation was not as beneficial as training on the line, due to the inability of interpreters to speak sufficient Spanish.[10]

The language difference also affected pilot training, and probably flight safety. One fatal training accident in the U.S. was probably due to communication problems. A pilot died during a take-off accident, when after receiving clearance to use the runway, he attempted to get airborne on a short taxiway. The tail wheel and the big engine on the P-47 forward visibility difficult on the ground. One pilot was eliminated during unit training for his limited knowledge of the English language; a problem that could not be solved completely even with bilingual instructors.[11] The check sheet for the ground training in the S.W.P.A. recommended: "Since only about 40 percent of the 201st Squadron personnel are English speaking, the use of posters, photos, maps and other visual aids is indicated. An interpreter will also be present to assist you in presenting your material."[12]

Most pilots agreed that the P-47 was not an easy plane to fly. Marvin Bledsoe, a P-47 fighter pilot, mentions in his book *Thunderbolt* that several inexperienced pilots were killed in this aircraft, while others asked for transfers.[13] In addition to that, the very nature of combat training increases risk. One pilot died on air-to-air gunnery training when the aircraft went out of control right after he made a firing pass on the target. It was never known if something hit him, but that is a possible cause. Another pilot died in the S.W.P.A. during combat training, attempting to recover from a high-speed stall after a dive-bombing pass.[14]

Maintenance during training was excellent, but the war requirements imposed to operate were often barely within safety margins. It is natural for a unit engaged in combat to retain the best aircraft and give away war-weary equipment. This is one possible explanation for some of the accidents in P-47s loaned to the 201st Squadron in the S.W.P.A. Three forced-landings because of engine malfunctions happened from May 21–24, 1945. Flights stopped for a maintenance inspection, and some aircraft were replaced, reducing the accident rate.[15] Sometimes, it was necessary to use "alternate procedures" to accomplish the mission, such as wood boxes or oil drums on top of dollies for loading bombs. During take-off and landing training of Mexican pilots at Napier Field, Alabama, it was necessary during the summer to spray water on the old P-40 engines before take-off to allow sufficient cooling. These limitations highlight the operational performance of the M.E.A.F.

After finishing the unit training, the M.E.A.F., which received the Mexican flag on February 22, 1945, was ready to go overseas.[16] Cornelius Orsatti, of the U.S. Air Force, who was one of the training directors of the 201st, wrote about it:

When I was informed that we had to train the Mexicans in a period equal to what we needed to train the Americans, which was one year, I thought it would not be possible, because they did not know our language completely. Each week I had to make a report to the General Staff in Washington about the best sections of the Squadron and its advances and in a few weeks I had reported them all, so I started to report to the most advanced individuals and I can say with satisfaction that I did not miss none to be mentioned for its use and the unit graduated in just nine months, with an excellent rating.[17]

The Mexican government granted its members two salaries: one in Mexican currency, covered by a special pay, which was paid to the attorneys appointed by each of them, in accordance with the expenditures budget in force in the Mexico; the other was paid in U.S. dollars that, in addition to the previous one, they received monthly, in the United States or in the Far East.[18]

Deployment to the Philippines

All 201st Squadron ground personnel left Greenville by rail at 8 a.m. on March 18, 1945, bound for Camp Stoneman at Pittsburgh, California. The pilots left Kansas City for California on March 19, traveling by rail along the northern rail route. From Majors Field, the 201st went through Dallas, San Antonio, Del Rio, and El Paso to Phoenix, Yuma, and Los Angeles and into Pittsburgh, California. Their special train consisted of five sleeping cars, a diner, and another car for luggage. For security reasons, their traveling orders prohibited them from wearing any symbol on their uniforms that could identify them as a Mexican squadron. Their orders also stated that all curtains on the train must remain closed during the entire journey. The military presumably issued this directive to prevent civilians from knowledge of their travel. Nonetheless, at stops along the way, the Mexicans got off the train, although they did not talk with civilians or send letters home. These precautions seemed pointless to the Mexicans with the war in Europe virtually at an end, but in the Pacific, the conflict forcefully raged on. The trip took three days, and they arrived at 10 a.m. on March 21.[1]

Camp Stoneman, located near Pittsburg on the east side of the San Francisco Bay in western Contra Costa County, served as a staging point for troops going to the Pacific. Military units, shipping out from Camp Stoneman, commonly used ferries to take them through Suisun Bay, San Pablo Bay, and San Francisco Bay to their embarkation point.[2]

At Camp Stoneman, the squadron continued preparations for deployment overseas. Besides filling their supply and equipment needs, the men received orders concerned with rules, regulations, procedures, and health matters. They also received information about their salaries, availability of life insurance, and mail censorship. They were told to remember the old adage that "loose lips sink ships," and not to talk about the squadron or its destination. They were told not to write letters home that disclosed their location or discuss military issues, routes, convoys, or anything relating to troop activity. They even received guidelines concerning navy shipboard practices and routines, including general quarters' battle station duties. They also received procedural instructions for embarkation, landing, abandoning ship, and utilization of gas masks. In order for them to avoid the health dangers of the Pacific Theater, they met with medical specialists who discussed hygiene and sickness prevention techniques.[3]

Several days before their departure from Camp Stoneman, all personnel received one more complete physical examination. This included immunization shots against common diseases in the Philippines such as smallpox, typhoid, typhus, tetanus, yellow fever, and the bubonic plague. The vaccinations and physical evaluations caused the elimination of two members of the troop, who returned to Mexico. Otherwise, no significant problems occurred with the health of the men. A brief itching epidemic tormented part of the troop. It first surfaced during their stay in Brownsville and the affected men required quarantine measures to prevent it from spreading. Fortunately, medication solved this problem by the time they left Camp Stoneman.[4]

The morale of the 201st Squadron personnel was sky high as they prepared to leave for combat. Not one case of desertion occurred, nor any instance of disobedience or dereliction of duty. The Mexican command expressed profound satisfaction with the high sense of responsibility and the great concept of duty of the men who formed the Mexican Expeditionary Air Force.[5]

Two days prior to their departure to the Far East, the squadron command laboriously went over all phases of their departure preparation plan, leaving nothing to chance. With this done and with the armament and equipment on its way to the cargo holds of their troop transport, the men turned to other activities. One last and important activity concerned the payment of troop salaries. Before their departure, all squadron members received an advance in pay so that they could have the banks in the San Francisco area transfer funds to relatives back home. Finally, the men also completed arrangements relating to their life insurance.[6]

The day before their scheduled departure on March 27, the 201st crews worked around the clock getting ready for departure. Early the next morning, the entire unit departed foggy Camp Stoneman. At 8 a.m., they boarded a ferry for a four-hour trip to San Francisco. As they left Pittsburg, a large billboard reminded them: "The best troops in the world have passed through this place."[7]

In San Francisco, they transferred to the troop transport S.S. *Fairisle*, a 10,000-ton Liberty ship anchored off Wharf Number 6. Finally, they began their trip to the island of Luzon in the Philippines. General Luis Alamillo Flores, military liaison, came to offer his assistance and see them off. Two U.S. Air Force squadron liaison officers, Lieutenant Colonel Gurza and Lieutenant Colonel Kellond, accompanied them from Majors Field, but did not come aboard the Liberty ship. Instead, they flew on to the Philippines to establish a link with the command of the Allied forces at that front. Wartime secrecy surrounded the departure of the ship. Few knew anything regarding this contingent of troops leaving for the Pacific except the port employees and some members of the Red Cross who distributed coffee and donuts to the troops before their departure.[8]

Shipboard life tested the Mexicans. Héctor Espinosa Galván's feelings about the *Fairisle* appeared to be a mixture of disappointment and approval. He wrote in his diary:

> We imagined a Queen Mary or a Leviathan but it was a relatively small ship conditioned by the needs of war, but it did have a sailor's taste. My cabin was small. Inside [referring to their topside compartment] we accommodated five officers and another eight people in front. In my cabin were Castro, Espinosa Fuentes and Amadeo—all lieutenants. We found the bathroom (called the head in the Navy) had showers, toilets and a sink; all tile. We went to the dinner room at 1730 hours, and when we finished dinner, I noticed the ship began to move. This was the beginning of a great adventure for us. Every one of us left something dear in Mexico. I left a beautiful young wife, a daughter of five months, my father and my mother. After all that natural pain, deep inside I wanted the adventure. I know the danger, but I trusted my abilities and God.[9]

The S.S. *Fairisle* left San Francisco at approximately 6 p.m. on March 27. Passing under the Golden Gate Bridge, it set sail for the Philippines. In his diary, Héctor Espinosa wrote: "At dusk, we left the pier of San Francisco. We went through the majestically engineered Golden Gate and as the night came upon us, small lights far away were shining like the coastal fireflies of our gulf." The *Fairisle's* sailing orders directed it to take an indirect route from San Francisco to its first stopping point—New Guinea. Route instructions required the ship to sail southwest through the Coral Sea—part of the Southern Pacific Ocean that lies between the northeast coast of Australia, the Solomon Islands, and the New Hebrides Islands—to the second largest island in the world, New Guinea.[10] Héctor Espinosa continued to describe their first night and next day at sea:

> The rules of the ship prohibited smoking or leaving lights visible to the outside. After turning away from civilization, we quietly went to our new home and since we were on cold waters, I slept pleasantly. At 0700 in the morning, we got up for breakfast, now away from any contact with America; we had the chance to study the new faces among us. Next to our group, the *crujía* [the talkers], a nickname that we decided to call ourselves, other Americans were sitting at the table #4 in the first shift. Because we were so many, two shifts were needed. Afterwards I learned that we were 140 officers in the ship and about 2,500 soldiers aboard. After breakfast, we went to the topside to admire the view and the immensity of the Pacific Ocean. We chatted between us and had fun watching the *gaviotas* [sea gulls]. From time to time, we took a snooze close to the warehouse walls (these are main deck hatch covers that sits above the holds). At 1130, we had lunch, by then we had a few seasick people. Fortunately, I still have not had the misfortune to be seasick. After lunch, we went back to the topside to see the ocean, smoke and make friends with other officers, etc. Again, at 1700, we had dinner and back to the topside to see the immensity of the ocean. Afterwards at night we watched the stars.[11]

Beside the M.E.A.F., other units of North American soldiers sailed with the *Fairisle*. Altogether, the ship carried approximately 2,800 troops, independent of the ship's crew. The American troops' commander issued shipboard guidelines that governed the conduct of all aboard the ship. The Mexicans rigorously followed these rules from the time they came on board until they left the ship. Colonel Cárdenas received a special mention for their good conduct.[12]

Only a few members of the Mexican troops previously had experienced sea travel before this voyage. A new world opened to them. All activity aboard a U.S. Naval vessel at sea followed a strict routine for the ship's company and a less stringent one for the passengers. These included sea watch and other usual duties for the crew. A timetable for meals, designation of general quarters' stations for all aboard, sleeping quarter assignments, and recreation and educational times. Second Sergeant Alfonso Cueller organized the Mexicans' sleeping arrangements aboard ship. Their quarters complied with shipboard principles of organization. Commanders and officers slept in special collective cabins topside. Enlisted quarters, below decks, contained canvas bunks— three to four lined one above the other and attached to the bulkhead. Some slept on folding bunks in the ship's stern. Cuellar took a bunk near the propeller shaft alley. Justino Reyes Retana selected the top bunk in quarters for the officers. He considered this a choice selection.[13]

With few exceptions, all facilities for the enlisted men remained below decks. These included mess halls, shower facilities, heads, and a ship's canteen, which sold toothpaste, shaving equipment, cigarettes, and candy. All of the troops used a special soap that neutralized salt water when they showered. The dining room had tall tables attached to the deck and the men stood while eating. Even so, when the ship rolled in the sea, trays often flew to the floor. At times, the men looked like jugglers walking from the food line to the table, carefully balancing their trays with the motion of the ship. Everyone on board had some duty: some cleaned the sleeping quarters; some washed the deck; while others had special assignments.[14]

The weather changed from cold to warm to hot as they sailed west for a short time and then turned south. Sailing without escort, they changed course frequently to prevent being an easy target for submarines. Colonel Justino Reyes Retana recalled the ship being cold as they first put out to sea, then he said that they turned south, and the weather became warm. Seven days out from San Francisco, on April 4, the *Fairisle* was in the same latitude as the Hawaiian Islands.[15] Lieutenant Héctor Espinosa wrote about his first week at sea:

Like any other thing, we began to get bored. Others began to play cards and dice to a point that after dinner, it was a well-organized game, like a Casino…. I have not done too badly. In addition, the Chaplain began to organize boxing matches, where our people overcame the Americans, two groups were formed, the amateur and the professional. We also had a group of Mexican guitarists and singers. Thanks to them, the journey was less tiresome. The 8th day of travel, we learned that we were 200 miles away from Hawaii when we passed the night before. We are still asking, when is our first stop. Some have said Midway, others Samoa or Fiji and like that, the days, hours went by. We saw two whales, dolphins and more. We saw far away to [*sic.*] ships, but we continue alone the immensity of the trip. At last, on April 6, we had a change in our lives on board; we were going to cross the equator.[16]

Troops received information every day about activities in the rest of the world. The ship radio provided daily news. A ship newspaper furnished periodic news, and a small library provided a limited selection of magazines. The April 4, 1945 edition of the S.S. *Fairisle* newspaper reminded the troops and crew that the greatest war in history still raged around the world. In Okinawa, the paper reported, Marines and soldiers had driven another wedge across the island and had taken firm control of the south-central section of the strategic Ryukyu Island. General MacArthur announced that the 45th Division had completed three years of overseas service, with twenty-two months spent in combat. The Americans on southeast Luzon drove 22 miles northwest of Legazpi on Bicol peninsula. In Europe, the U.S. Army, in a 19-mile sweep across wooded Thuringia, smashed into the outskirts of Gotha, 149 miles from Berlin. A section called the Chaplain's Office reminded everyone to please pass the magazines on to the next man, as they were scarce.[17]

As S.S. *Fairisle* steamed southward, the weather became increasingly warm. Lieutenant Justino Reyes Retana had trouble sleeping at night because the ventilation outlets in his compartment did not produce sufficient air to cool him. He took his mattress and went on to the top deck to sleep but even this did not prevent him from being drenched in perspiration. This problem did not confine itself to him alone. Many of the Mexican soldiers tried to sleep topside, particularly those with bunk space in compartments below decks. Continuing southward into an even warmer climate, the ship crossed the 180th meridian, the International Date Line, on April 8. Any ship that crosses this meridian going east loses a day. On this voyage, the passengers lost Monday, April 9, which became Tuesday, April 10.[18]

The Mexicans experienced their first general quarters' alarm at night with a sudden alarm. For this purpose, the ship command assigned everyone a specific general quarters' muster area. The men had orders to keep their life jackets near them. Captain Manuel Cervantes remembered that the jackets became their constant companions. After recovering their wits and grabbing their life jackets, the men went quickly to their general quarters' battle stations. Colonel Justino Reyes Retana remembered that the ship had no lights anywhere when the alarm sounded. During the war, the navy used blackout lights below decks while running at sea. The ability to see in this muted red light diminished into darkness as one moves away from the dim light. This unique safety feature allowed the ship's crew to operate within the ship and yet not allow light to seep out for a submarine or another vessel to see. Lieutenant Justino Reyes Retana skinned his shins hurrying around trying to find his life jacket. He also remembered that at first he ran to his battle station, after that he walked.[19]

This was the first of several general quarters' drills during the trip. At the first alarm, the Mexicans acted with a great haste to get topside and find their assigned battle stations. As the alarms continued, the men gradually slowed until, during the last drills, they walked to their stations. Some squadron members paid no attention to the claxon horn's frantic call to quarters. They remained in their quarters even when they heard the sound of machine guns and 20-mm cannon firing. General Sánchez Rebollo remembered being scared at first. During the first four drills, he went to his battle station, but after that, he ignored the signal for general quarters. He and several others stayed below and played poker.[20]

Early on the morning of April 12, an island appeared on the starboard side of the *Fairisle*. The Mexicans identified it as Guadalcanal. For whatever reason, they assumed that the ship would stop there, revealing that many Mexican soldiers had no idea of their first port. Although they hoped this was to be the port, their elation soon turned to disappointment. The ship continued on its course to Hollandia, New Guinea.[21]

The next day, while sailing between New Britain and the Solomon Islands, southwest toward New Guinea, the ship received news of the death of President Roosevelt. The Mexicans considered him one of the greatest men in contemporary times and one of Mexico's best friends. When the M.E.A.F. members learned the news, they dispatched messages of condolence to Mrs. Roosevelt and to the U.S. government.[22]

Two days later, at 8 p.m., S.S. *Fairisle* dropped anchor in the port of Hollandia. It remained at anchor for four days to refuel and for a naval convoy to form. Finally, one developed, made up of three destroyers and twelve troop transports. Two of the merchant ships carried the names *Mexico* and *Monterrey*. Although the officers went ashore, all of the other personnel remained on board, with no opportunity to go ashore even for a brief liberty break. Wartime recreational facilities ashore offered little except an opportunity to get off the ship, a place possibly to get a beer, and a place to gamble. The pilots went ashore one day for lunch at the base's officers' club. Afterwards, they enjoyed a movie, *The Fighting Lady*, a film about the U.S. aircraft carrier *Lexington*. Later that afternoon, they visited the officers' club bar. This facility contained a bar made from the wings of airplanes. Ice and beer were stored in 50-gallon drums, with the tops cut off. They took full advantage of this bar that offered them about anything they wanted to drink. Later that night, they returned to their ship. A rope ladder provided the normal manner of ingress and egress from their ship. That night, many of them required help from the ship's winch to come aboard because of their inability to scale the rope ladder.[23]

On April 20, the *Fairisle* pulled up anchor and sailed from the port of Hollandia. From the time they left San Francisco until reaching Hollandia, the *Fairisle* traveled unescorted. The Mexicans were quite relieved when their ship joined a convoy with three destroyers bound for the Philippine Islands. Operating now in more dangerous waters, the convoy exercised greater precautions, although its cruising speed did not exceed more than 6–7 knots. Soon after they left Hollandia, the Mexican soldiers noticed that many soldiers climbed the mast of their ship or stood at the railing with binoculars looking at the *Monterrey*. They found out later that it carried a troop of

W.A.C.S. (Women Army Corps Service) and the hot weather caused many of the women to come on deck in bathing suits or light clothing. After steaming north for four days, they joined with a slightly smaller convoy, forming a fleet of forty-six Liberty ships and three destroyers. They continued together toward the Philippines.[24]

Colonel Cárdenas' comments regarding their Pacific crossing suggested his great satisfaction concerning the treatment accorded his forces. He remarked that they received the finest consideration and attention. Cárdenas believed that this good treatment arose in part because they were foreigners and partly because of the rigorous discipline and order that his personnel displayed.[25]

The daily routine onboard ship continued, monotonous at times, but with some diversions. Sometimes the men spent their time talking on deck, and sometimes playing dice or cards below deck. At times, the sea was so calm that it looked like a mirror. Occasionally, the men went forward to the bow of the ship and watched the flying fish break out of the waves caused by the ship. They also saw whales and sharks. The men enjoyed such entertainment as movies, music, radio, lecture halls, a small club, and even sports events. Organized boxing, with participants from the various troop companies, provided another energy outlet. Manuel Cervantes, then a second sergeant and a former bantamweight boxing champion in college, fought a Mexican-American marine and lost. The ship's canteen provided candies, soft drinks, cleaning articles, cigarettes, and the many trifles that enhanced their monotonous daily life.[26]

At night, the Mexican aviators gathered on deck and reminisced about home. A Spanish guitar, never far away, played many favorite songs: "*Me voy soldado razo,*" "*Nochecita,*" "*Que lejos estoy,*" and "*Amor, Amor.*" One member of their squadron, Bemadino Mendoza, an accomplished guitar player known as *El Verde* (The Green), played "*Babalu.*" The men sang many other songs from different regions of their country. Often, American soldiers joined in the gaiety of the music, requesting Mexican songs, especially "*Cielito Undo*" and "*Alla en el Rancho Grande.*"[27]

The *Fairisle* crossed the equator twice during its trip. First, it crossed on April 6 while on their way to Hollandia, New Guinea. It crossed a second time on April 21 while *en route* to the Philippines. The U.S. Navy held the act of crossing the equator as a traditional time of celebration for the crews of all their ships. The ritual involved the appearance of King Neptune, who minutes before reaching the equator arose from the depths of the ocean to initiate neophytes—Polliwogs—who had not previously crossed the equator. Invested with wide mythical powers, King Neptune came aboard ship to chair a tribunal that selected some form of humiliating judgment or punishment for being a Polliwog. Those who had crossed before were called "Shellbacks" and were especially privileged. Shellbacks wore strange and picturesque clothing and helped King Neptune in his initiation ceremonies, including humiliation of the neophyte Polliwogs. The historically prearranged sentences, applied and executed publicly in an atmosphere of enthusiasm and happiness, were both comical and festive. Normally the initial punishment involved being soaked with a fire hose while being hit with a canvas belt stuffed with cotton. No living being who passed on the deck escaped the royal hose.

Other punishment ranged from kissing the royal baby (this involved pushing a Polliwog's face against the oiled stomach of the fattest sailor aboard ship) to drinking a royal toast (orange juice and coffee grounds). The culminating indignation, after being given an egg and tomato sauce shampoo, involved being thrown into a salt-water bath consisting of rotten eggs, smashed tomatoes, and peppery, coffee-laced oil. All Mexican Polliwogs, including Doctor Blanco, Captain Blanco Ledezma, and Captain Carranza, endured their initiation. Second Sergeant Manuel Cervantes expressed his great delight at being included in the ceremonies. These solemn ceremonies ended with all Polliwogs being certified as Shellbacks. At that time, the ship captain and members of the mythically celebrated imperial tribunal authenticated the newly consecrated Shellbacks. Each was presented with a document containing his name, the name of his vessel, and the time he crossed the equator, thus certifying that he was a Shellback.[28]

Beyond fire, abandon ship, and general quarters' drills, the 201st personnel occupied their time attending lectures on enemy organization and tactics. They also learned about the characteristics and customs of the inhabitants of the Philippines. These talks included geographical and statistical data and information about sanitary matters appropriate for those latitudes.[29]

The health of the 201st remained good except for some small skin infections caused by the climate. The Mexicans could acquire toiletries, sweets, cigarettes, and other things. In addition, the American Red Cross gifted to all a case containing toiletries, writing paper, some literature, games, and some tools for the repair of clothes.

During their first days at sea, the ancient malady commonly called seasickness affected most of the airmen. Seasickness became endemic and Colonel Cárdenas wrote that about 75 percent of the men endured the illness. Their seasickness ended soon after they became accustomed to the constant rolling of the ship. During the last days of the trip, Cárdenas remarked that they began to feel like old sea wolves (salts).[30] On Monday April 30, 1945, after thirty-three days at sea, at approximately 4 p.m., the *Fairisle* dropped anchor in Manila Bay.[31]

In spite of the fact that a navy salvage unit had earlier removed 350 sunken vessels from the harbor, a large number of half-sunken Japanese ships still remained in the bay. Unrecovered floating mines in the harbor also presented a safety hazard. These obstacles, the late arrival hour, and the many Allied naval ships in the harbor presented maneuvering and berthing difficulties. Consequently, the *Fairisle* anchored some distance out from Manila Bay.[32]

Preparations to disembark began early on May 1. Members of the 201st Squadron awoke to a hot, damp, tropical morning, went topside to survey their new surroundings, and made ready to go ashore. As they gathered along the railing of their ship, they looked out over a harbor filled with all types of war and merchant ships. Their sweat-soaked uniforms attested to the heat and humidity as they left the ship carrying backpacks, duffel bags, and weapons. They disembarked on to floating pontoons by climbing down netting thrown over the side of the ship. Navy landing crafts then came alongside and took them ashore.[33]

The Mexican force transported their entire troop to Manila's Glamour Pier Number 7 by 9 a.m., and General George C. Kenney, commanding officer of the Far East Air Force, greeted Colonel Cárdenas and the rest of the 210st Squadron as they came ashore. U.S. Air Force liaison personnel, Lieutenant Colonel Kellond and Lieutenant Colonel Alfredo Carmelo, also greeted them. The Philippine General Consul for Mexico and his three daughters, all dressed in typical Mexican costumes called *China Poblanas* or Chinese Pueblan (the traditional style of dress of women in the Mexican Republic), welcomed them. A military band played the U.S. and Mexican national anthems. In *A Personal History of the Pacific War*, General Kenney wrote:

> After a reception at the pier, I took Cárdenas over to see General MacArthur, and after the official exchange of greeting, the Mexicans were officially assigned to my command. They then proceeded to Clark Field, where I turned them over to Brigadier General Freddy Smith with instructions to outfit them with P-47s and give them a course of advance combat training before putting them into action. Both officers and enlisted men were a fine–looking lot and seemed anxious to get to work against the Japs as soon as possible.[34]

A short distance inland from where the 201st landed was the destroyed city of Manila. During the fight to retake the city, the Japanese set fire to virtually everything along the Pasig River's north bank, mined the streets, and destroyed many buildings. Most of the city was in ruins. Only shattered steel and fire-blackened walls remained of the city once called "the Pearl of the Orient." The Japanese razed hotels, theaters, banks, and department stores. General George Kenney wrote:

> The Japanese earned the undying hatred of the Filipinos for all time by their senseless orgy of pillage, murder and rape of the civilian population as they evacuated the city and suburbs. People in the houses were called out and shot in the streets, the houses searched for liquor and loot and then set on fire. Crazed with alcohol, Japanese officers and men raged through the city in an orgy of lust and destruction. The systematic looting by the Japanese created a critical food shortage. Besides the thousands of Filipinos killed indiscriminately, as the Japanese pulled out of Manila, additional hundreds died daily from hunger.[35]

At 12 p.m., members of the 201st Squadron boarded a narrow-gauge railway train that took them to Florida Blanca just south of Clark Field. They then boarded trucks for Porac field. Upon arrival, after six hours of travel and transfer time, they were welcomed by members of the 58th Fighter Group. They were told to expect to stay at this location after their admitting procedures. The 201st slept out in the open on cots on their first night in Luzon, in a camp near a forest infiltrated with stray Japanese. As a security measure, an U.S. Army infantry unit and the Philippine Scouts stood guard over the campground. That night, the guard unit killed three Japanese in disguise trying to sneak into the encampment for food.[36]

The Aztec Eagles passed the next eight days at Porac, waiting for their unit to be called to Clark Field for processing. They soon recognized their location as being subject to the danger caused by roving Japanese soldiers. Early on the morning of their first full day, they awoke to the sound of machine-gun fire. The Philippine Scouts killed a Japanese soldier 500 meters from the camp. That night, they killed another found hiding in the passageway between the tents. While the 201st remained at Florida Blanca, a night did not pass that either the American infantry watchdogs or the Philippine Scouts did not kill one or more Japanese soldiers. The sound of gunfire became routine. They soon learned to distinguish between the sounds of American and Japanese gunfire.[37]

While at Porac, the 201st celebrated *Cinco de Mayo*. The event commemorates a great Mexican victory at Puebla when the defending forces, led by General Ignacio Zaragoza, defeated an invading French force on May 5, 1862. For the first time, the 201st raised their tricolor flag in a combat zone.[38]

On each of the last two days of processing, the Mexican squadron departed early for Clark Field. The one-hour trip took them through areas strewn with hundreds of destroyed Japanese aircraft. During break times, they were able to purchase V stamps* and a chaplain provided them with wrapping paper for shipping items home. They returned at about 5 p.m. each day without incident.[39]

General Orders Number 67, dated April 5, 1945, assigned the 210st Squadron to the Fifth Air Force, 5th Fighter Command, and the 58th Fighter Group. After completing all processing procedures at Clark Field on May 7, Fighter Command permanently assigned the 201st to a camp area with the 58th Fighter Group at nearby Porac Field. The 210st Squadron became actively attached to the 58th Fighter Group during the first week in May.[40]

*Note: V, or Victory mail, was a valuable tool for the military during World War II. The process, which originated in England, was the microfilming of specially designed letter sheets. Instead of using valuable cargo space to ship whole letters overseas, microfilmed copies were sent in their stead and then enlarged at the destination before being delivered to the intended recipient.

Flight Training in the Philippines

Colonel Cárdenas with the M.E.A.F. command personnel established at Fort Stotsenburg in Clark Field, located about 40 miles northwest of Manila. Some M.E.A.F. elements were assigned to the Fifth Air Force Fighter Command as Liaison officers. The 201st Squadron established in Porac, in the Clark Field area, and was attached to the 58th Fighter Group, Fifth Fighter Command, Fifth Air Force, U.S. Far East Air Forces. Porac Airfield is a World War II airfield located at Porac to the east of the Porac River in the province of Pampanga on the island of Luzon in the Philippines. Porac Airfield was a single runway airfield prior to the war. A taxiway ran parallel to the runway, with a dispersal area near the northern end of the strip. It was used by the Japanese during their occupation. After the airfield was liberated, it was used by combined Filipino and American military units.

A vast complex of prewar and Japanese-constructed paved and unpaved runways, taxiways, dispersal areas, air craft revetments, and associated installations comprised the Clark Field Air Center. The whole extending from Barmban Airfield south along both sides of Route 3 for almost 15 miles. There were fifteen separate landing strips, with but three exceptions all located west of the highway. Clark Field proper, with six separate strips, lay on the west side of Route 3 in an open area about four miles wide, east to west, and extending from Mabalacat, 4 miles south of Bamban, south another 6 miles. In the western section of this airfield region was Fort Stotsenburg, prewar home of various Philippine Scout units, including the 26th Cavalry.[1]

East of Route 3, the flat, hot terrain gives way to rice paddies that are dry in January and farmlands that are cut by many irrigation ditches and small, tree-lined streams. The only prominent terrain feature is wooded Mount Arayat, rising in isolation above the floor of the Central Plains to a height of 3,350 feet. West of Clark Field, the bare foothills of the Zambales Mountains rise sharply, forming a series of parallel ridges, oriented northeast to southwest and separated by the Bamban River and many lesser wet-weather streams. Its source deep in the mountains behind Fort Stotsenburg, the Bamban River, called the Sacobia along its western reaches, flows generally northeastward past the northern side of the Clark Field strips.

About 1½ miles west of Mabalacat, the stream turns northward for 3 miles, its western bank formed by the steep noses of parallel ridges rising southwestward into the Zambales Mountains. A mile south of Bamban, an unnamed stream comes in from the west to join the Bamban River. Here, under the cliff-like southern side of another sharp ridge, the Bamban River makes a right-angled turn to the east, ultimately feeding into the Rio Chico de la Pampanga River off the northeastern slopes of Mount Arayat. Just east of the river bend south of Bamban, the Manila Railroad crosses the river and, about 200 yards further east, Route 3 goes over the Bamban River.

The ridges at the river bend south of Bamban and along the north–south stretch of the Bamban River rise steeply to a height of some 600 feet within 250 yards of the river's banks. West of Fort Stotsenburg bare, dominating hills shoot quickly and sharply up to a height of over 1,000 feet scarcely half a mile beyond the camp's western gate.[2]

Company "B," 803rd Engineer Battalion, began work on what was originally known as Del Carmen Field in mid-November 1941. It was to be major airdrome with multiple runways designed to serve heavy bombers that was to be assigned to the Philippines prior to the start of World War II. The engineers were not able to complete the field, and only the 34th Pursuit Squadron, Far East Air Force (F.E.A.F.), with its P-35 aircraft operated from there. Several P-40s from other F.E.A.F. pursuit squadrons used Del Carmen as an emergency landing strip after the bombing of Clark and Iba Fields on December 8, 1941.[3]

In late December 1941, during the early stages of World War II, the facility was successfully captured and taken over by the Japanese Army. The base was used by the Japanese as an auxiliary airfield. It was in this aerodrome complex of Clark, Floridablanca, Porac, and Mabalacat airfield where the scheme to employ *kamikaze* fighters was first conceived and launched by the Japanese.

In January 1945, the U.S. Air Force re-established a presence at the airfield when the United States Sixth Army cleared the area of Japanese forces. The 312th Bombardment Group based A-20 Havocs from April 19 through August 13, 1945 and the 348th Fighter Group based P-47 Thunderbolts and P-51 Mustangs at the airfield from May 15 through July 6, 1945. In 1945, during the period of Philippine liberation, the U.S. Army Air Forces enlarged the airfield further to accommodate B-17s and B-24s, which were used for air strikes against Japan.

The 201st Fighter Squadron began pre-combat orientation operating out of Porac Field as members of the 58th Fighter Group on May 7, 1945. The initial indoctrination phase consisted of terrain familiarization, weather briefing, location of troops fighting on the ground, air-sea rescue, escape and evasion, support air parties, and sectors of action. Following their indoctrination, each pilot observed practical demonstrations at the 51st Fighter sector and pre-combat ground training during a four-day rotating training phase. However, for nine days beginning May 7, no fighter group operated out of Porac because of the need to resurface the runways.[4] Nos. 69, 201, and 311 Squadrons remained inactive. No. 310 Squadron operated out of Clark Field. Although trained in air-to-air combat, the Mexican Fighter squadron's assignment in the Philippines called for them to fly ground support missions. To gain experience in flying this type of mission, the squadron spent the remainder of May flying with the "battle-seasoned" Thunderbolt pilots of the 58th Fighter Group.

The Fifth Air Force decided that the 201st Squadron would take training, which was considered necessary to complete its preparation to be able to participate in the operations. Advanced combat training in theater was a normal procedure for newly arrived replacements, and it involved ground and flight training. The training program for the 201st Squadron established by the Fifth Air Force from May 7–12, 1945 included ground and air training covering lectures, ground training before combat, air training, and theater training.

Lectures

1. General summary about the war fronts. Speaker: A. P. Hollyday, Assistant A-2. Time: Twenty minutes.
2. Aerial warfare in the South-Western Pacific Area. Speaker: Mayor C. O. Hicker, History, V.F.C. (Fighter Squadron Composite). Time: forty minutes.
3. Land warfare in the South-Western Pacific Area. Speaker: Major F. H. McCallie, Infantry Officer. Time: forty minutes.
4. The atmospheric conditions in the South-Western Pacific Area. Speaker: Captain F. S. Tuttle, Officer Meterorologist V.F.C. Time: thirty minutes.
5. Guidance on the Fighting Sector. Speaker: Captain M. Williams, Chief Controller, V.F.C. Time: forty minutes.
6. Air-Sea Rescue. Speaker: Captain R. C. Suehr, Rescue Officer, Air-Sea Rescue V.F.C.
7. Escape and evasion. Speaker: Captain F. Fulz, A-2, Mis-X, V.F.C.
8. Action areas. Speaker: Captain Hollyday, Assistant A-2, V.F.C.
9. Friendly ground situation. Speaker: Major F. McCallie, Infantry Liaison Officer with V.F.C.
10. Support detachments of aerial elements on the ground to harmonize air support. Speaker: Captain W. Binkley, Ground Enforcement Officer for air support, 5th Air Force.

Ground Training before Combat
Operations Officer, 58th Fight Group
1. Intelligence.
2. Transmissions.
3. Operations.
4. Long–range navigation.
5. Principles of recognition and observation (operations and intelligence).

Air Training
1. Familiarization and orientation (six hours).
2. Air tactics and fighting technique in the air (four hours).
3. Simulated combat missions (four hours).
4. Combat missions (twelve hours).

Theater Training
1. Familiarization with the airfield:
   a. radio procedures.
   b. orientation.
   c. individual flights.
2. Battle navigation at high altitude:
   a. simulated combat formation.
   b. aids to navigation.
   c. squadron formations of four aircraft.
3. Other training
   a. aids to navigation.
   b. individual flights.
   c. recognition and observation.
   d. simulated inclined bombardment.
   e. simulated strafing.
   f. squad formation four aircraft. [5]

The pre-combat training period for the Aztec Eagles extended from May 12 through June 7. After this guidance period, the 201st began flying with American units and participating in flights over the combat zones.[6]

Over 262,000 Japanese troops occupied Luzon when General MacArthur's forces attacked the island on January 9, 1945. The Japanese Kembu Group had 30,000 of these soldiers and was led by Major General Rikichi Tsukada, concentrated around the Clark Field–Bataan sector. The Mexican air squadron arrived on Luzon four months after the American invasion. By then, the American forces had forced the majority of the Japanese out of the southern Luzon and Clark Field area into northern Luzon.[7]

In Europe, the war now began to wind down, but circumstances and timing allowed the 201st to stand as warriors for a time in the war against Japan. They almost arrived too late to participate in the war. The day before the 201st arrived in Luzon, the Italians executed Benito Mussolini in Milan Square. The next day, Russian shock troops occupied Anhalter Station and 117 city blocks in the center of Berlin and American Seventh Army tanks and infantry poured into Munich. The U.S. Third Army liberated 27,000 Allied prisoners of war—mostly American flyers. On Luzon, the 37th Division thrust east and south to secure the enemy strongpoint at Topside and Loacon

Airfield. On Mindanao, the American 24th Division advanced to within 17 miles of Davao City.[8]

The 58th Fighter Group personnel displayed doubt and misgivings about the capability of the Mexican pilots soon after the 201st arrived in Porac. Although initially the American attitudes appeared to be racist, other reasons existed. For two years, the 58th, a seasoned combat unit, had fought the Japanese from New Guinea to the Philippines. They flew aircraft that gradually had become old from continual use. Along with a lifestyle with few amenities, they battled adverse climatic conditions, bad food, plagues (like scrub fever), and dirt runways.

Tested in battle and found to be not wanting, pilots of the 58th displayed an attitude of superiority. They possessed an overwhelming arrogant conviction in their own ability. The insertion of a new, untried, and untested unit into their old framework created resentment. Their feelings about the ability of any newcomers would have been the true even if they had been U.S. flyers. The fact that the Fifth Air Force separated the Mexicans from the rest of the squadron had little bearing on this attitude. Each of the squadrons maintained a separate tent and eating area. The situation was that the Mexicans were new, and untested, whose principal language was Spanish. Although the 201st pilots spoke English, less than half of the enlisted men did. The American personnel did not speak Spanish and they found it difficult to develop close relationships. With this exception, the skill of the Mexicans pilots granted them the right to be integrated into the other squadrons. Under wartime conditions, associations with those who were your counterparts tended to help develop friendships. The 69th Squadron Staff Sergeant Ned Ailes wrote to a colleague recalling an unpleasant first encounter with the Mexican unit:

> Our first knowledge of the 201st was when a detail was assigned to erect tents for an incoming squadron (I ducked it). When they arrived, their C.O. called ours and asked for a detail to dig the latrine pit. Our C.O., can't your men dig the pit? Their C.O., our men are specialists, they can't do that kind of work. Our C.O., you get your "blanket-blank" specialists some shovels and I'll bring a shovel and personally show them how to dig a hole.[9]

Ailes' impression of the Mexicans was somewhat different from that given in an interview by the 58th Fighter Group commander, Colonel Edward F. Roddy, and pilot, 1st Lieutenant Winston Handworker, No. 311 Squadron. Both men only dealt with the officers and pilots. Roddy said that the pilots of the 201st were knowledgeable, affable, and friendly. Roddy and Handworker affirmed that the pilots of the 201st were well behaved and they never had any negative impressions of them. Handworker added that toward him and the other pilots in his group the 201st pilots were friendly and outgoing with no display of arrogance.[10]

The insertion of the 201st into the 58th Fighter Group also created mixed feelings between the American pilots and their ground crews. Apart from all other overtones of disaffection with the Mexicans, the greatest discord developed over the assignment of aircraft to the 201st. According to Anthony J. Kupferer, the historian for the 58th, U.S. pilots complained that the Mexicans received the best aircraft. Technical Sergeant John Miller, 69th Squadron, related that the Mexican getting the choice aircraft did not set well with the American enlisted men. On the other hand, he noted that his relationship with the Mexican ground crews was good, although none of them spoke English to him. An example of their attitude toward the Mexicans was found in a quote by Staff Sergeant George E. Mayer:

> When we were operating off the fighter strip at Porac on Luzon … the 201st Mexican Fighter Squadron was attached to the group and did a lot of flying with our pilots. At first they had no aircraft so some were selected from our outfit and transferred to the Mexicans for use until they received their own aircraft. They had American Army Air Force personnel with them acting as advisors and these people performed the acceptance inspections. For some reason, they were extremely meticulous and we really had to work to get this equipment ready for the Mexicans. As it was, the Mexican squadron had nothing but nice, shiny new vehicles (cars and trucks) and lots of equipment that we didn't have and then to add further insult, we were tagged with these fanatical inspectors. Then when the Mexicans got their nice, shiny new aircraft, with the bubble canopies, the equipment that we had loaned was returned to us. [Author's note: The 201st did not receive the new bubble canopy P–47s until after the other 58th Fighter units had moved to Okinawa. These were flown back from Biak in July 1945]. The Mexicans earlier rejection of several P-47s was a decision of their mechanics and not the pilots who were prepared to fly the older aircraft.[11]

Several of the Mexican airmen disagreed with the stories that they initially received good aircraft equipment. Lieutenant Héctor Espinosa wrote in his diary:

> Unlucky day for the squadron due to the bad condition of the gears [aircraft] that was lent to us while ours is awaiting delivery. Again, Graco was forced to land in Loagag after losing the engine, fortunately without incidents. García Ramos, Estrada, Hernández Vega, Moreno, and Cal y Mayor landed in Mindoro due to mechanical problems. Only Hernández Vega came back but landed in Porac airstrip, a tire blew up and the gear (aircraft) was destroyed but without injuries. On May 23 and 24, Espinosa again recorded problems with the aircraft. In Porac, García Ramos was forced to land due to engine failure, fortunately without injuries. Barbosa and Cal y Mayor still in Mindoro. Captain Legorreta blew a tire on landing but nothing happened other than the scare. There are so many engine failures that an investigation is opened to determine if we could fly those old gears again.[12]

The borrowed aircraft represented a nightmare from the technical point of view, since they failed continuously, although the mechanics worked hard on the line, punished by an infernal heat, as Genaro Romero Parra, a mechanic of the squadron, said:

Our obligation was to keep these machines as efficient as possible, although many times the hoppers of the engines were so hot that we could not touch them, but we had to do the job very well, since at only five centimeters of height they change.[13]

Staff Sergeant Ned Ailes, 69th Fighter Squadron, remembered the argument over the quality of the P-47s given to the 201st Squadron:

We had to give them our best planes—mine was one of them. They flew it only once. It had a peculiarity—the cylinder head temperature hand would hang near the "red line" while in flight, but never go over. Guess they didn't like that. They raised such a fuss about us giving them junk that a 5th Air Force inspector came down and personally checked out the next batch. The Flight Chief asked if I wanted my old plane back and I said sure. I then had two planes to take care of for quite a while.[14]

Captain Joe Madison, No. 311 Squadron, contradicted others who stated that the Mexicans received the best aircraft. He said: "When the 201st Mexican Air Force Squadron attached to us … we had to supply planes to them, and gave them our worst planes, which they wouldn't accept. We then were forced to give them our best planes." Tech sergeant and squadron technical inspector Robert C. Duvall, 311 Fighter Squadron, received the assignment to see personally that the aircraft given to the 201st had no mechanical problems. He did not know who initiated this convention, but he was told that his orders came from the top. He said: "My orders were to turn the P-47s over to the Mexicans in 100 percent condition." Because of Roosevelt's interest in the Mexican squadron, the assumption was that all top commanders knew that they must be very evenhanded with the Mexican squadron.[15]

The 201st received old planes with new paint jobs. The red, white, and green Mexican Air Force emblem and the insignia of the U.S. Air Force reflected alternately on each wing tip, top and bottom. A white U.S. Air Force star within a black circular panel marked each side of the rear fuselage. Painted on the movable, vertical tail surface in stripes was the red, white, and green colors of the Mexican flag. The 201st painted the noses of their aircraft white, consequently someone referred to their planes as *Las Palomas* (The Doves).[16]

First Lieutenant Fred Clark, 69th Squadron, among the first to indoctrinate the 201st pilots, had reservations from the beginning over the insertion of the Mexicans into the 58th Fighter Squadron. This uncertainty continued as he later familiarized three or four of the Mexican pilots with the conditions around Porac by flying them around the field. Clark had difficulty understanding the accented English spoken by the Mexicans and thus regarded language differences as the greatest hindrance to mutual understanding. His skepticism never waned.[17]

The training problems with the 201st at Porac concerned many pilots in the 58th Fighter Group. First Lieutenant Joe Madison, 311 Squadron, expressed his view of these problems:

When they started flying, I looked over the strip one day, and have never seen so many red flares before. It looked like the 4th of July. The Mexicans were landing from one end of the strip and we were landing from the other. Later, one of the Mexicans came in for a landing, and overshot, and went around again with prop set wrong. He went around the strip just above the parked planes and when he approached, again he was off to one side, but turned and lined up with the strip with one wing almost on the ground, landed on one wheel and stopped on the runway safe. Immediately, a jeep drove onto the strip, and I understand, the commander of the Mexicans court–martialed him right on the spot. But really, the fellow was very lucky to be alive.[18]

Members of the 201st Squadron did not concur with Joe Madison's statement concerning the court-martial incident. He had only made a supposition. Ned Ailes, former staff sergeant, 69th Squadron, gave an opinion on some initial flights made by the 201st pilots. He wrote:

It took a while to smooth out their approach for a landing. A flight of four would come in over the field, but instead of peeling off 1, 2, 3, 4, they would sort of "explode" and scatter. When taxiing the planes, they had a mechanic riding on the wing and one by the cockpit to guide them—not a bad idea.[19]

Other American pilots and enlisted personnel also voiced concern in regard to operating with the Mexican unit. Many expressed baseless fears that the language barrier might spell trouble when the Mexican pilots flew in close ground support 1st Lieutenant Ken G. Larsen, a 69th Squadron pilot, expressed a judgment that the Mexican pilots were too macho; wanting to prove their skill, they took unnecessary chances. Larsen cited as an example that, quite often for thrills, P-47 pilots flew just off the choppy waves in Manila bay, kicking up a spray behind their aircraft as their big propellers picked up water. On May 24, Larson and his wingman, 201 Squadron pilot López Portillo, came down into the bay to kick up a little spray. As they thundered across the bay, Portillo positioned his plane slightly below Larson. When Larson brought his plane closer to the whitecaps, Portillo, as if challenged, dropped still closer. Finally, Portillo dropped so low that he flew his plane into the water. Fortunately, it did not kill him and he was rescued, but he lost a valuable plane.

For whatever reason, Lieutenant Héctor Espinosa Galván believed that the Portillo incident came about because of engine failure. There are no accident reports to verify this supposition, however. On May 24, Espinosa wrote in his diary: "Portillo suffered another accident due to engine failure in the Bay of Manila but miraculous came without injuries. There are so many engine failures that an investigation is opened to determine if we could fly those old gears [airplanes] again." The next day Espinosa wrote: "Portillo still has not come back from Manila." Two days later, he added:

Today, for the first time, I had to go to a commission in the city of Manila, which was totally destroyed. The purpose of the commission was to locate Portillo who went down in the bay and nobody knew about it. At midnight, I finally found him at the 80 [*sic.*] general hospital where he was resting. Fortunately, he had minor injuries in the face and by the end of the week he should be back again in Porac.[20]

Unfounded rumors circulated within the American forces about the training of the 201st Squadron. In a letter to the author, Ned Ailes wrote: "I don't know the extent of training that the 201 had, but rumor had it that their families had to have wealth or social standing to get them into pilot training. We were not very enthused to hear that they had brought their wives and were getting paid by both the Mexican and U.S. governments." These foolish rumors were, of course, wrong. The Mexican pilots did not bring their wives to Luzon. Several pilots from the 69th Squadron said that they thought that all of the Mexican pilots came from wealthy families. One veteran 69th pilot said that a Mexican pilot, whose name he did not remember, told him that his family owned half of Mexico City and if he came to visit in Mexico City, he would be treated to a swell time. The rumors arose through gossip, but the last story could well be a macho statement to a gullible "*gringo*."[21]

The U.S. Air Force inserted an inexperienced 201st Squadron into a veteran group of P-47 pilots, who long ago adapted to living in combat conditions foreign to the new arrivals. The initial indoctrination training for the Mexican pilots emphasized the importance of aircraft identification, weather and terrain recognition, and formation flying conformity. Because of their inexperience in a combat area, a common complaint among the American 58th Fighter Group pilots concerned their flying discipline. Russ Geisy, a retired 310 Squadron fighter pilot, helped to train the Mexicans after they reached the Philippines. Geisy remarked that initially the Mexicans lacked regimentation. He said: "Coming into training, Mexico's finest aviators were rusty by U.S. Air Force combat standards … the toughest part of training was getting the pilots used to the strict laws of combat flying." He went on to say:

> They didn't believe in radio silence. They always wanted to talk on the radio. They also wrecked more airplanes during training than anyone I can remember. The 58th Fighter Group referred to the newly arrived Mexican pilots as green pilots. Since replacement pilots from the U.S. had no combat experience, they were called green pilots. Staff Sergeant Ned Ailes thought they were overly anxious and nervous. On one occasion, he said, a Mexican pilot, while attempting to land kept coming in too high and repeatedly had to go around. After watching him make several failed attempts to land, Ailes' CO got on the radio and said, "Set it down the next time or I'll come up and shoot you down." On his next attempt Niles said, "I watched as he came in high but he set it down—in a rice paddy off the end of the runway. Mud and water flew, but I don't believe that the pilot was hurt.[22]

Others credit the Mexican pilots as being quite worthy, disregarding the criticism against them. U.S. Air Force Lieutenant Colonel Howard Tuman, commanding officer of 301 Squadron, highly praised their ability. Tuman trained the Mexicans after they arrived in Porac. He remarked: "… the Mexicans were only in the war for a short time, but it was enough to make them heroes for a lifetime back home. They were super pilots for a super plane. Their ability to accurately drop 1,000-pound bombs in difficult conditions was the stamp that made them legends."[23]

Captain Art Marston, 311 Squadron pilot, expressed the same unfounded fears as Lieutenant Clark that language difficulty might be big trouble when the Mexicans were used in close ground support:

While at Porac, they attached the 201st Mexican Fighter Squadron to our group for orientation. About half could speak English and the other half weak in its use. This produced a problem for a while. We had many dive-bombing missions in the Balete Pass underground control bombing on fortified positions in front of our troops. The ground controllers would time their target makers after the Japanese shot smoke shells into our lines. There was some concern whether the Mexicans could understand this without hitting our troops, but they apparently did well.[24]

Flying training did not start until May 17, due to bad weather the previous days. The 201st Squadron used P-47s on loan from the 58th Fighter Group units. Flight training included familiarization and orientation, fighter tactics and techniques, simulated combat missions, and combat missions.

Advanced flight training finished on June 3, and the Aztec Eagles was ready for combat in the S.W.P.A. The pilots began flying missions with U.S. formations, increasing the number of Mexican pilots until the formation was completely from the 201st Squadron. However, during most operations of the Mexican squadron, one American pilot was included in the formation. In addition, the squadron flew some more training missions in the S.W.P.A., especially in the air-to-air arena.

The Lend-Lease agreement permitted the Mexican squadron to use airplanes, equipment, instructors, and training facilities in the U.S. It also contemplated the equipment of the unit overseas, in the same manner that an American unit. Initially, the unit received in the Philippines used aircraft and other equipment on loan. The 201st Squadron's aircraft had U.S. markings in addition to the Mexican markings, and they had a white band painted on the nose.[25]

After the additional training, the 201st Squadron was ready to fly the P-47 aircraft, officially known as Thunderbolt, but nicknamed "Jug" due to its bulky shape that resembled a milk jug. It was a big and heavy airplane, weighting almost 7 tons, but it was powerful and fast. There were many series of this aircraft—of which 15,682 were built.[23] Initially it was used as an air superiority fighter, a role later taken by the P-51 Mustang, an aircraft with better endurance and range. The P-47 could carry up to two 1,000-lb.

bombs, and with its eight .50-cal. machine guns, it was an excellent aircraft for close air support and air-to-ground missions in general, especially at short range.

The unit started operations with fifteen P-47D aircraft and was able to maintain around twelve operational aircraft at all times. Adequate training and integration in the U.S. logistical system contributed to these numbers, in spite of losses. Spare parts were available and the 58th Fighter Group retained the P-47 aircraft, while other units changed to the P-51. Access to higher-level maintenance facilities also contributed to the squadron's operational status.[26]

10

Life at Porac Airfield

The 58th Fighter Group had transferred to Porac only a short time before the 201st Squadron arrived. Between April 5 and 8, the 58th Fighter Group moved its headquarters and three fighter squadrons from Mindoro to Mangaldan, Luzon. Seven days later, the unit prepared to move again. Although the unit members did not rejoice over the possibility of another move, they could not operate out of Mangaldan because the incessant rains had made a quagmire out of the dirt runways. They located a 5,000-foot, hard, dirt-surface runway at Porac Field, formerly called Clark Number 5, situated just south of Clark Field. At Porac Field, they set up a temporary camp near the airstrip. Once lumber became available, they relocated their camp to higher ground with better drainage and away from the airstrip.[1]

When the 201st Squadron reached Porac, the men began setting up camp in an area separated from the Americans and surrounded by hills and jungle. The stifling heat and the incessant mosquitoes made the work hard. They raised tents while constructing an operation's office, septic tanks, latrines, medical quarters, dining area, and a flag pole to display their national flag.[2]

Sleeping quarters at Porac enjoyed only wartime amenities. Most of the Allied airmen slept in tents. Mexican officers slept four to a tent, as did the enlisted men. The tents had dirt floors, though the floors were eventually upgraded to lumber. The occupants dug a drainage ditch around their tents to channel water away from the dirt floor. Water drainage was absolutely necessary because of the incessant rain in the Philippines. Each airman had mosquito netting to protect against the swarms of insects. Some Mexican airmen sought more comfortable sleeping quarters. Second Sergeant Alfonso Cuellar Ponce de Ledn and his tent mates paid a group of Filipinos to build them a tent with wooden floors. They also planted flowers and other plants outside their tents. In the passageways in between, they posted signs with the names of Mexican streets, such as *16 de Septiembre*, or *Madero*, and others. One sign had an arrow pointing east that read *Zócalo 10,000 km*.[3]

When they first arrived at Porac, the 201st Squadron commander, Captain Gaxiola Andrade, expressed anxiety about the welfare of his men. He had special concern over a malady called scrub fever. Ticks borne by rats carried typhus, and Gaxiola learned several American service members were dying from the sickness. Many described the initial effects of scrub fever as similar to that of malaria, but it became much worse as the disease progressed. In New Guinea, almost 70 percent of infected American soldiers died. Those who succumbed to scrub typhus ran extremely high fevers along with severe headaches. The effects of the fever were so bad that those infected could not sleep or eat. Second Lieutenant Jack Mathis, a 310 Squadron pilot from Texas, almost died of the fever. Mathis reported that he lost almost 35 lb. of body weight in ten days because of the heat and his inability to sleep and ingest food. The debilitating aftereffects of the fever prevented pilots from flying for four to six months. Mathis never again flew with the 310th, and his squadron sent him back the United States to convalesce. All clothing belonging to the Mexican airmen received a liberal dousing of chemicals when they came on to the base as a small measure of protection.[4]

As an additional health measure, Gaxiola wanted his men to have floors in their tents. Floors provided added protection from the scrub typhus and helped the men maintain cleaner and cooler sleeping quarters. Later he appealed to Lieutenant Colonel Edward F. Roddy, commander of the 58th Fighter Group, to supply flooring for the tents of his men. Although lumber was not easily obtained, Roddy found a source. He discovered that a nearby Navy Construction Battalion (C.B.) operated a sawmill near Porac from 6 a.m. until midnight. He then negotiated a deal to provide C-47 aircraft to bring in supplies for them in exchange for use of the sawmill from midnight until 6 a.m.[5] The latrine and shower arrangements at Porac were primitive. The Mexican latrine area lay some distance away from the tent area—and down wind. Their much closer open-air general shower facility provided no privacy. When rain fell, the men abandoned the military showers, removed their clothing, stepped out naked into the downpour with a bar of soap, and bathed. The more ingenious Mexican squadron members created their personal shower facilities in their tents. They made special showers by hoisting empty, specially fabricated 175-gallon fuel tanks on to 7-foot-high scuffles built in one of the corners of their tents. Filipino workers filled the tanks with water each day. Although most tents utilized wood as flooring material, the men sometimes used bamboo for the shower floor area because moisture did not cause it to rot.[6]

As with the sleeping quarters area, the Mexican airmen had eating facilities apart from the Americans. They ate together under a tent. The soldiers walked to and from the mess hall that was located more than a mile from their camp. Not accustomed to the intense tropical heat, the men suffered. All food supplies came from a general supply depot. American food was standard fare for the entire camp and the Mexican cooks were trained in its preparation. For breakfast, the 201st had powdered milk and eggs, butter, cereal, toast, coffee, sugar, and tomato juice. Lunch included beef stew, vegetables, onions, cheese, spiced apples, mashed potatoes, tea, and bread. Dinner consisted of meat stews, vegetables, French fries, bread, and apple pie or chocolate cake.

With the exception of the hot dog, the usual American G.I. food soon seemed bland to the Mexican's palate. In an attempt to spice up their meals, Mexican cooks foraged for fruit and foods native to their country.

Most Mexican food products were not available in Luzon, but fruits and vegetables were plentiful. Indigenous mangoes and coconuts grew profusely in the hot, moist Luzon climate. Pineapple, papayas, and bananas were also available. The Mexicans rejected the oranges grown in the Philippines, choosing instead those that came from the American supply depot. Many Filipinos came to their camp selling fruits and other foodstuffs. The Mexicans initially bought only coconuts, after being warned against eating anything that might be contaminated by the waters. An addition to their food supply and their morale came was when young Filipino maidens came around to their tents selling bananas, fresh eggs, chickens, and mangoes. Lieutenant Colonel H. A. Tuman, former commanding officer of 310 Squadron, remembered that, when U.S. Air Force cooks received a large supply of pinto beans, they traded them to the Mexican cooks for other food products.[7]

The war-torn Philippines offered few conveniences but did have an abundant supply of willing and able workers. The resourceful Mexican soldiers lost no time in taking advantage of this convenience. Every tent had from one to four houseboys. Privates as well as officers luxuriated in this help. Filipino youngsters filled helmets and canteens with water, raked up cigarette butts, cleaned the tent area, and ran errands. Women did the laundry for the Mexican soldiers. Most of the work was done by hand. It was typical, on a sunny day in the Mexican compound, to see many women and girls working at cleaning and laundry. All these chores were not free, Philippine civil authorities maintained a pricing policy that kept the cost within reason.[8]

Initial war impressions aroused deep emotions among the Mexican air squadron running from horror and fear to sadness. One particular anguish remained forever with Sergeant Pedro Martínez Pérez who was concerned about children. As the Japanese retreated, they killed or destroyed much in their path. They left little food for the civilian population. Many children, left on their own to obtain food, roamed camp areas searching and begging for something to eat. Several 201st Squadron members saw young Filipinos naked and going through every piece of trash for food. Soldiers received orders to forgo giving food to children because of the scarcity of supplies for the troops. Martínez, however, could not deny the small, emaciated children who came into camp pleading for food. He more or less adopted two or three, providing them with food but requiring them to eat it there. Sergeant Manuel Cervantes remembered that, although the food was not bad, sometimes it was not very appetizing. However, he felt it unjust to ask for something more when he could see how Filipino women and children dug through trashcans, hoping to find leftovers that the soldiers threw away. He remembered with great sadness watching little children, who could barely reach the lids of the trashcans, reaching in with their little hands to find something to eat. Many times, young women offered themselves to the soldiers, in return for a few cigarettes, candy, or cookies, items found only on the black market.[9]

The off-duty life for a Mexicans during the time they were at Porac and after their transfer to Clark was no different from other Allied aviators. On base, the men passed the time at sports during the daylight hours and the movies, cards, or reading at night. They played baseball and basketball or jogged. Although they played soccer at home, they did not play it in the Philippines. Every week each man received a carton containing twelve beers. With no refrigeration to cool it, they dug a hole in the ground near their tent and put the beer in it. Each morning they would pour some water into the hole, hoping the evaporation would cool the beer.[10]

When they could leave the base on personal and leisure time, some airmen, seeking excitement, went to Manila or other nearby towns. During the war, Manila was the place to go for more than 100,000 soldiers. The city was saturated with women, prostitutes, and soldiers with plenty of money. A few went to Manila only to have a bottle of Spanish cognac. One soldier reported that he and his friends drank much more than their share. Others went to Manila looking only for women. One Mexican soldier wrote that it was imperative that a young man be sexually satisfied. He mentioned a Filipino woman named Dolores that he thought looked like a Mexican. She liked Mexicans and the young soldier recalled that her father or another woman collected the money. Dolores was in love with a young Mexican officer. One Mexican soldier with the nickname "Bullets" spent his free time seeing girls in the small towns surrounding Manila. The $5 he spent on a drink did not go far as he earned only $101 a month. Allied personnel of all races and colors went into the small towns nearby to drink and make love to the girls. A single girl sometimes made love to more than fifty men in one night. "Comfort" or "pro" stations were set up by the medical corps at various locations around the towns to assist the men in sanitizing themselves and to prevent them from catching a venereal disease.[11]

Other towns located near the base also offered an escape from the war. In the town of San Fernando, for three or four Filipino pesos, a soldier could buy a roasted chicken. In this town and many others, the Mexicans found people who spoke fluent Spanish. They identified well with these people who were Spaniards or descendants of Spaniards. Some of these people had money before the war but now found themselves starving. In Angelos, another town close by, liquor stores sold a whiskey called Panequi. Soldiers were forbidden to drink it because it was made out of wood alcohol and could lead to blindness. Allied soldiers of all races visited these towns and those of the 201st Squadron had to be careful because someone was always looking for a fight.[12]

Racism generally did not intrude on the lives of the 201st Squadron in the Philippines. Colonel Edward F. Roddy did recall an incident when a very upset Captain Gaxiola came to see him with a racial complaint. The Mexican captain stated that signs in several of the Filipino bars read "No Negros or Mexicans allowed." He wanted Roddy to do something about it, but Roddy told him that this was out of his jurisdiction and referred him to Colonel Cárdenas, liaison to the U.S. military at Fort Stotsenburg, located about 10 miles from Clark Field. None of the other 201st members interviewed knew about this incident. They expressed surprise and skepticism when told about it.[13]

The 201st Squadron ground support personnel saw no combat. They sometimes stood guard to protect the camp perimeter, prepared the planes, and supported the pilots for combat. Ground support for their pilots and the aircraft they flew required ten or more different specialties—from mechanics and armorers to cooks and clerks. Many Mexican soldiers felt a keen disappointment that they could not go into combat against the Japanese. Some satisfied their urge to see warfare in differing ways. Intelligence officer Captain Blanco Ledesma fulfilled his yearning for action when he hitched a ride, on June 19, with a Fifth Air Force bombing mission to Formosa. Lieutenant Colonel Alfonso Gurza Farfan and Major Enrique Sandoval Castarrica observed the 33rd Infantry Division airborne operations in the region of Baguio.[14]

Other soldiers sought different types of excitement. In his article "Prisoners of War," Corporal Quintal Pinzon wrote that they heard many stories about soldiers or Filipinos finding a box of gold, a rare Japanese flag, or a beautiful Samurai sword encrusted with precious stones. These stories, he wrote, inspired several to venture out in search of treasure. On August 26, they planned their adventure. Equipped with .30-caliber weapons, plenty of ammunition, and food, they left early in the morning heading north. Their path took them through many native villages, where they rested and quenched their thirst. They passed out of the areas considered safe into areas of danger. Entering the jungle, they saw only paths, which previously served as roads, full of bomb holes and destroyed Japanese equipment. They saw skeletons of Japanese soldiers with parts of their uniforms still clinging to their bones. With great care, they did nothing to disturb the remains, as they knew the danger of booby traps left by the Japanese. After rounding one sloping hill, they saw a shack. Quickly preparing their weapons, they inched closer to the building and, finally, with their weapons, pushed open a door with the hinge broken. Quintal Pinzon jumped to one side and fired a round into the building. He waited a moment and then called to his companions. The building was empty and had a sickening odor that turned out to be two badly decayed Japanese soldiers' bodies. They did not stay inside the building any longer than necessary.[15]

At 2 p.m., the soldiers realized that they were many miles from their camp, so they decided to start back toward their base. After discovering a river near the shack, they followed it for a distance. As they walked along the edge of the river, they discovered fresh footprints disappearing into the water. Immediately, they hid in some foliage that grew along the bank of the river. After advancing in the leafage for about 50 yards, they discovered Japanese soldiers. Breaking up, two men stayed on the right bank and Quintal Pinzon and another companion crossed to the left side. Using hand signals to communicate with the others, Pinzon indicated that he saw eight Japanese soldiers in camp preparing their food. He also saw that the soldiers were armed with large caliber weapons. Quickly, he moved his friends to his side. Then suddenly he saw the silhouette of a man coming toward him. Fearful that if he fired it would alert the other Japanese; he crouched, with his gun ready, and waited as the man came toward him. After a minute, Pinzon lost sight of the man, so he retreated and hid again. Suddenly the man with a sword in his left hand and a grenade in his right appeared about 15 meters from him and yelled. Pinzon fired five shots at the figure and saw him go down. His other companions started attacking the Japanese camp.[16]

Looking around for the other Japanese, Pinzon discovered that they had ran into a cave on the side of the mountain. He then went over to the man he shot, who was still alive but bleeding profusely. They thought about killing him but decided against it. After Corporal Olegario climbed a mound to see into the mouth of the cave, a man came running out and fell when Olegario opened fire at him. They found the soldier alive but bleeding from a foot wound. Leaving one of their group to guard the two prisoners, the other three men headed for the cave to capture or kill the other Japanese.

At the entrance was a rifle with the bayonet stuck in the ground, and a torn Japanese flag. They threw hand grenades into the cave, but no one came out. The cave was small and had an opening at the other end. Looking inside, they found many sacks of rice and sugar, bags of tea, and bad odors because of the many dead bodies. With a group of fugitive Japanese soldiers on the loose, they decided to continue on to their base. On their way back, they came on some Filipino soldiers and told them of the shooting incident. Hours later, they returned to camp with their prisoners of war.[17]

A. J. Kupferer recorded in *No Glamor... No Glory* that "pilots and ground crew members of the Fifth Air Force Fighter Command organized a spare time hunting patrol and accounted for 45 Japs in one week near their advance base on Luzon."[18]

Early on, the Mexican Air Force received warnings of possible attacks by bombing or assaults by Japanese soldiers. When occasional night alarms alerted the quiet Mexican camp, the men quickly prepared to repel any efforts by the Japanese to take over the base. They spent numerous nights in this manner during their time at Porac and Clark. During August, many groups of Japanese soldiers still occupied the mountains and jungles around Clark Field. The mountains reminded the Mexican airmen of the area around Vera Cruz and Tabasco, as well as the jungle of Lacandona. They knew that the Japanese carved tunnels in the mountains to protect their armament, their headquarters, offices, and even hospitals. Although not a threat to the American army, the Japanese presented a problem when organized into guerrilla groups searching for food. They attacked towns for anything they could find to support their life in the jungle, but they sought mostly food.[19]

11

Missions over Luzon

The situation in the Pacific was already different from that which produced the Japanese offensive of 1942. Since the battles that took place on the Salomon Island in August 1943, the control of the situation was in the hands of the American forces. The memorable actions of Guadalcanal, Bougainville, the Gilberts, and Tarawa provide an interesting page of military history, written in November of the same year, as well as the battles in the Marshalls and Kwajalein of February 1944. American control had thus been imposed in the Central and Southwestern Pacific.

By April 1944, Australia was no longer in danger. When the F.A.E.M. crossed the Pacific, and the B-29s from Guam began attacking the Japanese cities, Formosa had already been the object of the guns of the American Navy. American forces had disembarked in Leyte, Manila had been captured, and Okinawa invaded. The decisive Battle of the Sea of the Philippines was fought.

The F.A.E.M. route was not expeditious and when leaving Hollandia, the *Fairisle* was framed in the YLN122 convoy and, faced with the danger of aerial attacks, the staff was no longer allowed to sleep on deck as they had been doing to escape from heat. When the F.A.E.M. arrived in the Philippines, the Japanese island of Okinawa had been invaded (on April 1), a landing was made in Legazpi, Luzon, another in Mindanao on the 18th, and Cebu was conquered. In addition, another similar operation was taking place in the Palawan group, north of Borneo, but the Malay, Indochinese, and Chinese coasts were still hostile.[1]

In the Philippine Islands, friendly forces only occupied a small part of Luzon, which was reduced to the valley that extended from Dagupan and San Fernando, in the Gulf of Lingayen, to Manila, adding to this area the peninsula of Bataan, Corregidor, and other points of the latter region. Some operation extended to Lucena, in the Province of Batangas, south of Manila. A portion of Marinduque Island was also occupied, as was Cebu and a part of Panay. With these sole exceptions, all the islands were in the power of the enemy, or at least out of the control of the American troops, although some areas of northern Luzon and Mindananao were under the control of the Philippine Army.[2]

Overview of the Battle of Luzon

"The Philippine theater of operations is the locus of victory or defeat," argued General Douglas MacArthur, as Japanese planes strafed and bombed key installations around Manila on December 8, 1941. Although overwhelming Japanese strength ultimately forced the United States to relinquish the Philippines, MacArthur began planning his return almost immediately from bases in Australia. Throughout the long campaign to push the Japanese out of their Pacific bastions, these islands remained his crucial objective. "The President of the United States ordered me to break through the Japanese lines … for the purpose, as I understand it, of organizing the American offensive against Japan, a primary object of which is the relief of the Philippines," MacArthur said when he took over as Allied commander in the Southwest Pacific, "I came through and I shall return." As the Pacific campaign dragged on, MacArthur never strayed far from that goal, and every move he made was aimed ultimately at recapturing the lost archipelago.

In March 1942, a Joint Chiefs of Staff directive established two U.S. military commands in the Pacific: the Southwest Pacific Area, headed by General MacArthur, and the Pacific Ocean Areas, under Admiral Chester W. Nimitz. The decision clearly violated the principle of unity of command. However, with naval officers objecting to MacArthur, the senior officer in the region, as overall Pacific commander and with MacArthur unlikely to subordinate himself to another, the ensuing division of authority seemed a workable compromise. Given the size of the theater and the different national contingents involved, it may even have been a blessing. However, it left no single authority in the Pacific to decide between conflicting plans or to coordinate between the two. MacArthur later wrote:

> … of all the faulty decisions of the war, perhaps the most unexplainable one was the failure to unify the command in the Pacific, [which] … resulted in divided effort; the waste, diffusion, and duplication of force; and the consequent extension of the war with added casualties and cost.[3]

From a strategic perspective, this divided command had a direct impact on decisions leading up to the invasion of the Philippines.

During the spring of 1944, the Joint Chiefs debated the merits of seizing Luzon or the Chinese island of Formosa as an initial point for direct operations against Japan. Admiral Ernest J. King, the Chief of Naval Operations, had long objected to landings in the Philippines, and by May 1944, he was joined by Army Chief of Staff General George C. Marshall and Army Air Force Chief of Staff General Henry H. Arnold. Marshall felt that MacArthur's Luzon plan would be the slow way and that it made more sense to cut across from the Mariana Islands to Formosa. MacArthur, on the other hand, argued that the Formosa route was militarily unsound and that the Philippine Islands provided a more sensible staging area for the final assault against the Japanese home islands. As commander of the Philippine defenses in 1941, MacArthur felt a strong moral responsibility to free the entire archipelago of the brutal Japanese occupation. Making the Philippines a major Pacific objective gave his Southwest Pacific command a key mission.

By July 1944, most planners agreed that an invasion of Formosa was not logistically feasible in the near future. In September, the Joint Chiefs thus approved a December starting date for MacArthur's invasion of Leyte Island in the central Philippines. The invasion would be followed by an assault on either Luzon—the large, northernmost Philippine island—on February 20 or Formosa on March 1. However, it was not until October that Admiral King finally agreed that Luzon was the better choice.

From the Japanese perspective, control of the islands was vital. Loss of the Philippines would threaten Japan's overseas access to foodstuffs and critical raw materials, especially oil, from the East Indies and Southeast Asia. Thus, Tokyo's naval and army leaders vowed to make the defense of the Philippines their major war effort for 1943–44. For these purposes, the commander of Japanese land forces in the Philippines, General Tomoyuki Yamashita, the former conqueror of British Malaya and Singapore, had some 430,000 troops stationed all across the islands, while Japanese naval leaders were prepared to commit the entire battle fleet. If the Americans could be stopped here, then perhaps the entire tide of the war could be changed or, at least, Japan's position greatly strengthened.

MacArthur's return to the Philippines began on the island of Leyte in October 1944. Prior to the amphibious assault, the Japanese carrier force had been decimated in the Battle of the Philippine Sea on June 19–20 of the same year. Moreover, the Battle of Leyte Gulf in October saw most of the Japanese surface fleet destroyed with little to show for its sacrifice. Japan's once formidable air force was also decimated, leaving the skies over the Philippines open to American air power. Yet the primary objective of assaulting Leyte was to provide a staging area for a much larger effort, the assault against the island of Luzon where most of the Japanese land defenses lay. The operations on Leyte in December gave the Americans little more than a foothold in the Philippines.[4]

Before Luzon could be attacked, MacArthur needed a base of operations closer to his objective than Leyte. He picked Mindoro, an island with minimal Japanese defenses just south of Luzon. About half the size of New Jersey, Mindoro is blanketed by mountains, with a few narrow plains along the coast. The high peaks trap clouds moving up from the south, causing almost daily rains and high humidity and making the island a breeding ground for malaria and other tropical diseases.

From MacArthur's point of view, Mindoro was important only for its potential airfields could supplement the unsatisfactory ones recently constructed on Leyte. Landing areas in the northeastern part of the island were best, but constant inclement weather and the airfields' proximity to what was left of Japanese air power on Luzon ruled them out. Instead, planners chose to secure beachhead and airfield sites near

San José, in the southwest corner of the island. Although not ideal, the region lay near Mangarin Bay, Mindoro's best anchorage. This location would provide a base for the amphibious invasion fleet and allow land-based American aircraft to intensify their attacks against the Japanese on Luzon.

MacArthur assigned the seizure of Mindoro to Lieutenant General Walter Krueger's Sixth Army. Krueger, in turn, gave the task to Major General Roscoe B. Woodruff, commander of the 24th Infantry Division, who was to employ one organic regiment, the 19th Infantry, and the separate 503rd Parachute Regimental Combat Team. Although the airborne unit was originally scheduled to jump into the battle area, the limited capacity of the Leyte airfields dictated that they arrive by sea, alongside the infantry. In any case, naval support for the small landing was substantial, with six escort carriers, three battleships, six cruisers, and many small warships providing direct support.

For the amphibious assault vessels and supporting warships, the main threat came from Japanese land-based *kamikaze* (divine wind) suicide planes. The Japanese had begun the practice as a desperate measure during the final stages of the Leyte Campaign, perfecting it during December. On the 13th, two days before the scheduled assault on Mindoro, the light cruiser *Nashville* was hit by a *kamikaze*, killing over 130 men and wounding another 190.[5]

Among the injured was Brigadier General William C. Dunkel, commander of the landing force. Later *kamikaze* attacks damaged two L.S.T.s (landing ships, tank) and disabled several other ships. U.S. Army and Navy aviation did what they could during the first weeks of December. The army claimed to have destroyed about 450 Japanese planes in the air and on the ground throughout the Philippines and the navy 270 more.

The invasion of Mindoro began on December 15. Clear weather allowed full use of U.S. air and naval power against virtually no Japanese resistance. The ensuing landings were also unopposed. With only about 1,000 Japanese troops on the large island, plus some 200 survivors from ships sunk off Mindoro while on their way to Leyte, the defenders could do little. By the end of the first day, Army engineers were hard at work preparing airfields for the invasion of Luzon. The first was completed in five days; a second was ready in thirteen. Together the airfields allowed American aircraft to provide more direct support for the planned Luzon beachhead, striking *kamikaze* airfields before aircraft could take off and harrying Japanese shipping between Luzon, Formosa, and southern Japan.[6]

From his headquarters in Manila, General Yamashita realized that he could expect little outside support. The Japanese naval and air arms had done their best in the preceding months but to no avail, and they had been largely destroyed in the process. Moreover, Yamashita's forces on Luzon, some 260,000 strong, were weak in artillery, transport, armor, and other modern equipment. They would be unable to face the well-equipped American Army units in open warfare. Thus, Yamashita decided to fight a delaying action, keeping his army in the field as long as possible. During his 1941–42 defense of the Philippines, MacArthur had considered Manila, the central Luzon plains, and the Bataan Peninsula critical, with their harbors and airfields. The Japanese commander, however, had no intention of defending these sites. Instead, Yamashita planned to withdraw the bulk of his forces into three widely separated mountain strongholds and settle down for a long battle of attrition.

Long before the American invasion began, General Yamashita divided his Luzon forces into three groups, each centered around a remote geographical region. The largest of these groups and under the direct command of Yamashita was Shobu Group, located in northern Luzon with about 152,000 troops. A much smaller force, Kembu Group, with approximately 30,000 troops, occupied the Clark Air Field complex as well as the Bataan Peninsula and Corridor. The third major force, Shimbu Group, consisted of some 80,000 soldiers occupying the southern sections of Luzon, an area that included the island's long Bicol Peninsula as well as the mountains immediately east of Manila. Most Shimbu units were in the latter area and controlled the vital reservoirs that provided most of the capital area's water supply.

On the American side, General MacArthur intended to strike first at Lingayen Gulf, an area of sheltered beaches on the northwestern coast of Luzon. A landing there would place his troops close to the best roads and railways on the island, all of which ran through the central plains south to Manila, his main objective. In addition, by landing that far north of the capital, MacArthur allowed himself maneuvering room for the large force he intended to use on Luzon. However, once the beachhead was secure, his initial effort would focus on a southern drive to the Filipino capital. Possession of this central core, as well as Manila Bay, would allow his forces to dominate the island and make a further coordinated defense by the Japanese exceedingly difficult. Ultimately, ten U.S. divisions and five independent regiments would see action on Luzon, making it the largest campaign of the Pacific war and involving more troops than the United States had used in North Africa, Italy, or southern France.[7,8]

The weather on January 9 (called S-Day) was ideal. A light overcast dappled the predawn sky, and gentle waves promised a smooth ride onto the beach. At 7 a.m., the pre-assault bombardment began and was followed an hour later by the landings. With little initial Japanese opposition, General Krueger's Sixth Army landed almost 175,000 men along a 20-mile beachhead within a few days. While the I Corps, commanded by Lieutenant General Innis P. Swift, protected the beachhead's flanks, Lieutenant General Oscar W. Griswold's XIV Corps prepared to drive south, first to Clark Field and then to Manila. Only after the Manila area had been secured was Swift's I Corps to push north and east to seize the vital road junctions leading from the coast into the mountains of northern Luzon.

Almost from the beginning, there was friction between MacArthur and some of his subordinates. Krueger wanted the I Corps to secure the roads leading east into the mountains before the XIV Corps advanced south. Already, he pointed out, I Corps had encountered opposition on the beachhead's northern (or left) flank, while the XIV Corps had found little resistance to the south. Cautious, Krueger hesitated before committing his army to a narrow thrust directly toward Manila with his eastern flank open to a possible Japanese attack.

MacArthur disagreed. He thought it unlikely that the Japanese were capable of mounting an attack in Sixth Army's rear flank and directed Krueger to follow his prearranged plans, seizing Clark Air Field and the port facilities at Manila as soon as possible. So, on January 18, Griswold's XIV Corps moved south with the 37th and 40th Infantry Divisions, leaving Sixth Army's eastern flank undefended as it proceeded from the beachhead area. With Yamashita's Shobu Group relatively inactive, Krueger's concerns proved unwarranted. As at the beachhead, the Japanese put up little opposition to the drive south, having evacuated the central plains earlier. Only when Griswold's troops reached the outskirts of Clark Field on January 23 did they run up against determined resistance, and it came from the relatively weak Kembu Group. For more than a week, the Japanese fought a stubborn battle against the advancing Americans, and it was not until the end of January that the airfield was in American hands. Leaving the 40th Division behind to occupy the area, Krueger regrouped the XIV Corps and on February 2 continued south toward the capital.

From the beginning, MacArthur remained unhappy with the pace of the advance. He personally drove up and down the advancing line, inspecting units and making suggestions.[9, 10]

On January 30, after visiting the 37th Division as it advanced south from San Fernando toward Calumpit, MacArthur sent off a message to Krueger criticizing "the noticeable lack of drive and aggressive initiative." Later, while visiting the 1st Cavalry Division, which had just arrived in Luzon to reinforce the XIV Corps, he told the division commander, Major General Verne D. Mudge, to "Go to Manila, go around the Nips, bounce off the Nips, but go to Manila." In response, Mudge formed a mechanized task force under the 1st Cavalry Brigade commander, Brigadier General William C. Chase, commanding two motorized cavalry squadrons reinforced with armor and motorized artillery and support units. This "flying column" rushed toward Manila while the rest of the division followed and mopped up.

At the same time, MacArthur added additional forces to the drive on the capital. On January 15, he launched Operation MIKE VI, a second amphibious assault some 45 miles southwest of Manila. On January 31, X-ray Day, two regiments of the 11th Airborne Division, under the command of Major General Joseph M. Swing, landed unopposed. The paratroopers seized a nearby bridge before the surprised Japanese defenders had a chance to demolish it, and then the paratroopers turned toward Manila. The division's third regiment, the 511th Parachute, dropped in by air to join the advance, which by the following day was speeding north along the paved highway toward the capital to the cheers of throngs of grateful Filipino civilians along the way.

Originally, the 11th Airborne Division, one of Lieutenant General Robert L. Eichelberger's Eighth Army units, had been slated to contain Japanese troops throughout southwestern Luzon. However, acting on MacArthur's orders, Eichelberger pushed the division north. On February 3, one battalion of the 511th encountered determined Japanese resistance near the town of Imus, 5 miles south of Manila, where some fifty defenders clung to an old stone building despite a fierce bombardment by the battalion's

75-mm. howitzers. Observing that the artillery had had little effect, Tech Sergeant Robert C. Steel climbed onto the building's roof, knocked a hole through it, poured in gasoline, and then threw in a phosphorous grenade. As the Japanese dashed out, Steel's men shot them down.

Another 3 miles up the road lay the Las Piñas River Bridge. It was set for demolition and guarded by a small detachment of Japanese who were dug in along the north bank. Despite the fierce firefight less than an hour before at Imus, the Japanese were surprised by the appearance of the Americans. The paratroopers secured the span before it could be blown. With one battalion guarding the bridge, another passed over on trucks toward Manila, hoping to enter the city from the south.[11]

It was not to be. By dawn on February 4, the paratroopers ran into increasingly heavy and harassing fire from Japanese riflemen and machine gunners. At the Paranaque River, just south of the Manila city limits, the battalion halted at a badly damaged bridge only to be battered by Japanese artillery fire from Nichols Field. The 11th Airborne Division had reached the main Japanese defenses south of the capital and could go no further.

The race for Manila was now between the 37th Division and the 1st Cavalry Division, with the cavalry in the lead. Since the operation had begun in late January, its units had been fortunate enough to find bridges and fordable crossings almost everywhere they went. On February 2, Chase's flying column was dashing toward Manila, sometimes at speeds of 50 mph, with individual units competing for the honor of reaching the city first. The 37th Division, on the other hand, was slowed down by difficult crossings, which forced it to either ferry its artillery and tanks across or wait for the engineers to build bridges.

On February 3, elements of the 1st Cavalry Division pushed into the northern outskirts of Manila, with only the steep-sided Tuliahan River separating them from the city proper. A squadron of the 8th Cavalry reached the bridge just moments after Japanese soldiers had finished preparing it for demolition. As the two sides opened fire on one another, the Japanese lit the fuse leading to the carefully placed explosives. Without hesitation, Lieutenant James P. Sutton, a Navy demolitions expert attached to the division, dashed through the enemy fire and cut the burning fuse. The way to Manila was clear.

That evening, the 8th Cavalry passed through the northern suburbs and into the city itself. The troopers had won the race to Manila. As the sun set over the ocean behind the advancing Americans, a single tank named "Battling Basic" crashed through the walls surrounding Santo Tomas University, the site of a camp holding almost 4,000 civilian prisoners. The Japanese guards put up little resistance, and soon the inmates, many of whom had been incarcerated for nearly two years, were liberated.

Despite the initial American euphoria, much fighting remained. Although the approach to the city had been relatively easy, wresting the capital from the Japanese proved far more difficult. Manila, a city of 800,000, was one of the largest in Southeast Asia. While much of it consisted of ramshackle huts, the downtown section boasted massive reinforced concrete buildings built to withstand earthquakes and old Spanish stone fortresses of equal size and strength. Most were located south of the Pasig River, which bisects the capital, requiring that the Americans cross over before closing with the enemy.[12]

Even a half-hearted defense was bound to make Manila's recapture difficult. Regarding Manila as indefensible, General Yamashita had originally ordered the commander of Shimbu Group, General Yokoyama Shizuo, to destroy all bridges and other vital installations and evacuate the city as soon as strong American forces made their appearance. However, Rear Admiral Iwabachi Sanji, the naval commander for the Manila area, vowed to resist the Americans and countermanded the order. Determined to support the admiral as best he could, Yokoyama contributed three Army battalions to Iwabachi's 16,000 men Manila Naval Defense Force and prepared for battle. The sailors knew little about infantry tactics or street fighting, but they were well armed and entrenched throughout the capital. Iwabachi resolved to fight to the last man.

On February 4, 1945, General MacArthur announced the imminent recapture of the capital while his staff planned a victory parade. However, the Battle for Manila had barely begun. Almost at once, the 1st Cavalry Division in the north and the 11th Airborne Division in the south reported stiffening Japanese resistance to further advances into the city. As one airborne company commander remarked in mock seriousness, "Tell Halsey to stop looking for the Jap Fleet; it's dying on Nichols Field." All thoughts of a parade had to be put aside.[13]

Following the initial American breakthrough on the 4th, fighting raged throughout the city for almost a month. The battle quickly came down to a series of bitter street-to-street and house-to-house struggles. In an attempt to protect the city and its civilians, MacArthur placed stringent restrictions on U.S. artillery and air support. However, massive devastation to the urban area could not be avoided. In the north, General Griswold continued to push elements of the XIV Corps south from Santo Tomas University toward the Pasig River. Late on the afternoon of February 4, he ordered the 2nd Squadron, 5th Cavalry, to seize Quezon Bridge, the only crossing over the Pasig that the Japanese had not destroyed. As the squadron approached the bridge, enemy heavy machine guns opened up from a formidable roadblock thrown up across Quezon Boulevard. The Japanese had pounded steel stakes into the pavement, sown the area with mines, and lined up old truck bodies across the road. Unable to advance farther, the cavalry withdrew after nightfall. As the Americans pulled back, the Japanese blew up the bridge.

The next day, February 5, went more smoothly. Once the 37th Division began to move into Manila, Griswold divided the northern section of the city into two sectors, with the 37th responsible for the western half and the 1st Cavalry responsible for the eastern part.[14]

By the afternoon of the 8th, 37th Division units had cleared most Japanese from their sector, although the damage done to the residential districts was extensive. The Japanese added to the destruction by demolishing buildings and military installations as they withdrew. However, the division's costliest fighting occurred on Provisor Island, a small industrial center on the Pasig River. The Japanese garrison, probably less than a battalion, held off elements of the division until February 11.

The 1st Cavalry Division had an easier time, encountering little opposition in the suburbs east of Manila. Although the 7th and 8th Cavalry fought pitched battles near two water supply installations north of the city, by February 10, the cavalry had extended its control south of the river. That night, the XIV Corps established, for the first time, separate bridgeheads on both banks of the Pasig River.

The final attack on the outer Japanese defenses came from the 11th Airborne Division, under the XIV Corps control since February 10. The division had been halted at Nichols Field on the 4th and since then had been battling firmly entrenched Japanese naval troops, backed up by heavy fire from concealed artillery.[15]

Only on February 11 did the airfield finally fall to the paratroopers, but the acquisition allowed the 11th Airborne Division to complete the American encirclement of Manila on the night of the 12th.[16]

For the rest of the month the Americans and their Filipino allies mopped up enemy resistance throughout the city. Due to the state of Japanese communications, Yamashita did not learn of the efforts of his subordinates in defending Manila until about February 17, when it was too late to countermand the order. The final weeks of fighting were thus bloody, but the results were inevitable. On March 4, with the capture of the giant Finance Building in the city center, Griswold reported that enemy resistance had ceased. Manila was officially liberated. But it was a city no more. Some observers commented that the destruction was more complete than in Cologne, Hamburg, or even London. Amid the devastation, Manila's residents tried to resume their lives. Just before the last fighting ended, MacArthur summoned a provisional assembly of prominent Filipinos to Malacañang Palace and in their presence declared the Commonwealth of the Philippines to be permanently reestablished. "My country kept the faith," he told the gathered assembly. "Your capital city, cruelly punished though it be, has regained its rightful place–citadel of democracy in the East."[17]

Securing Manila was significant for both military and psychological reasons, but from a logistical point of view, the seizure of Manila Bay was especially crucial. The supply lines at Lingayen Bay, which had so ably supported the American advance south on the capital, were strained almost to the breaking point. Yet, even though Manila's world-class harbor was in American hands, it could not be used unless the Bataan Peninsula, which encompassed the bay's western shore, was secure.

Even as XIV Corps forces drove on Manila, MacArthur had thus ordered Krueger's Sixth Army to seize Bataan, including Corregidor, the small island fortress at its southern tip. Since Griswold's troops were fully occupied, MacArthur supplemented Sixth Army with the XI Corps from Leyte, commanded by Major General Charles P. Hall. With the 38th Infantry Division and the 24th Division's 34th Infantry, the XI Corps was to land on the Zambales coast some 25 miles northwest of Bataan and drive rapidly east across the base of the peninsula, and then sweep south, clearing the entire peninsula including its eastern coast.[18]

Prior to the assault, American intelligence had badly overestimated enemy strength, predicting that the Japanese had nearly 13,000 soldiers on Bataan. However, having decided that the defense of Manila Bay was also beyond the capabilities of his forces, General Yamashita had the Kembu Group commander, Major General Rikichi Tsukada, place fewer than 4,000 of his troops on the peninsula. The main defensive force was Nagayoshi Detachment, a regiment from the 10th Division under Colonel Nagayoshi Sanenobu.

On the morning of January 29, nearly 35,000 U.S. troops landed just northwest of the peninsula. Elements of the 38th Division immediately dashed inland to take the San Marcelino airstrip but found that Filipino guerrillas under the command of Captain Ramon Magsaysay, later president of the Republic of the Philippines, had secured the field three days earlier. Elsewhere, surprise was complete. In fact, the only casualty on that first day was an American enlisted man, who was gored by an ornery bull. The next day, Subic Bay and Olongapo were occupied.

The Japanese chose to make a stand in the rugged Zambales mountains at the northern base of the peninsula, which Americans dubbed the "Zig Zag Pass." Colonel Nagayoshi had plenty of supplies and ammunition for a long battle, but his main defensive line was a mere 2,000 yards long, leaving his position open to flanking maneuvers. On January 31, Hall's forces advanced east, seeking out both Japanese flanks. But unfavorable terrain and determined resistance by the Japanese made it difficult. During the next two weeks, elements of the 38th Division struggled to open the Zig Zag Pass, and by February 8, they had overrun the main Japanese positions, killing more than 2,400 defenders. Colonel Nagayoshi and 300 of his men escaped farther south and joined other defenders who held out until the middle of February. But, before then, the vital shoreline of Manila Bay had been secured.

Although Corregidor lacked the importance to the Japanese defense that it had held for the Americans in 1942, it merited a separate attack. MacArthur's plan involved a combined amphibious and airborne assault, the most difficult of all modern military maneuvers. The airborne attack was obviously risky. At just over 5 square miles, Corregidor made a small target for a parachute drop. To make matters more difficult, the paratroopers were required to land on a hill known as Topside, the dominant terrain feature on the island. On the other hand, there was little choice. From Topside, the Japanese could dominate all possible amphibious landing sites. In addition, the Japanese would certainly not expect an airborne landing on such an unlikely target.[19]

The planners were correct in their assumptions. On the morning of February 16, the 503rd Parachute Regimental Combat Team floated down on the surprised defenders while a battalion of the 34th Infantry stormed ashore. During fierce fighting, the Japanese tried to regroup, and at one point, on the morning of February 16, they threatened to drive a salient into the paratroopers' tenuous foothold on Topside. Private Lloyd G. McCarter charged a key enemy position and destroyed a machine-gun nest with hand grenades. For his bravery, McCarter was awarded the Medal of Honor. His actions and those of many other paratroopers and infantrymen during the nine days that followed helped defeat the Japanese on Corregidor. The island fell on February 26, and, six days later, MacArthur returned to the fortress he had been forced to leave in disgrace three years before.

The battles for Manila, Bataan, and Corregidor were only the beginning of the Luzon Campaign. Both Shobu Group, securing northern Luzon, and the bulk of Shimbu Group, defending the south, remained intact. With about 50,000 men at his disposal, the Shimbu Group commander, General Yokoyama, had deployed some 30,000 of them immediately east and south of Manila, with the remainder arrayed along the narrow Bicol Peninsula to the southwest. The main Japanese defenses near the capital were built around the 8th and 105th Divisions, with the rest of the manpower drawn from a jumble of other units and provisional organizations. East of Manila, their positions were organized in considerable depth but lacked good lines of supply and reinforcement. Shimbu Group's eastern defenses obviously presented the most immediate threat to American control of the Manila area and would have to be dealt with first.

By mid-February, Krueger's Sixth Army staff had begun planning operations against those Shimbu Group forces closest to Manila. Although still concerned about Shobu Group troop concentrations in northern Luzon, both Krueger and MacArthur agreed that the Manila area, the potential logistical base for all American activities on Luzon, still had first priority. Nevertheless, MacArthur made Krueger's task more difficult in the coming weeks by continually detaching troop units from Sixth Army control and sending them to the southern and central Philippines, which had been bypassed earlier. These diversions greatly impaired Krueger's ability to deal with both Shobu and Shimbu Groups at the same time.[20]

By February 20, Krueger had positioned the 6th and 43rd Infantry Divisions, the 1st Cavalry Division, and the 112th Cavalry Regimental Combat Team for an offensive in the rolling hills east of Manila. In addition, as soon as Manila was secured, he wanted the 11th Airborne Division to clear the area south of the capital, assisted by the independent 158th Infantry. He hoped that the first effort could begin immediately and that the second would start by the first week in March.[21]

The main objective of XIV Corps' attack against Shimbu Group was to gain control of the Manila water supply, most of which came from dams along the Angat and Marikina Rivers some 20 miles northeast of the city. Here the coastal plains gave way to rolling mountains and plunging valleys carved by rivers flowing toward the sea. Nevertheless, two crucial errors affected the operation before it even began. First, the Americans did not realize that the Wawa Dam, thought to be one of Manila's sources of water, had been abandoned in 1938 in favor of the larger Ipo Dam in the Marikina Valley.

The Wawa Dam could have been bypassed, but Krueger did not realize his error for almost two months. Second, intelligence badly underestimated Shimbu Group's strength, reckoning that there were fewer than 20,000 Japanese troops east of Manila when; in reality, there were about 30,000. Enemy defensive positions were strung out along a thin line about 30 miles long running from Ipo Dam in the north to the town of Antipolo in the south. The Japanese positions alone were of little strategic value, but together they commanded all the high ground east of Manila.

On the afternoon of February 20, the XIV Corps launched its attack. Griswold assigned the 6th Division the task of capturing the dams in the north and ordered the 2nd Cavalry Brigade, 1st Cavalry Division, to attack the southern half of the Japanese defenses and secure the town of Antipolo. Both units traversed the broad Marikina Valley unmolested but encountered fierce resistance as they moved into the hills and mountains forming the valley's eastern wall. There the Japanese had honeycombed the area with subterranean strongholds and machine-gun positions covering all avenues of approach. Despite massive Allied air support, the cavalry advanced slowly, on some days measuring progress in mere yards. Not until March 4, did the troops reach Antipolo. However, success was bittersweet. The brigade had lost nearly sixty men killed and 315 wounded, among them the 1st Cavalry Division commander, General Mudge.

To the north, the 6th Infantry Division fared only slightly better. Its initial objectives were Mount Pacawagan and Mount Mataba, two strategic high points crucial to capturing the Wawa Dam. Both mountains were defended by extensive Japanese artillery and infantry positions. By March 4, the infantry's southernmost elements had gained a precarious foothold on the crest of Mount Pacawagan, but they could go no farther. Just to the north, the Japanese continued to deny the Americans any gains in the Mount Mataba area. Not until March 8 did the infantry regain its momentum, gouging the Japanese defenders from their positions as they advanced.[22]

From his vantage point in the mountains, General Yokoyama was concerned by these advances that threatened to envelop both his flanks. Unwilling to abandon his excellent defensive positions on Mataba and Pacawagan, he decided instead to launch a counterattack aimed at the advancing 6th Division. His plans and their subsequent execution typified major Japanese tactical weaknesses throughout the war. Yokoyama scheduled a series of complicated maneuvers that required meticulous coordination in difficult terrain, necessitating sophisticated communications that Shimbu Group lacked. In addition, the Japanese artillery was neither strong enough nor suitably deployed to provide proper support. Still, the counterattack began on March 12 with three reserve battalions assaulting three widely dispersed positions along the American line. How Yokoyama expected these scattered attacks to succeed is unclear, but to make matters worse, they ran straight into another major offensive of the 6th Division. In fact, the counterattacks were so weak that the Americans had no idea they were even under attack. The entire effort demonstrated only that Shimbu Group was incapable of effective offensive action and that the original defensive strategy was the best course. However, the Japanese were irretrievably weakened by the failed counterattack, and to Yokoyama the ultimate fate of Shimbu Group was a foregone conclusion. All he could do now was trade lives for terrain and time.

For the next two days, March 13–14, the Americans battered through Japanese positions, bolstered in the south by a regiment of the 43rd Division sent in as reserve for the 1st Cavalry Division. The 6th Division successfully cleaned out the extreme northern

Japanese positions, securing a strong foothold on Mount Mataba. The cost, however, continued to be high. On the morning of March 14, a burst from a hidden Japanese machine-gun position caught a group of officers bunched together at a regimental forward command post, mortally wounding the division commander, Major General Edwin D. Patrick, and one of the regimental commanders. Still, the dual offensives had begun to cave in the Japanese defensive line at both the northern and southern flanks, killing an estimated 3,350 enemy troops. On the American side, the XIV Corps lost almost 300 dead and over 1,000 wounded in less than a month of fighting.

On March 14, General Hall's XI Corps took over responsibility for operations against Shimbu Group. With the 38th and 43rd Infantry Divisions, Hall decided to continue XIV Corps' strategy, although he intended to concentrate more heavily on destroying the Japanese left or southern, flank.[23]

On March 15, American forces resumed the attack, and by the 22nd, to avoid complete encirclement, the Japanese had begun withdrawing to the northeast. The Americans followed up quickly, and by March 27, they had penetrated the hasty Japanese defenses, completely destroying Shimbu Group's left flank. On May 17, the 43rd Division, aided by guerrilla forces and air strikes that delivered the heaviest concentration of napalm ever used in the Southwest Pacific, captured the Ipo Dam intact and restored Manila's water supply. Wawa Dam was captured, also undamaged, on May 28 against comparatively light resistance. Continued pressure forced the Japanese to withdraw deep into the Sierra Madre mountains in eastern Luzon where starvation, disease, and guerrilla attacks gradually decimated their ranks during the remainder of the war.[24]

Shimbu Group's southern positions along the Bicol Peninsula fared no better. After the XI Corps had relieved the XIV Corps in mid-March, the latter concentrated on rooting the Japanese out of southern Luzon. On March 15, the 6th Division, with the 112th Regimental Combat Team attached, passed to the control of the XI Corps, and the 37th Division was placed in the Sixth Army reserve and given the mission of patrolling Manila. The XIV Corps now included the 1st Cavalry Division and the 11th Airborne Division with the 158th Regimental Combat Team attached. The corps held a line stretching from Laguna de Bay, a huge lake at the northern edge of the Bicol Peninsula, to Batangas Bay on the southern coast. Between the bays lay Lake Taal, a smaller body of water, and a crucial road junction at the town of Santo Tomas. On March 19, the 1st Cavalry Division on the northern edge of the line and the 11th Airborne Division on the south edge began a double enveloping drive around Japanese positions near Lake Taal. The purpose of the drive was to open the highway between Santo Tomas and Batangas, a move that was successfully completed by month's end. On March 24, the 158th Regimental Combat Team was taken from the 11th Airborne Division and ordered to prepare for an amphibious landing at Legaspi on the southeast coast of the Bicol Peninsula.

By April 19, the Americans had completed their encirclement and driven all the way to Luzon's east coast. The 11th Airborne Division cut all routes leading to the Bicol Peninsula, while the 1st Cavalry Division turned north into the Santa Maria Valley in a move intended to turn Shimbu Group's southeast flank and prevent the Japanese from using any of the small coastal towns as concentration or evacuation points. By May 25, the cavalry, with substantial support from guerrilla units, had seized Infanta, the largest town along the coast.

The XIV Corps was now free to proceed with the liberation of the Bicol Peninsula. The campaign had actually begun on April 1 when the 158th Regimental Combat Team carried out its amphibious assault at Legapsi on the southeastern tip of Luzon. Resistance was light because the Japanese had transferred most of their troops to the northern Shimbu Group positions during January. Although the 158th Regimental Combat Team encountered many prepared defenses, the opposition consisted mainly of support troops and naval service troops, together with a few remnants that had escaped from Leyte. The Americans had little trouble handling this hodgepodge of Japanese defenders, and on May 2, they linked up with the 1st Cavalry Division, which had been advancing into the peninsula from the northwest. By May 31, all of southern Luzon was cleared of major enemy units, and on June 14, the XIV Corps was relieved of tactical responsibility in southern Luzon and transferred north.[25]

Despite the hard fighting in Manila, the Bataan Peninsula, and throughout southern Luzon, the main Japanese force was in the northern part of the island. It was there that General Yamashita's Shobu Group occupied a large region resembling an inverted triangle, with northern Luzon's rugged geography as a shield. In the east rose the Sierra Madre mountain range, to the west, the impressive hills of the Cordillera Central, and at the northern edge of the triangle, the Babuyan channel. In the center lay the Cagayan Valley, Luzon's rice bowl and a key supply area for the Japanese units. Yamashita had pieced together a defensive force made up of the 19th Division, the 23rd Division, and elements of three others: the 103rd and 10th Divisions and the 2nd Tank Division. Its main purpose was to harass the Americans rather than to defeat them. Yamashita expected the main attack to come from the Manila area where American forces were consolidating their gains, particularly among the handful of roads winding north through Bambang and Baguio and into the Cagayan Valley. And there was always the possibility of amphibious landings along the northern coastline.

In February, as American troops gradually pushed the enemy out of Manila, General Krueger alerted the I Corps for an offensive into northern Luzon against Shobu Group. Originally, Krueger had planned to use a total of six divisions to gradually push north through Bambang, but MacArthur's emphasis on securing the entire Manila area first made this impossible. Nevertheless, by the end of February, General Swift, the I Corps commander, had begun probing the area north of the original beachhead with the 33rd Division, which had replaced the battle-weary 43rd Division and the 158th Regimental Combat Team on February 13. Although Swift's forces were outnumbered two-to-one by the Japanese, the relative passivity of their foes encouraged the more aggressive Americans.[26]

In early March, Swift ordered the 33rd Division to push northeast along Route 11, the easiest road into the mountains, toward the town of Bambang. However, the attackers quickly discovered that this avenue was heavily defended and made little progress. Meanwhile, other elements of the division operating along the coast directly north from the Lingayen Gulf landing beaches found little resistance. After taking some small towns farther up the coast and turning inland Major General Percy W. Clarkson, the division commander, decided to dash along Route 9 and attack Baguio—the prewar summer capital of the Philippines and currently Yamashita's headquarters—from the northeast. To assist, Krueger added the 37th Infantry Division to the attack and with the aid of air strikes and guerrilla harassment, wore down the defenders until they were on the verge of starvation. A small garrison made a last stand at Irisan Gorge, where the road crossed the Irisan River some three miles west of Baguio, but on April 27, the town fell to American troops.

Shobu Group had lost one of the three legs of its defensive triangle, but the battle on northern Luzon was far from over. Until the end of the war, Sixth Army forces continued to push Yamashita's men farther into the mountains, taking heavy casualties in the process. The 32rd Division, which had also seen heavy fighting on Leyte, was worn down to almost nothing, but the defenders suffered even heavier battle casualties as well as losses to starvation and disease. By the end of the war, the Japanese were still holding out in the rugged Asin Valley of the Sierra Madre in north-central Luzon, enduring the drenching summer monsoons. Nevertheless, General Yamashita and about 50,500 of his men surrendered only after the close of hostilities on August 15.

On June 30, 1945, Krueger's Sixth Army was relieved by the Eighth Army, whose task was to mop up scattered Japanese positions. By the end of March, however, the Allies controlled all of Luzon that had any strategic or economic significance.[27]

The 201st Fighter Squadron Mission Support

Throughout June 1945, the Japanese Fourteenth Army was conducting delaying actions in the key mountain redoubts of Luzon in the Philippines. The U.S. Sixth Army troops advanced through rugged mountain passes in pursuit of the determined Japanese Shobu Group. The fighting was a brutal mixture of jungle and mountain warfare. According to General Douglas MacArthur, the close air support proved by the 201st Squadron of the Mexican Expeditionary Air Force was crucial as the 25th Division conducted its breakthrough from Balete pass and Marikina Watershed area into the Cagayan Valley.[28]

In the first days of the month of June, the 201st ended the training to which it was submitted by the Fifth Fighting Command of the Fifth Force, in order to be able to take part in the operations. This period of final training included airplanes flights of the 201st Squadron framed in North American formations, sometimes with the purpose of knowing the combat zone and others with the one of acting against the adversary together with the formation in which they were framed. It began with an airplane and the number of them was increasing, until it was an exclusive formation of the 201st Squadron. In this work, three combat missions were properly fulfilled, finishing the training on June 3. On June 4, 1945, the squadron began to operate, sometimes with squadron elements in North American 58th formations and others with own formations taking an American leader. Shortly afterwards, the 201st managed by itself in the same combat missions. These operations were exclusively to support ground troops and during them the presence of enemy aviation was not recorded; eventually some aircraft returned to their base with light enemy weapons.

The situation in Luzon, within which it was operated, had not changed very noticeably from the one reported earlier, but deep penetrations of North American land forces towards the Northwest, in the Baguio region were recorded. The squadron flew right along with the 58th Fighter Group the rest of the month in ground support missions, often two flown per day, helping the 25th Division in its breakthrough from the Balete Pass and Marikana Watershed area into the Cagayan valley.[29]

Notes: The 58th Fighter Group filed no mission reports for squadron 201 activities until Mission Report Number 1-1, June 7, 1945. The 201st Squadron continued to make corollary mission reports. American and Mexican records do not record by name the American pilots from the liaison group or that of the 58th Fighter Group that flew in combat with the 201st Fighter Squadron. Documents only substantiate that they participated in twenty-six missions.

No. 201 Squadron, Mission Number 1

Date: June 4, 1945.
Mission: Bomb and strafe enemy positions along highway, targets 19, 20, and 21 in the Aritao area under direction of controller.
Pilots: Names not available.
Results: The bombs fell in the area of the target. The controller reported very good results from this mission. Four aircraft took off at 6.45 a.m., flew over the target until 7.30 a.m., and returned to base at 8.45 a.m.[30]

No. 201 Squadron. Mission Number 2

Date: June 4, 1945.
Mission: The planes contacted the Controller from the Aritao region, who ordered them to bomb and strafe South Aritao.
Pilots: Names not available.
Results: The bombs covered three-fourths of the objective. The Controller reported that the bombing and strafing had been good. Four aircraft took off at 7.15 a.m. and flew over the target from 8 a.m. until 8.30 a.m., returned to base at 9.15 a.m.[31]

Men of the Aztec Eagles marching before the National Palace upon their return. (*marcianosmx.com*)

Above left: The 201st Fighter Squadron unit patch. (*The Military Place*)

Above right: Captain Radamés Gaxiola stands in front of his P-47D with his maintenance team after he returned from a combat mission. (*U.S. Army Air Force*)

Left: Corporal Manuel Alcantar Torres, next to "Pancho Pistolas," the 201st Squadron's logo painted on the wing of a Japanese Zero. (*National Archives*)

Below: Members of the 201st Squadron standing before their planes. (*Los Angeles Times Magazine*)

Mexican pilots receiving a briefing in the Philippines. (*National Archives*)

Republic P-47D-30-RA Thunderbolt (U.S.A.A.F. s/n 44-33721) from the 201st Squadron over the Philippines during the summer of 1945. (*U.S. Army Air Force*)

The 201st Squadron on Porac Airstrip, Clark Field, Luzon, Philippines, August 27, 1945. (*U.S. Army Signal Corps*)

Above: P-47D of the 201st Mexican Fighter Squadron on mission over Philippines, 1945. (*U.S. Army Air Force*)

Below: Pilots of the Aztec Eagles walking the flight line. (*U.S. Army Air Force*)

Above left: Members of the 201st Fighter Squadron pose for a photo at an airfield. (*U.S. Army Air Force*)

Above right: Franklin D. Roosevelt and Mexican President Avila Camacho in Monterrey, Mexico. (*U.S. Army Air Force*)

The 201st Squadron display at the National Museum of the United States Air Force. (*U.S. Army Air Force*)

Armed with clubs, pipes, and bottles, this self-appointed posse of uniformed men was all set to settle the Zoot-suit War when the Navy Shore Patrol stepped in and broke it up. (*The Library of Congress*)

Above left: Crowds greet returning members of the 201st Squadron. (*Mexican Air Force*)

Above right: Mexican pilot on costal patrol, flying an America AT-6. (*Mexican Air Force*)

ht "A", 201st Mexican Fighter Squadron, FAEM, Clark
d, Luzon, P. I. Left to right: 1st Lt. Graco Ramirez,
o, D.F.; 1st Lt. Carlos Varela, Mexico, D.F.; 1st
Fernando from Jaurel, Mex., and Capt. Roberto Legurreta,
titlan, Mexico.

t No. SWPA-SigC-45-30343 rec'd 27 August 1945 from
al Corps. *Released 3 Oct. 45. Copied 30 Sept '60*

Above left: The 201st Mexican Fighter Squadron, World War II, Philippines. (*U.S. Army Signal Corps*)

Above right: Mexican pilot with Vought-Sikorsky Scout Plane. (*National Archives*)

000 lb bomb on a P-47 "Thunderbolt" of the 201st Mexican Fighter Squadron. Porac Airstrip, Philippine
26 June 1945.

Two of the first pilots to land after the first combat mission of the 201st Fighter squadron (Mexican
Keep a sharp lookout for others. They are Lt. J. Ramirez Vilchis, of Jalisco, Mexico, and Lt. Paul
Garcia, of Monterey, Mexico. They flew their first mission as wingmen to American pilots of the 5th
Fighter Command's 58th Group.

Prints rec'd 28 June 1945 from BPR, (Air
Forces Group). Copied 28 June 1945. Release
2 July 1945.

Above left: Loading 1,000-lb. bomb on a P-47 of the 201st Squadron. (*U.S. Army Signal Corps*)

Above right: Two of the first Mexican pilots to land after their first mission. (*U.S. Army Signal Corps*)

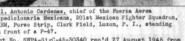

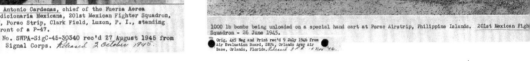

Above left: Colonel Antonio Cárdenas, Chief of the Mexican Expeditionary Force. (*U.S. Army Signal Corps*)

Above right: A 1,000-lb. bomb being unloaded on a special handcart at Porac Airstrip, Philippines. (*U.S. Army Signal Corps*)

Above left: Captain Pablo Rivas illustrates a combat mission. (*U.S. Army Signal Corps*)

Above right: Mechanics changing the engine on a P-47 Thunderbolt. (*U.S. Army Signal Corps*)

Above left: Second Lieutenant Raul Garcia Mercado and First Lieutenant Reinaldo Perez-Gallardo point skyward prior to their take-off. (*U.S. Army Air Force*)

Above right: Newly arrived in the Philippines, Mexican members of the 201st Fighter Squadron talk with a woman after recently disembarking from their ships. (*U.S. Army Air Force*)

Illustration of the 201st Squadron P-47 Thunderbolts on a bombing mission. (*War Thunder*)

Above left: The daughter of the honorary consul of Mexico in the Philippines, Alfredo Carmelo de las Casas, received the 201st Squadron. (*U.S. Army Signal Corps*)

Above right: A Mexican Air Force P-47D surmounts a monument at the Santa Lucia Air Base near Mexico City in memory of the seven Aztec Eagles who lost their lives in the line of duty during World War II. (*Mexican Air Force*)

The 201st Squadron sitting on the wing of a P-47 Thunderbolt. (*U.S. Army Signal Corps*)

Above left: Departure of the 201st Squadron of the Buena Vista station towards the U.S.A. to begin its training. (*Mexican Air Force*)

Above right: Member of the 201st Squadron returns home from the Philippines. (*Mexican Air Force*)

The Mexican tanker S.S. *Potrero del Llano* wrapped in flames after being torpedoed by the German submarine U-564 on May 13, 1942. (*Mexican Association of Veterans of World War II*)

The cockpit of the Republic P-47 Thunderbolt. (*Mexican Air Force*)

Above: Pilots of the 201st Mexican Fighter Squadron, M.E.A.F., fly in formation in front of P-47s during training, near Porac Strip, Clark Field, July 1945. (*Mexican Air Force*)

Below: A 201st Squadron P-47 in flight. (*Mexican Air Force*)

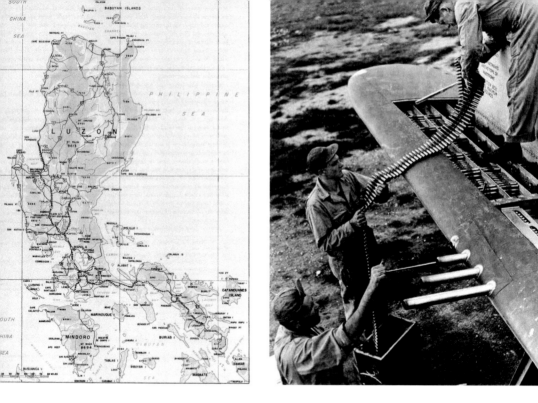

Above left: The Mindoro and Luzon operations. (*U.S. Army Center of Military History*)

Above right: Ground crew loading .50-caliber ammunition into a P-47. (*Mexican Air Force*)

Below: Location of Clark Field in Luzon. (*California State University*)

Above: The Sixth Army Landings on Luzon, January 9–17, 1945. (*U.S. Army Center of Military History*)

Below: S.S. *Potrero del Llano* burns off the Miami, Florida, coast after being torpedoed by a German U-boat.

Above left: Departure of the 201st Squadron of the Buena Vista Station, July 24, 1944. (*Mexican National Archives*)

Above right: A 201st Squadron pilot looks skyward before take-off. (*Mexican Air Force*)

Alberto Braniff with his Voisin airplane. (*Mexican Air Force*)

Above left: Squadron ground crew preparing a bomb. (*Mexican Air Force*)

Above right: Mexican Service in the Far East Medal. (*Mexican Air Force*)

Pilots of the F.A.E.M. 201st Squadron in the air base of Major's Field, Greenville, Texas, January 1945. (*Mexican Air Force*)

No. 201 Squadron, Mission Number 3

Date: June 4, 1945.
Mission: The flight was directed by the Controller to bomb and strafe the area to the west of Rio Santa Fe.
Pilots: Names not available.
Results: Bombs fell in the target area, damaging one building and wiping out a machine gun nest. Four aircraft took off at 11.15 a.m., flew over the target until 12.30 p.m. and returned to base at 1.15 p.m.[32]

No. 201 Squadron, Mission Number 4

Date: June 4, 1945.
Mission: The flight was directed by the Controller to bomb and strafe area to the west of the bridge of Rio Santa Fe.
Pilots: Names not available.
Results: The bombs fell in the target area but the results were not observed due to heavy foliage. Four aircraft took off at 11.45 a.m., flew over the target from 12 p.m. until 12.30 p.m. and returned to base at 1 p.m.[33]

No. 201 Squadron, Mission Number 5

Date: June 4, 1945.
Mission: The flight was directed by the Controller to bomb and strafe troop concentrations situated to the north of Rio Santa Fe.
Pilots: Names not available.
Results: Bombs fell in the target area but the results were not observed due to heavy underbrush. Four aircraft took off at 12.15 p.m.; flew over the target from 1 p.m. until 1.30 p.m.; returned to base at 2.15 p.m.[34]

No. 201 Squadron, Mission Number 6

Date: June 5, 1945.
Mission: The Controller had no observer at the initial target and ordered the squadron leader to bomb the town of Dupax, flying from south to north, dropping the bombs from an altitude of approximately 2,000 feet.
Pilots: Names not available.
Results: The bombs were well distributed in the western part of the town; two of them exploded in a good position in a large building located just south of the

intersection of two principal highways on the northwest side of Dupax the Aritao region. There was an explosion in the southwest corner of the building but it was not completely destroyed. Small fires were produced instantly and black smoke was observed in the point of the impact. The results were not observed due to the thickness of underbrush. Troops and vehicles were seen on Highway 5 to the south of the principal bridge, which crosses the southwest part of the town of Aritao. Four aircraft took off at 6.30 a.m., flew over the target from 7.10 a.m. until 7.50 a.m. at an altitude of 7,000 feet and returned to base at 8.30 a.m.[35]

No. 201 Squadron, Mission Number 7

Date: June 5, 1945.
Mission: The flight was directed by the Controller to bomb and strafe enemy positions on the western side of the canyon and on the north side of Highway 5 in Baganan, and at 4,000 yards from Aritao.
Pilots: Names not available.
Results: The bombs were dropped in the target area and on both sides of Highway 5 between Baganan and Indiana. No results were observed due to the thickness of trees and underbrush. The Controller said that it had been a good mission and reported that friendly troops had entered the town. Four aircraft took off at 7.15 a.m., flew over the target from 7.55 a.m. until 8.25 a.m. at an altitude of 6,000 feet and returned to base at 9.10 a.m.[36]

No. 201 Squadron, Mission Number 8

Date: June 5, 1945.
Mission: To give direct support to the ground forces in the Aritao area. The flight was directed by the Controller to bomb and strafe enemy artillery positions and possible tank concentrations in a ravine on the west side of Highway 5, about 1 mile to the north of the town of Indiana, and enemy troop concentrations on the west side of the Highway 5 in the same town.
Pilots: Names not available.
Results: The Controller reported that the target area was perfectly covered and very difficult to observe due to the great amounts of underbrush and dust over the objective. The aircraft strafed both targets and after passing, small fires of short duration broke out. The small enemy force, which was stationed in the buildings of the town of Indiana, was wiped out. Two aircraft took off at 7.45 a.m., flew over the target from 8.30 a.m. until 9 a.m. at an altitude of 6,000 feet and returned to base at 9.50 a.m.[37]

No. 201 Squadron, Mission Number 9

Date: June 5, 1945.
Mission: The Controller assigned the target on the southwest, in the region of
              Bayombong and this area was bombed to the northeast of Highway 5 and
              parallel to the main highway.
Pilots: Names not available.
Results: The bomb passes were made from south to north, dropping the bombs at
              approximately 1,500 feet. Two strafing passes were made in the area with
              the only visible results of bombing and strafing being various weeds on fire,
              which remained burning in the area. Two aircraft took off at 11.15 a.m., flew
              over the target from 12.15 p.m. until 12.55 p.m. at an altitude of 8,000 feet and
              returned to base at 1.30 p.m.[38]

No. 201 Squadron, Mission Number 10

Date: June 5, 1945.
Mission: The flight was directed by the Controller to bomb and strafe enemy positions
              on the east side of Highway 5 at 1,000 yards to the south of Bambang.
Pilots: Names not available.
Results: The bombs covered the area of the southwest regions and were dispersed in
              the summit of the hill. This region was heavily strafed and the results were
              not observed due to heaviness of the foliage. Two airplanes took off at 12.15
              p.m., flew over the target from 12.45 p.m. until 13.45 p.m. at an altitude of
              6,000 feet and returned to base at 2.15 p.m.[39]

No. 201 Squadron, Mission Number 11

Date: June 6, 1945.
Mission: The flight was directed by the Controller to bomb and strafe artillery positions
              situated 5,000 yards to the west of Highway 5, one mile southwest of the
              Bambang Highway.
Pilots: Names not available.
Results: The flight strafed opportune targets along the Main Highway, setting one
              building afire and destroying an antiaircraft position. Three airplanes took off
              at 12.15 p.m., flew over the target from 12.45 p.m. until 1.10 p.m. and returned
              to base at 2.20 p.m.[40]

No. 201 Squadron, Mission Number 12

Date: June 6, 1945.
Mission: The Controller instructed bombing and attacking enemy positions in a
           canyon covered with foliage, situated on the west side of the Highway 5, 1,000
           yards south of Bambang.
Pilots: Names not available.
Results: Bombs were dropped in the target area which was indicated to the aircraft by
           smoke. The buildings in the area of the objective were destroyed and smoke was
           observed coming from the buildings. The region was heavily strafed and damages
           were not seen due to darkness in the foliage. The only things which could be
           observed were some lights like explosions during the attack in Bambang. The
           ground patrols reported to the Controller that the bombs fell exactly where they
           were needed. Two airplanes took off at 6.20 a.m., flew over the target from 6.50
           a.m. until 7.55 a.m. at an altitude of 6,000 feet and returned to base at 8.20 a.m.[41]

No. 201 Squadron, Mission Number 13

Date: June 6, 1945.
Mission: The Controller directed bombing and strafing enemy positions along the
           canyon on the east side of Highway 5, at 1,000 yards south of Bambang.
Pilots: Names not available.
Results: One building within the target was destroyed, and debris and smoke were visible. This
           same region was heavily strafed, but the results were not observed due to thickness
           of foliage. The bombing and strafing passes were made from south to north at an
           altitude of 2,000 feet. Patrols of the ground forces reported to the Controller that the
           bombs fell exactly where they were needed. Two airplanes took off at 6.20 a.m., flew
           over the target at 7.10 a.m. until 7.40 a.m. and returned to base at 8.20 a.m.[42]

No. 201 Squadron, Mission Number 14

Date: June 6, 1945.
Mission: To give direct support to the ground troops in the Bambang area. The flight
           was directed by the Controller to strafe and bomb enemy troop and artillery
           positions, on the east side of the hills about one mile west of Banbang.
Pilots: Names not available.
Results: The bombs were dropped in the area of the objective. The region was heavily
           strafed and numerous small brush fires were started. The Controller reported
           very good bombing. Two airplanes took off at 7.15 a.m., flew over the target
           from 8 a.m. until 8.30 a.m. and returned to base at 9.15 a.m.[43]

No. 201 Squadron, Mission Number 15

Date: June 6, 1945.
Mission: The flight was directed by the Controller to bomb enemy troop concentrations located in the east hill in the decline of the mountain between 1,000 and 1,500 yards west-southwest of Bambang.
Pilots: Names not available.
Results: The bombing passes were made from southwest to northwest, releasing the bombs at an altitude of approximately 1,500 feet. The bombs were all distributed in the target area. Stores of recent construction were observed in the hills to the northwest of Bambang. The Controller said that the results were very good. Four airplanes took off at 7.50 a.m., flew over the target from 8.30 a.m. until 9 a.m. and returned to base at 9.50 a.m.[44]

No. 201 Squadron, Mission Number 16

Date: June 6, 1945.
Mission: The flight was directed by the Controller to bomb and strafe enemy positions located along the groves of the bridge on the south of Highway 5, 1,000 yards west of Bayombong.
Pilots: Names not available.
Results: All the bombs were released in the target area, covering the bridge and the side of the hills, but the results were not observed due to heavy foliage. The Controller ordered the strafing of a house hidden in the same region, and after their strafing; they saw that the house began to burn. They also strafed the groves on the west side of Highway 5, at 4,000 yards north of Polano. Three airplanes took off at 11.10 a.m., flew over the target from 11.40 a.m. until 12.20 p.m. at an altitude of 6,000 feet and returned to base at 1 p.m.[45]

No. 201 Squadron, Mission Number 17

Date: June 6, 1945.
Mission: Bomb enemy positions in the mountains northwest of Santo Domingo and in the hillsides of Bayombong.
Pilots: Names not available.
Results: The bombing passes were made from east to west, dropping the bombs at an altitude of approximately 2,000 feet. The bombs were well distributed in the target area but the results were not observed due to heavy foliage. Four airplanes took off at 12 p.m., flew over the target from 12.45 p.m. to 1.15 p.m. at an altitude of 9,000 feet and returned to base at 2.15 p.m.[46]

58th Fighter Group Mission Number 1-1 (No. 201 Squadron, Mission Number 18)

Date: June 7, 1945.

Mission: Bomb enemy troops concentrations at Infanta. (Infanta is located on the most Western coast of Luzon, just inland from Dasol Bay and South of Lingayen Gulf.)

Pilots: Captain Radamés Gaxiola Andrade; Lieutenant Jacobo Estrada Luna; and Second Lieutenants Raúl García Mercado, Roberto Urías Avelleyra, José Luis Pratt Ramos, and two American pilots.

Results: The mission was not completed due to bad weather. Seven airplanes took at off 9.30 a.m., were over the target at 10 a.m. and returned to base at 11.30 a.m. A total thirteen 1,000-lb. bombs were jettisoned in Lamon Bay.[47]

58th Fighter Group Mission Number 1-2 (No. 201 Squadron, Mission Number 19)

Date: June 7, 1945.

Mission: Bomb enemy troop concentrations in Infanta area.

Pilots: Captain Pablo L. Rivas Martínez; Lieutenants Amadeo Castro Almanza, José Luis Barbosa Cerda, and Reynaldo Pérez Gallardo; and Second Lieutenant Mario López Portillo, and two American pilots. The 58th Fighter Group Deputy Commander led the flight.

Results: Thirteen 1,000-lb. bombs fell directly in target area and one 1,000-lb. bomb fell approximately 300 yards southeast of target area. Heavy foliage obscured results. The 58th Fighter Group Deputy Commander commented that the bombing was excellent. Five Mexican pilots and two American pilots took off at 2 p.m., were over the target at 2.30 p.m. and returned to base at 4 p.m.[48]

58th Fighter Group Mission Number 1-3 (No. 201 Squadron, Mission Number 20)

Date: June 10, 1945.

Mission: Provide support for land forces in the Mariquina water shed area. The flight was directed by the Controller to bomb enemy positions located in the waterfall west of the Panas Mountains.

Pilots: Captain Roberto Legorreta Sicilia; Lieutenants Héctor Espinosa Galván, Joaquín Ramírez Vilchis, and Amador Sámano Piña; and Second Lieutenants José Miguel Uriarte Aguilar, and José Luis Pratt Ramos. An American pilot accompanied the mission.

Results: The mission was directed by the liaison element Coyote. The P-47s bombed
            enemy troops in the west side of a gorge west of Monte Panas. The effects
            of the bombardment could not be observed due to the heavy foliage and
            cloud cover the target. Eighteen 1,000-lb. were dropped on the target. Two
            planes strafed the target on the bomb run. Four 1,000-lb. were jettisoned
            in the South China Sea east of Manila Bay, by pilots who did not complete
            their mission. Seven aircraft took off at 7.10 a.m., were over the target at 7.40
            a.m. and returned to base at 9.40 a.m. At 8.15 a.m., Captain Legorreta and
            Lieutenant Ramírez Vilchis did not complete the mission due to the lack of
            fuel. Lieutenant Espinosa Galván took command of the formation until the
            fulfillment of the mission. The flight experienced mostly cloudy to broken
            cloud cover en route to the target with partly cloudy conditions over the
            target.[49]

58th Fighter Group Mission Number 1-4 (No. 201 Squadron, Mission Number 21)

Date: June 10, 1945.
Mission: Support for ground troops in the Marikina Watershed Area.
Pilots: Lieutenants Amadeo Castro Almanza, José Luis Barbosa Cerda, and Julio Cal
            y Mayor Sauz and Second Lieutenants Práxedis López Ramos, Jaime Zenizo
            Rojas, Angel Sánchez Rebollo, Mario López Portillo, and an American pilot.
Results: Arrived over primary target the Controller advised that an L-5 reconnaissance
            aircraft at 1,500 feet would spot new target. Clouds prohibited leader from
            spotting L-5 and the mission was not completed. Sixteen 1,000-lb. bombs
            were jettisoned in the vicinity of Tabones Island. Seven Mexican pilots and
            one American pilot took off at 12.20 p.m., were over the target at 12.50 p.m.,
            and returned to base at 2.30 p.m.[50]

58th Fighter Group Mission Number 1-5 (No. 201 Squadron, Mission Number 22)

Date: June 11, 1945.
Mission: As directed by Support Aircraft Party (S.A.P.) Bunny 2, planes were to bomb
            an area north of intersection of Highway 4 and Lamut River.
Pilots: Captain Pablo L. Rivas Martínez; Lieutenants Graco Ramirez Garrido
            Alvardo, and Julio Cal y Mayor Sauz; and Second Lieutenants José Luis Pratt
            Ramos, and three American pilots.
Results: The leader made dry run over target from northwest to the southeast to
            get S.A.P.'s approval and after receiving verification, the flight made two

more consecutive passes. The eight aircraft bombed and strafed area along Highway 4, south of bank of Lamut River—probably near friendly troops. S.A.P. reported no damage. Due to trees, bombing results were unobserved. One airplane received two impacts from enemy fire. The pilot, Lieutenant Pratt Ramos, was unhurt. Sixteen 1,000-lb. bombs were released and 540 rounds of .50-caliber rounds were fired at the target. Eight aircraft took off at 8 a.m., were over the target from 8.30 a.m. until 9.45 a.m. and an altitude of 5,000 feet, and returned to base at 10.35 a.m.[51]

58th Fighter Group Mission Number 1-6 (No. 201 Squadron, Mission Number 23)

Date: June 11, 1945.

Mission: As directed by S.A.P. Bunny 2, five aircraft were to bomb and strafe enemy troop concentrations blocking Highway 4, approximately 2,200 yards west northwest of Payawan.

Pilots: Lieutenants Joaquín Ramírez Vilchis and Carlos Rodríguez Corona and Second Lieutenants Mario López Portillo, Angel Sánchez Rebollo, and Miguel Moreno Arreola.

Results: The leader made dry run from southeast to northwest to get S.A.P.'s approval, and in two subsequent passes, the five aircraft dropped ten 1,000-lb. bombs and strafed both sides of highway. S.A.P. Bunny 2 said artillery observers reported impacts on both sides of highway with excellent results. The aircraft attacked in string formation from 8,000 feet. Five aircraft took off at 11.30 a.m., were over the target from 12 p.m. until 1 p.m. at an altitude of 7,500 feet, and returned to base at 1.35 p.m.[52]

58th Fighter Group Mission Number 1-7 (No. 201 Squadron, Mission Number 24)

Date: June 12, 1945.

Mission: As directed by S.A.P. Trophy 7, aircraft were to bomb and strafe enemy troop concentrations in Mt. Mapatad–Mt. Campana area.

Pilots: Captain Roberto Legorreta Sicilia; Lieutenants Carlos Varela Landini and Fernando Hernández Vega; and Second Lieutenants David Cerón Bedolla, and José Luis Pratt Ramos. An American pilot accompanied the formation.

Result: The leader made dry run from west to east identify bombing objective, and in two successive passes, the two flights dropped eleven bombs in target area. S.A.P. Trophy reported excellent results to the flight leader. The first flight, after bombing enemy troop concentrations, strafed positions marked by the L-5 making run from northeast to southwest. The second flight did not strafe. Pilots observed bombs striking in areas marked by white phosphorus. One 1,000-lb. bomb struck approximately 400 yards northwest of target on the south bank of the Manaolan River. Seven aircraft took off at 9 a.m., were over the target from 9.30 a.m. until 10.16 a.m. at an altitude of 5,000 feet, and returned to base at 11 a.m.[53]

58th Fighter Group Mission Number 1-8 (No. 201 Squadron, Mission Number 25)

Date: June 13, 1945.

Mission: Bomb troop convoys moving south from Bagabag–Lamut area on Highway 4.

Pilots: Lieutenants Amadeo Castro Almanza, Jacobo Estrada Luna and Reynaldo Pérez Gallardo and Second Lieutenants Angel Sánchez Rebollo, Miguel Moreno Arreola, and David Cerón Bedolla. An American pilot accompanied the mission.

Results: Mission not completed due to weather and lack of available targets. Immediately after flight was airborne, the Controller ordered the mission to proceed to Balete Pass area and contact Doodle Bug. Upon arrival at target, the leader was ordered to stand by and wait for another aircraft. When another aircraft joined formation, the flight leader called the Controller asking that the new aircraft to takeover mission. The Controller ordered the bombs jettisoned in the vicinity of Tabones Island. Seven aircraft took off at 2.50 p.m., were over the target from 3.35 p.m. until 3.55 p.m. at an altitude of 6,000–9,500 feet, and returned to base at 4.30 p.m.[54]

58th Fighter Group Mission Number 1-9 (No. 201 Squadron, Mission Number 26)

Date: June 13, 1945.

Mission: Provide support for troops in the Mariquina area. The unit was to bomb a ravine marked by white phosphorus, with the second aircraft of second element strafing during the bomb run.

Pilots: Captain Pablo Rivas Martínez; Lieutenant Graco Ramirez Garrido Alvarado; and Second Lieutenants David Cerón Bedolla, and José Miguel Uriarte Aguilar. Two American pilots accompanied the mission.

Results: Nine 1,000-lb. bombs fell direct in target area, one bomb fell 400 yards north-northwest of smoke marked target and two bombs hung up and were jettisoned in Laguna Bay. The results unobserved due to heavy foliage. Six aircraft took off at 8.30 a.m., were over the target at 9.10 a.m. at an altitude of 8,500 feet, and returned to base at 10.30 a.m.[55]

58th Fighter Group Mission Number 1-10 (No. 201 Squadron, Mission Number 27)

Date: June 13, 1945.
Mission: Air alert over Infanta.
Pilots: Second Lieutenants Raúl García Mercado, Jaime Zenizo Rojas, Roberto Urías Avelleyra, David Cerón Bedolla, and Pratt Ramos. Two American pilots accompanied the mission.
Results: The flight leader contacted S.A.P. Curless 2 upon arrival over Infanta area and was advised that there were no targets available in the area. S.A.P. Curless 2 said that he had notified proper authorities to that effect the previous night. Fourteen 1,000-lb. general-purpose bombs were jettisoned in safety zone at Bagag Bay. Seven aircraft took off at 12.40 p.m., were over the target from 1.15 p.m. to 1.20 p.m., and returned to base at 3 p.m.[56]

58th Fighter Group Mission Number 1-11 (No. 201 Squadron, Mission Number 28)

Date: June 14, 1945.
Mission: The area over Montalban was alerted.
Pilots: Captain Roberto Legorreta Sicilia; Lieutenants Carlos Varela Landini, Amador Sámano Piña, Graco Ramirez Garrido Almanza, Fernando Hernández Vega, and Carlos Rodríguez Corona; and Second Lieutenants David Cerón Bedolla, Guillermo García Ramos, Manuel Farías Rodríguez, and José Miguel Uriarte Aguilar. An American pilot accompanied the mission.
Results: The flight leader contacted S.A.P. Trophy upon arrival over Montalban area. S.A.P. Trophy advised mission leader to contact other S.A.P.s in area. Leader contacted S.A.P. Trophy 2 but could not read the target designation. Leader then attempted to contact Curless but radio communication was not possible. Seventeen 1,000-lb. bombs were jettisoned in the security area off the Island de Tabones. A bomb of the same class fell, due to mechanical failure, out of the Laguna Bay safety area without causing damage. Four bombs of the same class, corresponding to the two pilots who abandoned their mission, were jettisoned into the safety area of Manila Bay. The mission was incomplete due to unavailability of target and poor radio contact. Ten airplanes took off at 7.30 a.m., flew over the target at 6,000 feet from 8 a.m. to 8.45 a.m. and returned to base at 9.15 a.m.[57]

58th Fighter Group Mission Number 1-12 (No. 201 Squadron, Mission Number 29)

Date: June 15, 1945.

Mission: Bomb and strafe enemy concentrations, supplies and ammo dump at Tuguegarao, in the top northeast section of Luzon on Highway 5.

Pilots: Captain Radamés Gaxiola Andrade; Lieutenants Héctor Espinosa Galván, Joaquín Ramírez Vilchis, and Amadeo Castro Almanza; and Second Lieutenants Guillermo García Ramos, Roberto Urías Avelleyra, and Jaime Zenizo Rojas. Two American pilots joined the mission.

Results: The flight leader made two dry runs east to west over target and on following pass, bombed and strafed objective. One aircraft failed to release bombs over target due to mechanical failure and two 1,000-lb. bombs were jettisoned in Gulf of Lingayen. One direct hit with attendant explosion was observed one building of two designated as target. It was observed that one bomb fell directly on the west side of the building, which was one of the designated targets, another bomb was dropped on the objective and exploded approximately in the southeast corner of the intersection point at some 400 yards. Five minutes after strike, the flight leader noticed blue smoke approximately at 1,500 feet in the air over areas where two large explosions were reported. Nine aircraft took off at 8 a.m., flew over the target from 9 a.m. to 9.30 a.m. at an altitude of 5,000 feet, and returned to base at 10.30 a.m. One aircraft landed at 8.30 a.m. due to mechanical trouble.[58]

58th Fighter Group Mission Number 1-13 (No. 201 Squadron, Mission Number 30)

Date: June 15, 1945.

Mission: Bomb and strafe enemy positions approximately 1,200 feet, east southeast of San Andres.

Pilots: Lieutenants Carlos Garduño Núñez, Reynaldo Pérez Gallardo, Julio Cal y Mayor Sauz, Carlos Rodríguez Corona, and Amador Sámano Piña and Second Lieutenants Angel Sánchez Rebollo and Miguel Moreno Arreola. Two American pilots accompanied the mission, Lieutenant Sámano Piña and Second Lieutenant Angel Sánchez Rebollo; both returned to Porac without completing the mission.

Result: As directed by the Controller S.A.P. Curless 1, six aircraft bombed and strafed enemy positions approximately 1,200 yards east-southeast of San Andres, attacking the east side of the gorge of Antipolo. The results were not observed by pilots due to heavy foliage. S.A.P. Curless reported good bombing results. Nine aircraft took off at 12.30 p.m., flew over the target from 1.20 p.m. to 2 p.m. at an altitude of 7,000 feet, and returned to base at 2.30 p.m. Four 1,000-lb. bombs were jettisoned in Laguna de Bay and two 1,000-lb. bombs were jettisoned on Tabones Island.[59]

58th Fighter Group Mission Number 1-14 (No. 201 Squadron, Mission Number 31)

Date: June 16, 1946.
Mission: To bomb and strafe enemy concentration at Infanta.
Pilots: Captains Pablo L. Rivas Martínez and Roberto Legorreta Sicilia; Lieutenants Reynaldo Pérez, Gallardo, Héctor Es pines Galván, and Joss Luis Barbosa Cerda; and Second Lieutenants Luis Pratt Ramos, Jacobo Estrada Luna, Guillermo García Ramos, Mario López Portillo, and Manuel Farías Rodríguez. An American pilot accompanied the mission.
Results: The flight leader contacted the Controller of the Infanta region, who informed them that the assigned target was occupied by United States troops. The Controller assigned them to another target along Ikdan Creek where there were enemy concentrations. Eleven aircraft bombed enemy troop concentrations on the first run from northeast to southwest along Ikdan Creek. The pilots made three strafing runs on target. Pilots observed two large explosions, which produced brown smoke. S.A.P. Curless 2 reported good results. The flight received enemy fire from mortars and from small arms; the firing came from both sides of the river and along the beach. Two airplanes were hit—one from mortar fire and the other from small firearms. Eleven aircraft took off at 11.45 a.m., flew over the target from 12.45 p.m. to 1.15 p.m. at an altitude of 5,000 feet, and returned to base at 1.45 p.m.[60]
Note: Several of the reported 201st mission numbers are out of sequence.

58th Fighter Group Mission Number 1-15 (No. 201 Squadron, Mission Number 33)

Date: June 17, 1945.
Mission: Bomb enemy positions in the Zolanga area and in the vicinity of Bangbang.
Pilots: Lieutenants Amadeo Castro Almanza and Carlos Garduño Núñez and Second lieutenants Jacobo Estrada Luna, Jaime Zenizo Rojas, Práxedis López Ramos, and Roberto Urías Avelleyra. Lieutenant Garduño Núñez suffered an accident during the take-off from Porac. The plane caught fire, destroying itself completely. The pilot received burns. Second Lieutenant Jaime Zenizo Rojas returned to the field before completing the mission due to failure in his airplane.

Results: The Controller directed the flight to bomb enemy troop concentrations located approximately 6,500 yards west southwest of Bambang. The leader made a pass in order to familiarize himself with the object, and on the following passes the bombs were released in the area marked with phosphorous by the Controller; the pilots saw the bombs fall in the target area but they were not able to observe the results due to the thickness of the foliage. S.A.P. Bygone 1 reported first two 1,000-lb. bombs long, but into target area, and six 1,000-lb. bombs direct on target. Six aircraft took off at 7.30 a.m., flew over the target from 9.20 a.m. until 9.30 a.m., and returned to base at 10 a.m.[61]

58th Fighter Group Mission Number 1-16 (No. 201 Squadron, Mission Number 32)

Date: June 17, 1945.
Mission: Bomb enemy concentrations vicinity Payawan Rest House, north central Luzon.
Pilots: Lieutenants Carlos Varela Landini, Fernando Hernández Vega, Amador Sámano Piña, Héctor Espinosa Galván, and Joaquín Ramírez Vilchis and Second Lieutenants Miguel Uriarte Aguilar, Manuel Farías Ramos, and Raúl García Mercado. Lieutenant Fernando Hernández and his wingman, Second Lieutenant Miguel Uriarte Aguilar, left the formation before fulfilling the mission.
Results: As directed by S.A.P. Bygone with the aid of Daisy Blue leader, seven aircraft bombed and strafed enemy concentrations and a motor convoy, approximately 6,000 yards northeast of Payaman. Pilots observed twelve bomb hits on target. Two trucks were left burning after strafing passes. Two 1,000-lb. bombs fell in target area. The airplanes were fired at by large mortars and close-range guns. Two planes were hit but suffered only slight damage. Nine airplanes took off at 1.15 p.m., flew over the target at 5,000 feet from 2.30 p.m. to 3 p.m., and returned to base at 3.45 p.m. One airplane returned due to mechanical failure.[62]

58th Fighter Group Mission Number 1-17 (No. 201 Squadron, Mission Number 35)

Date: June 18, 1945.
Mission: Bomb and machine gun enemy positions east of the Lenatin River.
Pilots: Lieutenants Amadeo Castro Almanza, Julio Cal y Mayor Sauz, and José Luis Barhosi Cerda and Second Lieutenants Miguel Moreno Arreola, Jaime Zenizo Rojas, Mario López Portillo, and Angel Sánchez Rebollo. An American pilot accompanied the formation.

Results: Directed by the controller on land Curless 1, Lieutenant Castro Almanza led the flight to bomb enemy machine-gun positions east of the Lenatin River. The objective was marked by an L-5 aircraft. The pilots observed sixteen bombs making impact on a bunker. In four subsequent passes, the aircraft strafed the target occupied by enemy forces. Eight aircraft took off at 7.30 a.m. and landed at its base at 9.30 a.m. A plane landed with a flat tire when it reached Porac.[63]

58th Fighter Group Mission Number 1-18 (No. 201 Squadron, Mission Number 34)

Date: June 18, 1945.
Mission: Bomb enemy concentrations on both sides of the Lenatin River.
Pilots: Lieutenants Héctor Espinosa Galván and Graco Ramírez Gallardo and Second Lieutenants Guillermo García Ramos and Manuel Farías Rodriguez. An American pilot accompanied the mission.
Results: The flight leader contacted the Controller in the Lenatin River region, who directed them to bomb enemy positions in the bed of Said River. An L-5 type aircraft marked the target for them with a white phosphorous bomb. The bombs were released directly on target. The pilots did not see the results of the bombing due to the thickness of the underbrush. The Controller had ordered that they were not to strafe the area, which they bombed and marked a target to be strafed a mile south of the bombing. They made two subsequent passes from south to north, strafing both sides of the river bed beginning from the initial point of the bombing area. Two machine-gun nests were destroyed on their first pass, but when the airplanes began the second pass, enemy machine guns fired again. The Controller reported excellent results from this mission. Five aircraft took off at 12 p.m., flew over the target from 12.45 p.m. to 1.30 p.m. at an altitude of 4,000 feet, and returned to base at 2 p.m.[64]

58th Fighter Group Mission Number 1-19 (No. 201 Squadron, Mission Number 36)

Date: June 19, 1945.
Mission: Bomb enemy positions in the vicinity of Antipolo.
Pilots: Captains Pablo L. Rivas Martínez and Roberto Legorreta Sicilia and Lieutenants Graco Reynaldo Péres Gallardo and Carlos Rodríguez Corona. Two American pilots accompanied the formation.
Results: The pilots saw the L-5 spot the target with white phosphorus. The Controller ordered the flight leader to stand by since S.A.P. had lost radio contact

with L-5. S.A.P. Curless 1 ordered the leader to return flight to base and not to jettison bombs in the area. Twelve 1,000-lb. bombs were jettisoned in Laguna de Bay. Six aircraft took off at 8 a.m., flew over the target from 8.45 a.m. to 9.15 a.m. at an altitude of 7,000 feet, and returned to base at 10 a.m.[65]

58th Fighter Group Mission Number 1-20 (No. 201 Squadron, Mission Number 37)

Date: June 20, 1945.
Mission: Bomb and strafe enemy positions on the east side of Montalban River.
Pilots: Captain Radamés Gaxiola Andrade; Lieutenants Jacobo Estrada Luna, Graco Ramírez Gallardo, Fernando Hernández Vega, and Amador Sámano Piña; and Second Lieutenant José Luis Pratt Ramos. Two American pilots accompanied the mission.
Results: Directed by S.A.P. Curless 1, the flight leader made contact with an L-5 Captain Gaxiola Andrade, which marked the target with white smoke bombs. The aircraft bombed the target and also reported two additional strafing passes on both sides of the river. Controller Curless 1 reported satisfactory results. Eight aircraft took off at 7.30 a.m., flew over the target from 8.30 a.m. to 8.50 a.m. at an altitude of 7,000 feet, and returned to base at 9.30 a.m.[66]

58th Fighter Group Mission Number 1-21 (No. 201 Squadron, Mission Number 38)

Date: June 21, 1945.
Mission: Bomb and strafe concentrations of enemy troops in the vicinity of Antirolo.
Pilots: Lieutenants Amadeo Castro Almanza and José Luis Barbosa Cerda and Second Lieutenants Práxedis López Ramos, Miguel Moreno Arreola, Roberto Urías Avelleyra, and Mario López Portillo. An American pilot accompanied the mission.
Results: The flight leader contacted the Controller of the Antipolo region and was told to wait for an L-5, which marked the objective for them with white smoke. The leader made a reconnaissance pass over the target area and on subsequent passes released the bomb over the objective to the north of Montalban River. Three passes were made from south to north. On orders from the Controller, one plane strafed the area passing southwest to northeast. The results were not observed due to the thickness of foliage. One pilot reported that a machine-gun nest was silenced. There was enemy mortar fire and the Controller

reported that the bombing was good on this mission. Seven aircraft took off at 1 p.m., flew over the target from 1.45 p.m. to 2.14 p.m. at an altitude of 3,500 feet, and returned to base at 3 p.m.[67]

58th Fighter Group Mission Number 1-22 (No. 201 Squadron, Mission Number 39)

Date: June 21, 1945.
Mission: Bomb and strafe enemy positions approximately 150 yards from Malavite Mountain.
Pilots: Captains Pablo L. Rivas Martínez and Roberto Legorreta Sicilia; Lieutenants Héctor Espinosa Galván, Carlos Rodríguez Corona, and Joaquín Ramírez Vilchis; and Second Lieutenant Jaime Zenizo Rojas. A plane from 58 Group accompanied the mission
Results: Under the direction of Curless 1, the seven aircraft bombed and strafed an area of an approximate radius of 150 meters southwest near Malavite Mountain. The flight leader made a first recognition pass and in the second pass. Fourteen 1,000-lb. bombs were dropped on both sides of the river. Curless reported the attack as good. Seven aircraft took off at 8.30 a.m., flew over the target from 9.35 a.m. to 10 a.m., and returned to base at 10.30 a.m.[68]

58th Fighter Group Mission Number 1-23 (No. 201 Squadron, Mission Number 40)

Date: June 21, 1945.
Mission: Bomb and strafe enemy positions near Alealá.
Pilots: Lieutenants Amadeo Castro Almanza and Julio Cal y Mayor Sauz and Second Lieutenants Roberto Urías Avelleyra, Miguel Moreno Arreola, Angel Sánchez Rebollo, and Miguel Uriarte Aguilar. An American pilot of the 58th Group accompanied the mission.
Results: The leader contacted the Controller in the Llagan region, who directed the squadron toward the town of Alealá, to the south of Tuguegarao. The Controller ordered the bombs released on an unidentified town, thinking that it was part of Zalano. The Controller identified the town and told the leader that it was not their objective. He directed the flight to Penablanca and ordered them to bomb it. The bombs were released on the target, but the Controller did not report the results of this mission. Fourteen 1,000-lb. bombs were dropped on the target. Seven aircraft took off, flew over the target from 2 p.m. to 3 p.m., and landed at 4 p.m.[69]

58th Fighter Group Mission Number 1-24 (No. 201 Squadron, Mission Number 41)

Date: June 22, 1945.

Mission: Bomb and strafe a newly made enemy trail running north from the north bank of Agnos River, approximately 120 yards southwest of Infanta, on the western most edge of the South China Sea coast.

Pilots: Lieutenants Amadeo Castro Almanza, Reynaldo Pérez Gallardo, and José Luis Barbosa Cerda and Second Lieutenants Roberto Urías Avelleyra, Mario López Portillo, and José Luis Pratt Ramos.

Results: As directed by S.A.P. Curless 2, nine aircraft bombed and strafed enemy positions marked with white phosphorus by artillery. Results not observed by pilots due to heavy foliage. Sixteen 1,000-lb. bombs and 7,136 cartridges 0.50 were used in the mission. Anti-aircraft light weapons fire was observed. Eight aircraft took off at 8 a.m., flew over the target from 8.40 a.m. to 9.20 a.m., and returned to base at 10 a.m.[70]

58th Fighter Group Mission Number 1-25 (No. 201 Squadron, Mission Number 42)

Date: June 22, 1945.

Mission: Bomb and strafe enemy positions, which were marked for them with white phosphorous by artillery along the Agos River.

Pilots: Captains Radamés Gaxiola Andrade and Roberto Legorreta Sicilia; Lieutenants Carlos Varela Landini, Joaquín Ramírez Vilchis, Julio Cal y Mayor Sauz, and Graco Ramírez Garrido Alvarado; and Second Lieutenants Raúl García Mercado and Miguel Uriarte Aguilar. A pilot of the 58 Group accompanied the flight.

Results: Bombs were released in target area, but the Controller did not report the results of this mission due to the thickness of underbrush. Enemy troops fired at the formation. Nine airplanes took off at 12.45 p.m., flew over the target from 1.30 p.m. to 1.50 p.m. at 4,000 feet, and returned to base at 2.45 p.m.[71]

58th Fighter Group Mission Number 1-26 (No. 201 Squadron, Mission Number 43)

Date: June 23, 1945.

Mission: Bomb and strafe enemy positions located east of the Kanan River.

Pilots: Captain Pablo Rivas Martínez; Lieutenants Héctor Espinosa Galván, Carlos Rodríguez Corona, Amador Castro Almanza, Manuel Farías Rodríguez, and

Amador Sámano Piña; and Second Lieutenant Guillermo García Ramos. An American pilot accompany the formation.

Results: As reported by Curless 2, eight aircraft bombed and strafed enemy positions, making one bomb run and one strafing run from southwest to northeast with results unobserved by pilots due to heavy foliage. Four large explosions were observed south of secondary road. S.A.P. reported bombing and strafing results as very good, except for two bombs which were long. Two aircraft damaged on landing upon return from mission. One pilot was injured with a probably fracture of an arm. Eight aircraft took off at 7.30 a.m., flew over the target from 9 a.m. to 9.30 a.m. at an altitude of 9,000 feet, and returned to base at 10 a.m.[72]

58th Fighter Group Mission Number 1-27 (No. 201 Squadron, Mission Number 44)

Date: June 23, 1945.
Mission: Bomb enemy concentrations in map position 30.9-768 to 30.5-78.4 3555-111.
Pilots: Captain Radamés Gaxiola Andrade; Lieutenant Julio Cal y Major Sauz; and Second Lieutenants Jaime Zenizo Rojas, José Luis Pratt Ramos, and Mario López Portillo. An American pilot accompanied the formation.
Results: The Controller directed bombing enemy concentrations located on the topographical crest of a hill. They dropped their bombs on the target area and the Controller reported very good results from this mission. The leader of the squadron received orders from the Controller to contact the special Controller, who, in turn, ordered him to communicate with an L-5. The leader could not contact the aircraft L-5 and consequently the Controller ordered him to check with Controller No. 2, who designated the target for them. Ten 1,000-lb. bombs were dropped on enemy positions. Six aircraft took off at 11.30 a.m., flew over the target at 7,000 feet from 12.20 p.m. to 12.50 p.m., and returned to base at 1.30 p.m.[73]

58th Fighter Group Mission Number 1-28 (No. 201 Squadron, Mission Number 45)

Date: June 24, 1945.
Mission: Bomb and strafed enemy concentrations located on both sides of Kanan River ravine.
Pilots: Captains Pablo Rivas Martínez and Roberto Legorreta Sicilia; Lieutenant Amadeo Castro Almanza; and Second Lieutenants Angel Sánchez Rebollo and Mario López Portillo. An American plane joined the formation. Second

Lieutenant Rebollo returned to base thirty minutes after take-off due to high oil pressure.

Results: As directed by S.A.P. Curless 2, six aircraft bombed and strafed enemy concentrations located on both sides of ravine with results unobserved by pilots due to heavy foliage. The flight leader made a first run and one bombing pass. The flight made eight strafing passes from southwest to northeast and dropped ten 1,000-lb. bombs. They expended 10,060 round of .50-caliber ammunition on the target. S.A.P. Curless 2 was unable to observe results from his position. The U.S. pilot on mission reported very good bomb pattern. Six aircraft took off at 7.30 a.m., flew over the target from 8.15 a.m. to 8.45 a.m. at an altitude of 7,000 feet, and returned to base at 9.30 a.m.[74]

58th Fighter Group Mission Number 1-29 (No. 201 Squadron, Mission Number 46)

Date: June 24, 1945.

Mission: Bombard enemy concentrations marked by white phosphorous in map position 49.5-80.7 in the Infanta area.

Pilots: Lieutenants Amador Sámano Piña and Graco Ramírez Garrido Alvarado and Second lieutenants Mario López Portillo, José Luis Pratt Ramos, and Angel Sánchez Rebollo. An American pilot accompanied the mission.

Results: As directed by Curless 2, six aircraft bombed enemy concentrations marked by white phosphorous on east bank of ravine. Due to poor weather, the bombing was made in close formation, the flight leader led the flight through a small clearing in the clouds to begin their bombing passes. S.A.P. Curless 2 reported the bombing as good and that all twelve bombs had struck target area. Six aircraft took off at 12.45 p.m., flew over the target from 1.20 p.m. to 1.50 p.m. at an altitude of 3,500 feet, and returned to base at 2.45 p.m. One aircraft failed to take off due to a broken belly tank hose.[75]

58th Fighter Group Mission Number 1-30 (No. 201 Squadron, Mission Number 47)

Date: June 25, 1945.

Mission: Bomb and strafed enemy troop concentrations that were marked with white phosphorous, located on the south side of the Agos River at map position 49.5-80.7.

Pilots: Captain Pablo L. Rivas Martínez; Lieutenants Héctor Espinosa Galván, Joaquín Ramírez Vilchis, Carlos Rodriguez Corona, Amador Sámano Piña, and José L. Barbosa Cerda; and Second Lieutenants Guillermo García

Ramos, Jaime Zenizo Rojas, Mario López Portillo, Roberto Urías Avelleyra, and Angel Sánchez Rebollo, An American pilot accompanied the formation.

Results: The bombing and strafing passes were made from south to north. The bombs fell directly on the target and the Controller reported excellent results from this mission. Twelve aircraft took off at 9.15 a.m., flew over the target at 6,500 feet from 9.20 a.m. to 9.45 a.m., and landed at 10.45 a.m. The aircraft returned to base at 10.30 a.m.[76]

58th Fighter Group Mission Number 1-31 (No. 201 Squadron, Mission Number 48

Date: June 25, 1945.

Mission: Bomb and strafe enemy troop concentrations, which were marked with white phosphorous, located in the Infanta area at map position 51.5-79. 9.

Pilots: Captains Radamés Gaxiola Andrade and Roberto Legorreta Sicilia; Lieutenants José Luis Barbosa Cerda, Amadeo Castro Almanza, and Carlos Rodríguez Corona; and Second Lieutenants Práxedis López Arreola, Miguel Uriarte Aguilar, and José Luis Pratt Rebollo. An American pilot accompanied the mission.

Results: Under the direction of Curless 2, Captain Gaxiola attacked enemy positions dropping twenty-four 1,000-lb. bombs and machine-gunned the target. Curless reported the bombing and machine-gunning as good. Nine aircraft took off at 1 p.m., flew over the target at 6,500 feet from 1.30 p.m. to 1.45 p.m., and returned to base at 2 p.m.[77]

58th Fighter Group Mission Number 1-32 (No. 201 Squadron, Mission Number 49)

Date: June 26, 1945.

Mission: Bomb enemy concentrations in map position 49.5-89.7 in the Infanta area.

Pilots: Captains Pablo L. Rivas Martínez and Roberto Legorreta Sicilia; Lieutenants Héctor Espinosa Galván, Fernando Hernández Vega, Graco Ramírez Garrido Alvarado, Julio Cal y Mayor Sauz, Carlos Varela Landini, and Jacobo Estrada Luna; and Second Lieutenants José Miguel Uriarte Aguilar, José Luis Pratt Ramos, and Jaime Zenizo Rojas.

Results: Directed by Curless 2, the eleven aircraft bombed and strafed enemy concentrations. The target was marked by white was marked by white smoke grenades. Curless 2 reported good results of the attack. Eleven aircraft took off at 7.30 a.m., flew over the target from 8.15 a.m. to 0 a.m., and returned to base at 9.40 a.m. Eleven 1,000-lb. bombs were used on the target as well as 8,750 .50-caliber machine-gun ammunition. One 1,000-lb. bomb was jettisoned into the security zone at Camon Bay.[78]

58th Fighter Group Mission Number 1-33 (No. 201 Squadron, Mission Number 50)

Date: June 28, 1945.

Mission: Bomb and strafe enemy positions marked for them to the north of Limutan River.

Pilots: Captain Radamés Gaxiola Andrade; Lieutenants Carlos Varela Landini, Jacobo Estrada Luna, Graco Ramirez Garrido, and José Luis Barbosa Cerda; and Second Lieutenants Raúl García Mercado, Roberto Urías Avelleyra, Jaime Zenizo Rojas, and Manuel Farías Ramos. An American pilot accompanied the unit.

Results: Directed by the Curless, the ten P-47s bombarded and machine-gunned enemy positions in the target area, a bombing pass from north to south and three passes from south to north. Eighteen 1,000-lb. bombs were dropped on the target. The Liaison Detachment did not report the results. Ten aircraft took off at 1 p.m., flew over the target from 1.30 p.m. to 1.45 p.m., and returned to base at 2.20 p.m. Two 1,000-lb. bombs were jettisoned in the security zone, and 2,290 cartridges of .50-caliber machine-gun ammunition were shot at the target.[79]

58th Fighter Group Mission Number 1-34 (No. 201 Squadron, Mission Number 51)

Date: June 29, 1945.

Mission: Bomb and strafe enemy positions and concentrations located along Limutan River.

Pilots: Lieutenants Héctor Espinosa Galván, Carlos Varela Landini, Joaquín Ramírez Vilchis, and Jacobo Estrada Luna and Second Lieutenants José Miguel Uriarte Aguilar, Mario López Portillo, Manuel Farías Rodríguez, and Raúl García Mercado. Two American pilots accompanied the mission.

Results: As directed by S.A.P. Curless Special, ten aircraft bombed and strafed enemy positions and concentrations setting off two explosions and fires. The first and seventh planes attacking strafed approximately twenty-five Japanese soldiers lined up across the Limutan River and fired at airplanes with machine guns. Curless reported the fourth aircraft of first flight dropped two 1,000-lb. bombs directly on heavy troop concentrations and reported bombing and strafing results excellent with good coverage. Ten aircraft took off at 9.30 a.m., flew over the target from 10.05 a.m. to 10.50 a.m. at an altitude of 4,000 feet, and returned to base at 11.40 a.m.[80]

58th Fighter Group Mission Number 1-35 (No. 201 Squadron, Mission Number 52)

Date: June 30, 1945.
Mission: Bomb enemy positions located in the Cervanes area.
Pilots: Lieutenants Amadeo Castro Almanza, Reynaldo Pérez Gallardo, and Julio Cal y Major Sauz and Second Lieutenants Práxedis López Ramos, Jaime Zenizo Rojas, Angel Sánchez Rebollo, Raúl García Mercado, Roberto Urías Avelleyra, and Miguel Moreno Arreola.
Results: The leader received orders to make contact with Curless Special, who designated a target covered by bad weather. The Liaison Detachment reported that there were no targets at hand, so the formation jettisoned its bombs in the security zone at Isla de Tabones. Nine aircraft took off at 8 a.m., flew over the target from 8.30 a.m. to 8.50 a.m. at an altitude of 3,000 feet, and returned to base at 9.15 a.m.[81]

58th Fighter Group Mission Number 1-36 (No. 201 Squadron, Mission Number 53)

Date: July 4, 1945.
Mission: Bomb enemy positions in the Cervantes area.
Pilots: Captains Radamés Gaxiola Andrade and Pablo L. Rivas Martínez; Lieutenants Jacobo Estrada Luna, José Luis Barbosa Cerda, Joaquín Ramírez Vilchis, Carlos Rodríguez Corona, and Reynaldo Pérez Gallardo; and Second Lieutenants Raúl García Mercado, Justino Reyes Retana, and Jaime Zenizo Rojas. An American pilot accompanied the formation.
Results: The leader contacted the Controller in the Cervantes region, who ordered them to contact an L-5 at a town called Lana. The leader tried to communicate with the L-5, but due to poor radio contact, he could not communicate with the L-5. The controller ordered them to jettison their thirty-two 1,000-lb. bombs in the security zone in the South China Sea. Eleven aircraft took off at 7 a.m., flew over the target area from 8 a.m. to 8.10 a.m. at an altitude of 1,500 feet, and returned to base at 10 a.m. This is the last 58th Fighter Squadron Mission record for the 201st Squadron.[82]

In his memoirs, Lieutenant Amador Sámano Piña recounts one of his missions:

On June 17, over the Payawan Restlow region, our leader, Lieutenant Héctor Espinoza Galván, discovered an enemy convoy on one of the secondary roads and we were ordered to attack the seven planes; We launched ourselves directly at the target by machine-gunning, I took aim at a truck directly in front of me, we approached quickly while I released two machine gun bursts and almost immediately the flames caught the truck, we promptly rose to avoid the secondary explosions after launching our bombs, the enemy responded vigorously with light weapons fire, damaging two of our planes. This mission lasted from 1:30 p.m. to 3:45 p.m....[83]

But not only were there dangers to face for the pilots, there were numerous Japanese snipers in the vicinity of the camp of the 201st and several times there was direct contact with the enemy. On July 23, a group commanded by the Second Lieutenant of Administration Guillermo A. Robles, who was collecting wood, was attacked and a soldier was wounded in the arm. Later, on August 26, a Mexican contingent faced a group of Japanese in a skirmish, one of the Japanese died and two more were captured.

From June 27 and until the last of July, the squadron maintained two airplanes in "Immediate Alert Status" and two in "Alert in 30 Minutes Status." The Luzon Campaign end officially at midnight June 30 to July 1. U.S. Sixth Army turned over to U.S. Eight Army the task of concluding operations on Luzon and regrouped extensively for its next assignment, the invasion of Japan. Eighth Army took command of XIV Corps, which included the final mop up operations on Luzon. Two large pockets of enemy remain on north Luzon; about 11,000 Japanese were estimated to be concealed in Sierra Madre Mountains and an estimated 12,000 were established in the Kiangan–Bontoc area. Operations to eliminate these pockets continued until end of the war. Under XIV Corps command were 6th, 32rd, 37th, and 38th Infantry Divisions plus Filipino guerrilla forces on the island. The 24th Division was chosen for the final amphibious operations in the Philippines—a landing on Mindanao at Saragani Bay. On Mindanao, X Corps continued to mop up until end of war.[84]

12

Missions over Formosa

Shortly before the invasion of Leyte began, the Joint Chiefs of Staff directed MacArthur to invade Luzon on December 20, 1944, thus settling the argument as to whether Luzon or Formosa should be the next object of attack. It was not expected that Luzon would be easily reclaimed, but it was believed that the conquest of Formosa would be much more difficult and might require as many as nine divisions, more than were then available in the Pacific area. While construction of airfields on the muddy terrain of Leyte moved slowly forward, and while the fleet recovered from the Battle of Leyte Gulf, MacArthur decided to occupy the island of Mindoro, directly south of Luzon, for the construction of additional airfields. The attack on Mindoro began on December 15 and the invasion of Luzon was rescheduled for January 9, 1945. Both invasions were undertaken by the U.S. Sixth Army under Lieutenant General Walter Krueger, supported by the 3rd and 7th Fleets, and by the Army air forces in the area. After the preliminary air attacks on Luzon at the turn of the year, the 3rd Fleet moved into the South China Sea to strike the Indochina coast, Formosa, Hong Kong, and Chinese coastal points.[1]

Early in July, the 58th Fighter Group left for Okinawa. The 201st operated from Clark Field while it brought its P-47 inventory up to strength with new P-47D-30 models and awaited more squadrons. In the meantime, the aircraft were fitted with auxiliary wing tanks and prepared for long-range reconnaissance missions to Toko, Formosa. The distance to Toko was 700 miles. Early on July 6, eight Mexican Thunderbolts took off from Clark with a maximum load, barely clearing the runway. They traveled north hour after hour, with the blazing tropical sun beating down on their cramped cockpits, the pilots became drained and dehydrated. Adding to their discomfort was the tension of flying single-engined aircraft over hundreds of miles of water with only basic instruments. A small navigational error, bad weather or high fuel consumption could force them to ditch. After over seven hours in the air, in full survival gear, the men had to be helped from their cockpits. Each downed several ounces of hard liquor before debriefing to break the tension.

Over Formosa, the Mexicans encountered no challengers. The Aztec Eagles owned the air. The fighter sweeps were completed successfully, and all pilots managed to return safely to Clark except Lieutenant Pérez, who put down at Lingayen, out of fuel. The Mexican pilots also practiced combat tactics and ferried new P-47s from Biak Island, New Guinea, to Clark as well as flying war-weary aircraft to Biak for disposal. It was the height of the typhoon season by that time, and the weather conditions proved both unpredictable and treacherous. In the Philippines, there was almost no enemy air activity. Japanese aviation had concentrated in the defense of Japan, and only sporadic flights were seen over the Philippines. There was some enemy air activity over Formosa and the 201st Squadron received the opportunity to go after it from July 6 to 9, 1945.[2]

On July 6, 7, 8, and 9, two squadrons, of four aircraft each, carried out armed reconnaissance (American denomination "Fighter Sweep") over the island of Formosa. The squadron continued to record 58th Fighter Group mission number.

58th Fighter Group Mission Number 1-37 (No. 201 Squadron, Mission Number 54)

Date: July 6, 1945.
Mission: Long-range reconnaissance to Toko, Formosa.
Pilots: Captain Radamés Gaxiola Andrade; Lieutenants Amadeo Castro Almanza, Reynaldo Pérez Gallardo, and Jacobo Estrada Luna; and Second Lieutenants Miguel Moreno Arreola, Práxedis López Ramos, Mario López Portillo, and Jaime Zenizo Rojas.
Results: On this mission, nothing was observed due to poor meteorological conditions. No enemies were encountered to attack. During the return, Lieutenant Pérez Gallardo landed in Lingayen due to lack of fuel. Eight aircraft took off at 8.30 a.m., flew over the Formosa from 11 a.m. to 11.30 a.m. at an altitude of 12,000 feet, and returned to base at 1 p.m.[3]

58th Fighter Group Mission Number 1-38 (No. 201 Squadron, Mission Number 55)

Date: July 7, 1945.
Mission: Long-range reconnaissance to Toko, Formosa.
Pilots: Captains Pablo L. Rivas Martínez and Roberto Legorreta Sicilia; Lieutenants Héctor Espinosa Galván, Joaquín Ramírez Vilchis, and José L. Barbosa Cerda; and Second Lieutenants Guillermo García Ramos, Raúl García Mercado, and Roberto Urías Avelleyra.

Results: This mission did not record any enemy action. From the point of view of the operations, the mission was in general fulfilled and correctly conducted. Eight aircraft took off at 9 a.m., flew over the Formosa from 11.20 a.m. to 11.40 a.m., and landed at 2.15 p.m.[4]

58th Fighter Group Mission Number 1-39 (No. 201 Squadron, Mission Number 56)

Date: July 8, 1945.
Mission: Long-range reconnaissance to Toko, Formosa.
Pilots: Lieutenants Carlos Varela Landini, Fernando Hernández Vega, Graco Ramírez Garrido, Julio Cal y Mayor Sauz, Amador Sámano Piña, and Carlos Garduño Núñez and Second Lieutenants José Luis Pratt Ramos, José Miguel Uriarte Aguilar, and Manuel Farías Rodríguez.
Results: This mission did not record any enemy action. When they were returning from Formosa Island at approximately 1 p.m., they saw four unidentified planes on the east side of Byuku, flying north at 1,000 feet. The leader lost contact in the clouds. One squadron of P-38s and another of P-51s were seen flying to the south of Formosa *en route* to Luzon. One of the pilots of the squadron reported a submarine at approximately 22°10′N and 120°30′E. Nine aircraft took off at 9.25 a.m., flew over the Formosa from 11.05 a.m. to 12.10 p.m., and landed at 2.25 p.m.[5]

58th Fighter Group Mission Number 1-40 (No. 201 Squadron, Mission Number 57)

Date: July 9, 1945.
Mission: Long-range reconnaissance to Toko, Formosa.
Pilots: Captain Pablo Rivas Martínez; Lieutenants Amador Sámano Piña, Fernando Hernández Vega, and Reynaldo Pérez Gallardo; and Second Lieutenants Guillermo García Ramos, Manuel Farías Rodríguez, Angel Sánchez Rebollo, and Raúl García Mercado. An American pilot accompanied the mission.
Results: This time, the planes did not carry bombs. During flight, they encountered numerous B-24, B-33, P-51, and P-38 planes *en route* north, over the southern part of Formosa. Two enemy monoplanes were seen at Haite Airdrome to the south of Toko. They observed two destroyers and seven vessels of large floating surfaces, which were anchored in Tokyo Bay and three hydroplanes in the same bay with all their necessary equipment. The leader of the flight did not attack the ships because his mission was only to combat enemy aircraft or to intercept them. Nine aircraft took off at 9 a.m., flew over the

Formosa from 11.30 a.m. to 12 p.m. at an altitude of 12,000 feet, and landed at 2.15 p.m.[6]

Note: On August 7, the squadron carried out an interception-training mission with elements placed at the orders of Lieutenant Amadeo Castro Almanza. A squadron of four aircraft remained at base on alert status pending orders from the Fight Control Center. Upon receipt of orders, they left to fulfill the mission, which was ineffective due to difficulties of contact with the controllers. On the same day, seven aircraft left for Biak, New Guinea, with the mission of transporting old aircraft to Biak for disposal and new P-47s from there to Luzon. They return to Porac Field on the August 12 without incident.[7]

58th Fighter Group Mission Number 1-41 (No. 201 Squadron, Mission Number 58)

Date: August 8, 1945.
Mission: Bomb some building in the port of Karenko, Formosa.
Pilots: Captain Radamés Gaxiola Andrade; Lieutenants Amadeo Castro Almanza, Carlos Garduño Núñez, Reynaldo Pérez Gallardo, and Julio Cal y Mayor Sauz; and Second Lieutenants Justino Reyes Retana, Miguel Moreno Arreola, and Práxedis López Ramos.
Results: Six airplanes bombed the buildings designated as primary target, according to references from a photograph of Karenko, Formosa. The bombs fell between the river and the highway, which runs from north to south, leaving two fires and no damage to the buildings. Two airplanes after having participated in the mission, landed at Lingayen base, due to lack of fuel. The pilots reported that the bombing was not effective. Eight aircraft took off at 7.45 a.m., flew over the target from 10.30 a.m. to 10.40 a.m. at an altitude of 12,000 feet, and returned to base at 1.45 p.m. Two airplanes returned due to lack of gasoline and landed at Lingayen at 11.15 a.m. without participating in the mission. One airplane suffered an accident when landing in Porac, seriously damaging the airplane.[8]

Mission to Karenko

Despite the risks, the pilots carried out this dangerous long-range bombardment mission to Karenko, Formosa. Lieutenant Amadeo Castro Almanza, leader of the squadron, recalled what happened:

This mission had some degree of difficulty because it was necessary to fly a great distance over the sea, which implied that in case of being intercepted or of finding unfavorable meteorological conditions, the fuel consumption would be greater and there was the danger of falling short and fall. A submarine would be aware of our passage and would try to go to the rescue of the one that had to jump by parachute, besides that in a certain area there would be a Catalina seaplane to help if necessary. The start of the flight was at convenient heights thanks to the IFF, but at a certain distance from the target we had to descend to approach low altitude in order to evade the enemy radars and attack by surprise. We did not have any help for navigation and the silence on the radio was maintained throughout the journey; The experience that I obtained as a naval pilot before belonging to the 201 Squadron was very useful for me to lead it to its destination over that blue immensity. A factor that increased the difficulty of this mission was the fact that to reach the target, we required an additional external tank of fuel in the belly of the plane and another in the left semi-wing, being able to transport only one bomb in the semi-wing on the right. Because the fuel in the wing tank was consumed, the plane became heavy on the side that we had the bomb, forcing us to go compensating continuously. On the target, I started the attack followed by my companions, but when releasing my bomb, the plane jerked in the opposite direction to the wing that was carrying it, due to the imbalance provoked, which put me in an unexpected situation on the verge of colliding with the soil or penetrate the explosive wave. I was able to regain control of the plane and immediately alerted my colleagues to prevent this attitude of the plane, after the action we were waiting 600 miles over the sea, back to Luzon[9]

On August 15, on returning from a training flight, Captain Roberto Legorreta Sicilia suffered an accident in which the damaged plane was unharmed. On the 24th, an American transport plane was taxiing near the parking lot of the squadron and damaged two squadron P-47 planes. During the last days of the month, some local training flights were made and cataloged as isolated. Mission No. 59 was the last mission for the Aztec Eagles.[10]

No. 201 Squadron, Mission Number 59

Date: August 26, 1945.
Mission: Convoy to Okinawa.
Pilots: All the pilots of the squadron participated in the mission.
Results: The squadron departed with a convoy to Okinawa at 6 a.m. until they were relieved by Black Widows at 6 p.m. This mission took place due to the fact it was feared there would be an attack of suicide planes based at Formosa.[11]

The flights carried out during the month of August are as follows:

Local in combat zone: 118 hours, thirty minutes.
Route reconnaissance in combat zone: Eighteen hours.
Escort in combat zone: Eighty-nine hours, thirty minutes.
In combat mission: Forty-seven hours.
Total hours flown during the month: 273 hours.[12]

Of all the experiences of the 201st Squadron since becoming associated with the U.S. Army Air Force, the one they had the most trouble understanding was being left behind when the other squadrons moved to Okinawa. The Fifth Air Force decided as early as June 16 to move the 58th Fighter Group command out of the Philippines to forward combat positions at Okinawa. They left by convoy for the Ryukyu Islands on July 4, 1945; the 201st did not accompany them. The Mexicans did not know the reason why they did not accompany the rest of the Fighter Group to Okinawa. Both the U.S. and Mexico expended a considerable amount of time, effort, and money to train and bring them to the Philippines.

On June 24, Lieutenant Colonel A. W. Kellond submitted a report to Fifth Air Force Commander General George Kenney concerning conditions existing at that time, with respect to the Mexican fighter squadron. Kellond's report reflected an unprecedented number of non-combat losses of personnel and aircraft, crash landings, and taxiing accidents during a relatively short period of time. He noted five pilots had been lost and fourteen aircraft damaged or lost. The strength of the squadron had been reduced to twenty-three active pilots. Of the remaining pilots, he believed that only two could be called satisfactory leaders.[13]

After General Kenney received Lieutenant Colonel Kellond's report and recommendation, he commented on it in a lengthy letter to the Commanding General, Army Air Forces in Washington D.C. on July 5. Although he mentioned Kellond's comments on the squadron's strength, he focused mainly on several other matters. He wrote:

> It is believed that certain of the difficulties have become apparent in the functioning of this organization are and will remain incapable of solution as long as the Mexican liaison component (referring to Colonel Cárdenas) as in a position to interfere with the internal administration of the tactical squadron.[14]

Colonel Cárdenas had different thoughts concerning his authority. He believed it encompassed all activities within the squadron. In his translated version of his book *Mis Dos Misiones*, he writes:

> Outside the American continent, the commander of the Mexican Expeditionary Air Force is the representative of the Mexican Army to whom will be subordinated

all the elements integrated in the squadron, both in the relations with the American Army and in all those aspects that affect its' combat capacity and general welfare of the personnel under his orders.… Assisting the Commanding Group, the commander of the Mexican Expeditionary Air Force will resolve all those affairs related to military justice, pay and allowances.[15]

Before the 201st left Majors Field, Texas, for the Philippines, Captain Norman Sund, a veteran flight trainer told Lieutenant Amadeo Castro the command structure of the squadron must be changed. He pointed out that squadron command positions should be based on competency and not on rank alone. At that time, he said the squadron had more competent men than those assigned in command. By the time the squadron reached Luzon, those with capability filled command positions, and in the opinion of some 201st pilots, this could well be the cause of the conflict regarding squadron/command interference. On July 24, Brigadier General Freddie H. Smith, Jr., commander of the Fifth Fighter Group, recommended that the 201st Squadron be retained in the Philippines. In his opinion, they should remain there until such time as their operational efficiency was brought to a level to insure success in combat operations. For this reason, the 201st did not accompany the other units of the 58th Fighter Group to Okinawa.[16]

There was a question in the minds of the 201st pilots to the real reason why they remained in the Philippines. If the Mexican squadron had the capability to fly combat missions on Luzon, which they did in July and August, then they undoubtedly had the same ability to operate from Okinawa where all Japanese resistance had ceased. The Fifth Air Force did not send the 201st to Okinawa because of the perceived interference at the top command level. No other reasons were given for this decision. Perhaps the long-time conflict of ideologies between Mexico and the U.S. play a part in the pilots thinking that their flying ability was not respected. If anything, the war should have helped wash away many of the cultural differences.[17]

13

Returning Home to a Hero's Welcome

On August 26, just at dark, the 201st began to watch a movie when Captain Gaxiola Andrade stopped the film and asked for silence. Then, he said:

> I have great news. Although this news has not been verified, it does appear to be true. A radio operator at General headquarters has just received a radio message that Japan has surrendered to the Allies. Then he told them about the Hiroshima atomic bomb, "Headquarters," he told them, "is now attempting to officially confirm it. I do not want to celebrate until this information is found to be correct, so proceed with regular activities with caution. All operations will continue. That is all gentlemen."[1]

They looked at each other in disbelief. Not having heard about the atomic bomb, they could hardly believe what he told them, but they exploded with joy. Later the news was verified, and they celebrated long into the night, firing flares and their pistols. Sergeant Pedro Martínez said the news so overwhelmed him that he sat in silence for a long time. His thoughts stretched over many things, the war that brought him to this place and the possibility of going home.

The next day, Captain Gaxiola Andrade and the pilots discussed the possibility of going to Okinawa. Colonel Cárdenas said that he did not think they would be transferred there since the Japanese had given up. Of course, both also knew of the July 24 note from Brigadier General Freddie H. Smith, Jr., recommending that the 201st Squadron remain in the Philippines until such time as they could bring their operational efficiency to a higher level.[2]

After that, the war began to unwind, and everything slowed down. The Aztec Eagles enjoyed knowing that they were going home. Many began to gather souvenirs such as Japanese battle flags and guns. Sergeant Cervantes remembered that a Filipino gave him a Japanese machine gun. However, he did not bring it home because of his fear that it would be taken away from him at the U.S. port of entry and he would be charged with the violation of some military law.[3]

On September 2, 1945, General Douglas MacArthur presided over the Japanese surrender ceremonies in Tokyo harbor aboard the battleship U.S.S. *Missouri*. At 9.25 a.m. that day, as the last Japanese official signed the surrender documents, General MacArthur stepped forward and declared: "These proceedings are now closed."[4] That same day, General George C. Kenney sent the following telegram of recognition to the Commander of the Mexican Expeditionary Air Force:

1. It is with profound gratitude for your magnificent cooperation that I send this last message as Commander of the Allied Air Forces in the Pacific. For almost four years, we were confronted with one of the most arduous moments that either of our nations have ever experienced: our common civilization was threatened by an enemy that fought us, frantically, with all the might of his forces. Today, we can have the satisfaction of have defeated the enemy, having remained united and combating with the strength of our combined resources.

2. Directing a retrospective view, we can see that the Japanese capitulation was due, in large part, to the prolonged aerial allied offensive that had its start in the epic battles over Darwin, Port Moresby and Milne Bay. The success of the Allied force will remain in history as a tribute to the force that can be attained by free peoples, when those are united in a just cause. Americans, Australians, New Zealanders, Dutch and Mexicans, we have struggled together as comrades, depending upon each other for our lives, and together we have emerged victorious.

3. Each one of us fought with courage and without egotism, to restore peace among nations and liberty and justice for all men. Hopefully good faith, fomented by our common effort in the aerial war and by the very high degree of companionship displayed in the Pacific, will continue to encourage us in the peace years, like it has united us since the days of victory.[5]

The War Department actively began to reduce the size of the massive American forces in the Far East. General George C. Kenney, Commander of the 5th Air Force, wrote to the Commanding General, Army Air Forces in Washington, on September 9, 1945, with a request to relieve the 201st Fighter Squadron from further duty.[6]

Sometime before they received orders to go home, the pilots of the 201st began thinking of a way to remember their fallen comrades. They unanimously agreed to build a small monument. Arrangements were made with both military and local authorities and they secured a site location in Manila. This small monument still stands today, only a few hundred yards from the Macro Monument honoring the heroes of the Philippines.[7]

Soon after hostilities terminated, the Philippine government decorated five members of the Mexican Air Force for their valuable service and as a remembrance of the historic bonds with Mexico. President Truman awarded Colonel Antonio Cárdenas

Rodriguez and Captain Radamés Gaxiola Andrade the Legion of Merit medal.[8] Truman's citation read:

> Colonel Antonio Cárdenas Rodriguez, of the Mexican Expeditionary Air Force, demonstrated an exceptionally meritorious conduct in the discharge of outstanding services in the Southwest Area of the Pacific, during the period between April 5 and October 15, 1945. As Commanding Officer of the Mexican Expeditionary Air Force, he demonstrated exceptional aptitudes and abilities in the command of his unit, in combat operations against the Japanese. While supervising and participating in numerous attacks carried out against enemy positions, he guided his forces to victorious excursions, efficiently destroying enemy ships, installations and personnel. By exhibiting exceptional professional tact and aptitude, he managed to coordinate with a remarkable success the activities of his command with those of the Air Forces of the Far East. For his command aptitude, initiative and devotion in the fulfillment of his duties, Colonel Cárdenas raised very high his prestige and that of his country, and, his exemplary execution of his duties materially contributed to the success of the Allied Aerial operation in the Southwest Zone of the Pacific.[9]

On September 20, 1945, the United States Air Force issued orders to the Deputy Chief of Air Staff, 201st Fighter Squadron, returning them to the United States by the first available water transportation. The 201st members began preparations for their journey to the United States and back home to Mexico. Personnel medical examinations and the final packing of all their equipment and supplies delayed their exodus for several days.[10]

By October 21, they were ready to leave. At 3 a.m., the majority of the 201st personnel left Clark Field for Dau Station and a short ride to Manila. Lieutenant Carlos Garduño and thirty-eight men remained at the base to return all their motor vehicles. Others remaining included Captain Salido, a patient in Clark Field Hospital Number 427, and Lieutenant Velasco Cerón at Manila's general hospital. Both men had hepatitis. Four men remained in Japan.[11] By 9 a.m. on October 22, a tired and listless squadron assembled at the port of Manila; Wharf Number 2, waiting to go aboard the U.S.S. *Sea Martin*, a naval transport ship anchored in the bay. A launch transferred the airmen aboard the transport, but instead of weighing anchor and putting out to sea, the *Sea Martin* returned to Wharf Number 15 and tied up for the night. The next day, October 23, after completing its cargo loading, the transport put out to sea with a modest compliment of American and Mexican soldiers. By then Lieutenant Garduño and the thirty-eight men in his group arrived and sailed with them.[12]

Colonel Cárdenas knew that the United States Air Force intended to return the 201st to the United States some time before the official orders were out on September 20, 1945. He wrote in *Mis Dos Misiones*:

> In accordance with the instructions that I opportunely received, already by the middle of September, I had taken the necessary measures and issued the corresponding orders

to the personnel under my command to organize and carry out the displacement of the Mexican Expeditionary Air Force to America; but, I could not abandon the Pacific without before having the opportunity of saying good bye personally to General MacArthur and to thank him, in the name of Mexico and our army, for all the attentions and fineness.[13]

The *Sea Martin* first sailed west out of Manila bay and then north toward Formosa after entering the South China Sea. On the second day out, the ship changed course to the northeast and on the fourth day penetrated a parallel latitude line east of Tokyo. Rain, fog, and bad weather plagued the voyage. The seas ran high and the ship rolled and bucked, causing many objects to be thrown to the deck. The stormy ocean also caused a large number of the Aztec Eagles to become seasick.[14]

The weather in the North Pacific Ocean remained turbulent and cold as the *Sea Martin* navigated northeast along the great circle route—moving ever nearer colder temperatures—toward the Aleutians. For four days beginning November 4, the sea raged unabated with 30-foot waves pounding the ship. The men became seasick again. On November 5, ten days into their voyage home, the *Sea Martin* crossed the 180th meridian, the International Date Line. Because heavy weather kept the troops below decks, the ship held no ceremony to observe the crossing. On November 7, the sea calmed for two days. Seven days out the Mexicans found themselves at 42 degrees north latitude with the temperature continuing to drop. The low temperatures caused a rash of coughing and colds as most of the ship's passengers traveled without coats. When available, the men changed from cotton to wool clothing.[15]

After their bouts with seasickness, the Aztec Eagles tried to make the most of life aboard the ship for the remainder of the trip home. This journey held no fear of a possible enemy attack that gripped them on their voyage to the Philippines. Except for bad weather, colds, seasickness, and an endemic stomach condition brought on by eating frozen, canned, and dehydrated foods, the voyage proceeded without incident. Movies, shown almost daily on the main deck, helped the troops pass the time. Attendance at these shows remained good, despite the rolling motion of the ship and the cold blowing wind that penetrated their light clothing. Although standard ship's discipline prevailed for everyone on board, the daily routine called for no general quarters' drills and no target practices. No one mustered except for debarkation procedure meetings. Fewer troopers aboard meant less crowding at meal times. Eating arrangements aboard ship included the usual three meals a day. Although the quality and quantity of this food surpassed what they had on the trip over, they still wished for something better to eat.[16]

The Mexicans learned from the ship's company personnel a few things about being aboard a U.S. naval vessel. Colonel Justino Reyes Retana told how the sailors taught him an easy way to wash his clothing. He acquired some 100 yards of small, strong line, tying it on to an article of clothing (generally trousers and shirts) and throwing the line and clothing over the ship's stern into the water. An abrasive, cleaning process resulted from the ship pulling the clothing through the water. To be effective, the article needed to be left in the water for at least three to four hours. If one carelessly left the article in the water overnight, however, the corrosive effect left only shreds of cloth.[17]

During their voyage home, the sailors and other servicemen aboard the ship learned that the Mexicans were not innocents abroad. With preconceived thoughts of riches and with tongue-in-cheek, they gratuitously ventured to teach the Mexicans about gambling. To their dismay, they found that the Mexicans already knew how to gamble. In addition, the Mexicans already knew the subtle techniques used in the art of "midnight requisition," an old naval term describing a clandestine method for acquiring goods and supplies without proper authorization. Reyes Retana related that the Mexicans acquired sizable amounts of frozen canned orange juice. He did not know how they got the juice, but he said that soon a lively trade developed selling and bartering these cans. Garduño stated that they had access to canned cherries, which they also traded. Somehow the Mexican airmen gained access to the ship's cargo hold. Garduño related how they went down into the cargo holds and opened boxes of K-rations only for the chocolates and other goodies.[18]

Cárdenas learned through the Mexican Embassy, soon after his arrival in San Francisco, that the Navy had diverted the *Sea Marlin* to a port in the Los Angeles area. The ship received a radiogram on November 4, ordering it to change its port of entry from San Francisco to San Pedro. The reason for this change involved the time factor needed for the 201st Squadron to arrive in Mexico City precisely on November 18. Mexican President Ávila Camacho wanted their arrival to be in time for the commemoration of the twenty-fifth anniversary of the Mexican Revolution on November 20. They believed the logistical expediency of landing the troops from the *Sea Marlin* directly on to a troop train at San Pedro, with only one transfer at Laredo, Texas, gave them a time benefit.[19]

The ship newspaper, the *Marlin Spike*, issued its final edition the same day that Cárdenas landed in San Francisco. This souvenir-edition newspaper reported statistical voyage facts, current news releases, tongue-in-cheek editorial comments, and amusing fictitious stories. Statistical data showed the *Sea Marlin* to be eighteen days out from Manila; the ship traveled 381 miles from noon the day before; total distance traveled at the time of publication was 5,806 miles; distance to San Pedro 904 miles. It reported the ship's position at latitude 37°15′N, longitude 135°38′W. Another section entitled sports chatter, described how 76,000 cheering fans thronged Yankee Stadium to watch undefeated, untied Army move another step closer to its second undefeated season and a likely Rose Bowl bid. The Cadets beat Notre Dame in a 41–0 rout. In a lighter vein, one article included a humorous report on the "Influence of the barnacle on the speed of the *Sea Marlin*." Another reported the hazardous invasion landing procedures in San Pedro and how to handle the curious natives.[20]

After twenty-four days at sea, a journey covering 6,710 miles, the *Sea Marlin* dropped anchor in the bay just outside the port of San Pedro at 12.30 a.m. The day was November 13, 1945—231 days after leaving the shores of the United States, the 201st Squadron returned. Assignment completed, but five did not return: Captain Pablo Rivas Martínez;

First Lieutenant José Espinosa Fuentes; First Lieutenant Héctor Espinosa Galván; Second Lieutenant Mario López Portillo; and Second Lieutenant Fausto Vega Santander.

Early the next morning, after the men all received medical examinations, the ship began to move toward the port. A tugboat paid tribute to the Mexicans by circling the Sea Marlin in a salute of respect. Displaying a large banner "Welcome to your home," the tugboat broadcast Mexican military music over loudspeakers.[21]

A large throng of military and civilian dignitaries waited at the port of San Pedro. The military included General Guzmán Cárdenas who was Mexican military attach in Washington, General Cárdenas Rodriguez, the air defense commander at the port of San Pedro, American General Courland D. Parker, and from the North American High Command, Admiral I. C. Johnson. Civilians included the Consul of Mexico at Los Angeles and many legislative and prominent southern Californians of Mexican descent.[22]

After the men came ashore, an auto convoy took them to nearby Peck Park. Along the route, well-wishers threw flowers, confetti, and serpentines at them in a show of emotion. An estimated 30,000 citizens of Mexican ancestry, residents of California, from all social classes awaited them at the park. After a warm welcome by the military and local authorities, they ate a real Mexican lunch—to their delight. Their long term of eating dehydrated, frozen, and powdered foods ended.[23]

The ceremonies at Peck Park concluded around 4 p.m. The Mexicans then returned to the *Sea Marlin* to retrieve their equipment and personal gear. On the dock rail terminal, next to their ship, a special train stood by ready to take the Aztec Eagles home. It consisted of nine Pullman cars, a diner and two boxcars for their equipment. At 5.30 p.m., the train departed for Laredo.[24]

The route home took them east through southern California, Arizona, New Mexico, and finally into Texas. Publicity notices of their travel route preceded them and crowds of well-wishers, mostly Mexican, met them at various stops along the way. They arrived in El Paso at 5 a.m. on November 15. A light turnout of Texas Mexicans and Mexican citizens from Cuidad Juárez, Chihuahua, greeted them here in the cold early morning hours.[25]

After a change of train crews in El Paso, the journey home continued. At midnight that same day, eighteen travel hours later, they pulled into the train station at San Antonio, Texas. Despite the late hour, a large and enthusiastically festive crowd met them. Radio stations broadcast their arrival. A marching band played patriotic military music and various social groups earned banners welcoming them home. Their tight schedule did not permit a long stay in San Antonio and soon they were on their way to Laredo.[26]

Their unusual arrival hours continued as they reached Laredo early the next morning. With one eye on their tight time schedule, they began the transfer to the train station in Nuevo Laredo. Relocating all of the equipment and personal belongings of the Mexicans from the Laredo train station to the sister station in Nuevo Laredo had all the potential of a logistic nightmare. Fortunately, the transfer went well. Hard-working American and Mexican liaison officers provided the necessary means to move the equipment quickly. Trucks moved over 100 tons of material into Mexico.[27]

The 201st came home to a proud nation. Three days after crossing over the border into Nuevo Laredo, they reached Mexico City, stopping in major cities along the route to be welcomed as heroes. Arriving in the capital city on November 18 to a tumultuous welcome, they paraded down Madero Avenue to the *Zocalo* (the main square in central Mexico City) to meet President Manuel Ávila Camacho.[28]

From his platform in front of the national palace, President Camacho welcomed them back from the war in a speech filled with emotion and affection:

Citizen General, commanders, officers and troops of the Expeditionary Air Force: I receive with emotion the flag that the nation conferred upon you to be taken as a symbol of itself and of the ideals of humanity for which we fought in common cause with our allies. Glorious return and, with the dignity that you conducted it, from today it will pass to the gallery of our epic history, to be a war testimony of the contemporary generation, of our people that, like all, needs to revive its moral values symbolized whether in its heroes, its warriors, its artists or in its wise men. It has been your turn to fill this category in this epoch that in the name of the nation I recognize you. You return with glory because you discharged brilliantly your duty and, in these moments, in this our historic plaza, heart of the republic, receive the thanks of your people. Your companions: Lieutenant Fausto Vega Santander, Lieutenant José Espinosa Fuentes, Lieutenant Mario López Portillo, Captain Pablo Rivas Martínez, Lieutenant Crisóforo Salido Grijalva … are missing from your ranks because they have passed to the eternal veneration end the memory and honor of our people. You remain to live with that honor; be careful to conserve it with that devotion that today we render to you.[29]

By presidential decree, the *Fuerza Aérea Expedicionaria Mexicana* ended its existence on December 1, 1945. A simple declaration ended the force. The honor that the 201st Squadron brought to Mexico will live forever in the hearts of patriotic Mexicans. No other Latin American country, except Brazil, stood with the Allied nations whose citizens gave their lives for the cause of liberty. The names of the seven pilots, who gave their lives for liberty, are inscribed around the marble semicircular amphitheater below Chapultepec Castle in Mexico City. For the pilot group, their real heroes were the ones who died in the Philippines and symbols of patriotism for future generations of Mexicans who hopefully would understand why these pilots risk their lives for Mexico. A short distance down the road from the 201st monument is another revered memorial. It is the monument to *Los Niños* Heroes, the Boy Heroes. These teenage Chapultepec military cadets jumped to their deaths rather than surrender to invaders from the U.S., attacking the school during the U.S.–Mexican war. There are monuments to the 201st Squadron throughout Mexico.[30]

Epilogue

To assess the significance of the Mexican Expeditionary Air Force and the 201st Squadron, it is necessary to consider more than the simple participation in combat. Several aspects of the Mexican military benefited from the participation of this small but significant military force. Hence, the contributions of the M.E.A.F. can even be connected to emerging U.S.–Mexico relations after World War II.

The operations during the month of June were intense. The Japanese forces concentrated in the north of Luzon were relentlessly attacked. Fifty-two combat missions were carried out by the Aztec Eagles in support of the ground troops, helping the 25th Division to make its way to the Cagayan Valley using mainly general-purpose 1,000-lb. bombs. The close support missions consisted mainly of attacking enemy resistance points very close to the friendly troops, in the front line. Usually, a Stinson L-5 liaison aircraft from the 25th Squadron of the Tactical Reconnaissance Group 71, in coordination with the troops on the ground, marked the target with bombs of white phosphorus or smoke so that the P-47 of the 201st could unload on the enemy the fury of his machine guns and bombs. Many enemy pieces of artillery were silenced, as well as machine-gun nests, buildings, and vehicles destroyed. Many times, the pilots faced the anti-aircraft fire and the planes of the squadron were hit on several occasions, without consequences.

Fundamentally, the missions of the Mexican squadron were carried out in June 1945, and they concentrated on strafing and bombing in various targets indicated by vectoring (no air clashes were reported), and in supporting the ground troops in eastern Manila, on the Cagayan basin and in northern Luzon. The squadron flew ninety-five missions, fifty-three of which were of direct support to U.S. troops in Luzon, from June 4 to July 4, 1945. Among the most outstanding actions are the following: on June 16, 1945, in which eleven P-47 aircraft, led by Lieutenant Espinosa Galván and with the participation of Captain Radamés Gaxiola Andrade, bombed and machine-gunned the strong concentration of troops along the Idau Creek—they launched twenty-two 1,000-lb. bombs and fired 13,250 .50-caliber machine-gun rounds; on June 18, seven pilots bombed and machine-gunned occupied enemy positions east of the Lenatín River—they launched sixteen 1,000-lb. bombs and fired 4,360 .50-caliber machine-gun rounds; and on June 25, the Mexican pilots carried out a sweeping and strafing of enemy concentrations along the River Agos—the eleven aviators dropped twenty-four 1,000-lb. bombs and fired 9,200 .50-caliber machine-gun rounds.

The atomic bombings on Hiroshima and Nagasaki (August 6 and 9, 1945) forced Japan to surrender without conditions. With World War II over, the legendary 201st Squadron put an end to its operations. The performance of the Mexican squad obtained wide recognition from General MacArthur. He recommended the handing over of the Legion of Honor to Colonel P. A. Antonio Cárdenas Rodríguez and the Captain P. A. Radamés Gaxiola Andrade. However, the battle took a heavy toll on the Mexican squad. During the training and fighting, the F.A.E.M. suffered casualties. They had carried out more missions for the same time period than many American pilots, and the American high command looked highly at the F.A.E.M.

The number of effective missions is clearly greater than the ineffective ones, and the mission reports indicate accurate bombing and strafing. When assessing the impact of the unit in the war, clearly it was not essential for the Allied victory, but this was never the purpose of the Mexican force. It was only a small unit representing the Mexican military, and it was immersed in a new combat arena full of technical innovations.

In spite of the losses of lives and material, the overall cost of the M.E.A.F. was not excessive. Perhaps the lack of combat experience and the conditions in the S.W.P.A. contributed to a relatively high amount of casualties and accidents. Probably they could have been avoided with better training, conducted without time constraints. The M.E.A.F. program brought great political value. The people of Mexico united to receive and honor the returning M.E.A.F. personnel. Enormous groups of Mexicans gathered in the U.S. and Mexican cities to celebrate with the M.E.A.F. They were part of the forces of liberation that fought against the oppressor and attained victory. Mexico's participation in combat overseas brought international prestige and strengthened U.S.–Mexico relations.

Probably in the same way that the war contributed to better U.S.–Mexico relations, the M.E.A.F. also contributed to better relations between the military of both countries. The M.E.A.F. program fully developed from start to finish, and it contributed to a greater degree of cooperation between the U.S. and Mexican military. This cooperation contributed significantly to the modernization of the Mexican armed forces. Some of the equipment acquired during World War II remained in the inventory for many years. Some trainer aircraft were still flying almost forty years after the Mexican Air Force received them through the Lend-Lease agreement. The Mexican Air Force also received some B-25 bombers after the war. For a country with a reduced military budget, these were very important contributions.

The training of pilots in the U.S. was another positive result of this cooperation. Some 201st Squadron replacements continued training in twin-engined aircraft after the war finished. Many of them would later fly the transport and cargo aircraft of the Mexican Air Force, fulfilling an important role during peacetime. In addition, some Mexican Air Force pilots went on to civilian jobs in airline companies during the following years. This somewhat reduced capabilities of the armed forces but contributed to the development of Mexico's commercial aviation. The pilots graduating from flight training centers in the U.S. helped to improve the Mexican training programs. Since 1943, the Mexican Air Force pursued a reorganization of its training centers.

The participation of the M.E.A.F. in the South West Pacific Area in World War II is an important aspect in the history of Mexico's Armed Forces. The organization, equipment, and operations of this force, successful in spite of many obstacles, offer valuable lessons. The development and performance of this force are an example of trust, coordination, commitment, and cooperation between international allies for a worthy cause. The participation of this force in World War II was not an ordinary accomplishment, especially if we consider that this was the first occasion that Mexico's government sent forces to fight outside of the country's territory.

The pilots of the 201st returned to Mexico in November 1945 as national heroes. During the following nine months, the surviving pilots toured dozens of Mexican cities and towns where patriotic pride erupted everywhere. Town plazas were brightly decorated in red, white, and green banners as local townsfolk gathered to catch a glimpse of the famed unit. The Mexico City Metro Line 8 station *Metro Escuadrón* 201 is named after the squadron. They were also the subject of the Mexican film *Escuadrón 201*, directed by Jaime Salvador and released in 1945. On November 22, 2004, the squadron was awarded the Philippine Legion of Honor, with a rank of Legionnaire, by then-President Gloria Macapagal-Arroyo.

Many of the young aviators and ground support crews who flew and fought with the Allies became successful in academia, business, and aviation. The 201st Squadron's Republic P-47 Thunderbolts are long gone, but the battle flag the Aztec Eagles carried rests in the National History Museum in Mexico City. Five of those pilots became *Fuerza Aérea Mexicana* generals. Members of the 201st received the following awards and decorations: Air Medal, American Campaign Medal, Army Good Conduct Medal, Asiatic Pacific Campaign Medal, Legion of Merit, Philippine Liberation Medal, Philippine Presidential Unit Citation, and Service in the Far East Medal.

After the war, the Mexican government did not want to play up the accomplishments of the Aztec Eagles. One fear was that such attention would feed into the common Mexican perception that it had done the American's bidding in 1945. Moreover, if members of the 201st were celebrated as war heroes, and one or two became popular enough to run for office, it threatened the rigid, vertical, political structure in Mexico, where politicians were handpicked by the establishment. Still, the men of the 201st refuse to criticize their government for failing to adequately honor their sacrifice.

The Aztec Eagles helped the Allies defeat Japan. They helped end the isolationism of Mexico. They paved the way for important agreements between the United States and Mexico. They helped modernize the Mexican Air Force and demonstrated that Mexico could mount a successful expeditionary force. An enduring monument to the 201st Squadron is the school the Aztec Eagles built. The school still commands the center and heart of the village of Tepoztlán. More than 600 children enter the building each day to study. Significant as these achievements are, perhaps the unit's most important legacy is that the Aztec Eagles fought for honor and for Mexico as Allies in World War II, creating national pride throughout their homeland. That pride endures and is evident today as the story of the Aztec Eagles can be heard in towns and villages across the nation.

Transcription of
the Mexico–United States Agreement

(Source: Mexican Secretariat of National Defense)

Executive Order 9080—Joint Mexican-United States Defense Commission, February 27, 1942

By virtue of the authority vested in me by the Constitution and as President of the United States, and acting jointly and in full accord with His Excellency, the President of the Republic of Mexico, I hereby authorize, on the part of the Government of the United States, the creation of a joint commission to be known as the Joint Mexican–United States Defense Commission.

The purposes of the Commission shall be to study problems relating to the common defense of the United States and Mexico, to consider broad plans for the defense of Mexico and adjacent areas of the United States, and to propose to the respective governments the cooperative measures which, in its opinion should be adopted.

The United States membership of the Commission shall consist of an Army member, a Navy member, an Air Force member, and a Marine Corps member, each of whom shall be designated by the Secretary of Defense and serve during the pleasure of the Secretary. The Secretary shall designate from among the United States members the chairman thereof and may designate alternate United States members of the Commission.

The Commission will convene initially at a time and place agreeable to both governments, and may thereafter proceed at any time with its professional and clerical assistants to such place or places in Mexico, with the approval of the Government of Mexico, or in the United States as it may consider desirable or necessary to visit for the accomplishment or its purposes.

The United States members of the Commission, in agreement with their Mexican colleagues, may prescribe their own procedure. They are also empowered to employ such professional and clerical assistants as may be deemed necessary, and to incur such expenses for travel, services, supplies, and other purposes as may be required for the accomplishment of their mission.

Each of the United States members of the Commission and each of their professional assistants, including civilian advisers and any United States Army, Navy, or Marine Corps officers so employed, detailed, or assigned, shall receive, in lieu of subsistence while outside of the continental limits of the United States in connection with the business of the Commission, a per diem allowance of ten dollars.

All expenses incurred by the United States Section of the Commission shall be paid by Army disbursing officers from allocations to be made to the War Department for that purpose from the Emergency Fund for the President.

SIGNED:
FRANKLIN D. ROOSEVELT

AGREEMENT THAT HAS BEEN ARRIVED BETWEEN THE GOVERNMENTS OF THE UNITED MEXICAN STATES AND THE UNITED STATES OF AMERICA, WITH RESPECT TO THE PARTICIPATION OF THE SQUADRON MEXICAN AIRCRAFT OF FIGHTER 201, IN OVERSEAS.

I. The Governments of the United Mexican States and the United States of America, agree to the participation of a Mexican Fight Squadron, with the Army of the United States, under the following conditions, in which the Mexican Government and the United States Government:

1. The Mexican Fighter Squadron and Mexican deputy personnel will be, for all intents and purposes, managed as an integral part of the Army of the United States, with the following exceptions:

a) COMMAND:
The Mexican Fight Squadron can be accompanied by a Mexican Chief, whose degree does not exceed that of Coronel, with a small group of assistants, officers and troop, whose functions will be limited to those related to supervision, liaison and administration. The tactical commander of the Mexican Fight Squad, actually, will be a Mexican Official, classified to send in accordance with the requirements of the Air Forces of the United States.

b) ADMINISTRATION:
(1) The internal administration of Mexican personnel shall be exercised by an Official Mexican, and personnel subject to the regulations and codes of Mexican military laws.

(2) In its relations with civilian personnel in the area in which the personnel of the Squadron is stationed, in combat or at rest, the Mexican Command should adopt the modalities and rules currently in force, followed by the Army of the United States under the same circumstances.

(3) Officers of the Air Forces of the United States may be assigned, in liaison mission, with the Mexican Air Squadron in order to facilitate operations of the Squadron.

(4) If for some reason, the Operations Theater Commander estimates it convenient, any Mexican personnel can be returned to Mexico.

(5) The Mexican Government will provide replacements for personnel that require, upon notification made by the United States Air Forces for its training and sending to the unit.

(6) Official communications between the Mexican Fight Squadron, and the Mexican Government, will be through the Department of War of the States United.

(7) To avoid confusion, and for safety reasons, the airplanes of the Mexican Fighter Squadron will carry the regular identifications of the States United. The Mexican insignia must be registered, in addition and its placement subject to the approval of the Operations Theater Commander.

c) EXPENSES:

(1) The salaries, assignments, etc., of Mexican troops outside the limits of the United States, will be made in dollars or in any other unit money used by the United States Army in the same area, and in accordance with the distribution established by the Mexican Government. The funds for this object will be provided to the War Department by the Mexican Government, upon request

of the first. The initial advance to be made by the Mexican Government will amount to five hundred thousand dollars (500,000.00). The American Officials, payers in the Theaters of Operations, will receive convenient instructions to ensure the prompt payment of the Mexican personnel in campaign.

(2) EQUIPMENT AND SUPPLIES:

The initial ministerial items for a Fighting Squad, classification S.E. T/O & E [Table of Organization and Equipment] 1–27, will be provided by the United States under the agreement of Loans and Leases, currently existing between the two Governments, to the limit of equipment availability within operational priorities. Replacement items and maintenance for the unit will be provided through the conduits of normal supplies from the United States. Maintenance covers articles of standard administration, including subsistence and services normally provided to the units of the Air Forces of the United States. All articles by Initial administration, replacement and maintenance, will be charged according to the Loan and Lease procedures.

P-47D Republic Thunderbolt

(Sources: History—www.chuckhawks. com/index3.naval_military_history.htm. Reprinted with permission of Chuck Hawks and Rip Collins; No. 201 Squadron P-47 Aircraft— National Museum of the U.S.A.F.)

History

The Republic Aviation Corporation (previously Seversky Aircraft Corporation) had successfully designed and built the P-35 fighter for the U.S. Army Air Corps (U.S.A.A.C.) in 1937 and the EP-1 for the Swedish Air Force (known as the P-35A in the U.S.A.A.C.) in 1939. Chief engineer Alexander Kartveli followed these successes with the P-43 Lancer of 1940, which incorporated a turbo supercharger for its 1,200-hp Pratt & Whitney radial engine, and the similar P-44, with a 1,400-hp radial engine. The latter was overtaken by the advent of an entirely new fighter that became the P-47 and was never produced, but about 272 P-43s were built between September 1940 and April 1942. Fifty-one of these P-43s were supplied to China under the Lend-Lease program.

Although the P-43A was a high-performance airplane for its day, with a top speed of 356 mph at 20,000 feet, it was to be overshadowed by Alexander Kartveli's subsequent classic, the great P-47 Thunderbolt. The P-47 became one of the premier fighters of its day.

The first P-47 models were the XP-47 (AP-4) and the XP-47A (AP-10) of 1940. These were lightweight fighter projects contracted by the U.S.A.A.C., bearing no real resemblance to the later Thunderbolt. Both were canceled after studying combat reports from Europe, where the war had already begun. Instead, a new heavy fighter was designed; this was designated the XP-47B.

The XP-47B was designed around the 2,000-hp Pratt & Whitney R-2800 Double Wasp eighteen-cylinder radial with a very large turbo supercharger and a big three-bladed propeller. The armament was eight .50-caliber machine guns, four in each wing. The new fighter flew for the first time in May 1941. Because of its large radial engine and the turbo supercharger with its ducting, the P-47 was one of the largest single-engined fighters built during World War II.

The U.S. government ordered 171 P-47Bs, and 602 improved P-47Cs. The first P-47B was completed in March 1942 and entered combat in April 1943 with the 78th Fighter Group of the 8th Air Force. From that time on, the Thunderbolt began to change the history of the war in the air in favor of the Americans.

The P-47B and C models were fine high-altitude fighters. The P-47B had a top speed of 406 miles per hour at 27,000 feet, with an excellent rate of roll and could dive like a stone. The Thunderbolt had great survivability; it could absorb a lot of punishment and still get home. The best climb rate was unimpressive, however, at only 1,650 feet per minute.

By early 1943, the P-47D was coming off the production lines. The P-47D was produced in higher quantity than any other model and in many variations. Early D models were similar to the previous C model, with only detail improvements, but as production progressed the D model continued to be improved. Republic built a total of 12,602 P-47Ds. In addition, Curtis-Wright built 354 P-47Ds under license as the P-47G.

P47D-6-RE to P-47D-11-RE models came with an under-fuselage shackle for a 500-lb. bomb or a drop tank. Subsequent models, up to the P-47D-20-RE, had strengthened wings with under wing pylons and were able to carry a 1,000-lb. bomb under each wing. The universal wing, which could carry a variety of stores, was introduced with the P-47D-20-RE. A large four-bladed paddle propeller was also fitted. This, along with the water-injection R-2800-21 engine that had a war emergency rating of 2,300 hp, markedly improved the maximum rate of climb, which increased to 2,750 feet per minute at 5,000 feet.

The P-47D-25-RE and subsequent models had a cut down rear fuselage and a teardrop canopy, adapted from the British Typhoon fighter. Internal fuel capacity was also increased. The R-2800-59 engine had a war emergency rating of 2,535 hp. Climb rate was now up to 3,120 feet per minute and top speed was 426 mph at 30,000 feet. The Thunderbolt had basically reached full flower. The next variant to achieve series production was the P-47M. This was called the sprint model. It was a response to the jet powered German V-1 "Buzz Bomb" cruise missile and the German jet fighters. It had an uprated R-2800-57(C) engine and CH-5 turbocharger system, which gave a top speed of 470 mph at 30,000 feet. The initial climb rate was 3,500 feet per minute. Delivered beginning in December 1944, 130 were produced.

The last P-47 variant to achieve series production was the P-47N. This model was designed specifically for the pacific theatre, where very long range was a requirement. The N initially used the same engine as the M; late production models received the P-2800-77 engine. A new, stronger, wing with squared tips was designed, which incorporated eight internal fuel cells. The landing gear was strengthened to deal with the increased weight of the aircraft. From the P-47N-5-RE model on, zero length rocket launchers were added beneath the wings. Habitability improvements included an automatic pilot, an armchair seat and folding rudder pedals to give the pilot increased leg room. These improvements were intended to increase the pilot's comfort on long escort missions.

Maximum speed was 467 mph at 32,500 feet. The initial climb rate was 2,770 feet per minute and the range on maximum internal fuel was 2,350 miles. The P-47N saw extensive use in the last months of the Pacific War, as it had the range to escort the B-29s all the way from Saipan to Japan. Between December 1944 and December 1945, a total of 1,816 P-47Ns were manufactured.

A total of 15,683 P-47 Thunderbolts of all types were built before production ceased at the end of 1945; 9,087 were completed at the Farmingdale, New York, plant and 6,242 at the Evansville, Indiana, plant. The Curtiss plant at Buffalo, New York, produced 354 Thunderbolts under license.

More Thunderbolts were produced than any other U.S.A.A.F. fighter. (The P-51 was second with 15,386 produced; the P-40 was third with an even 15,000 produced; and the P-38 was fourth with 10,037 produced.) In addition to the U.S.A.A.F., during World War II, P-47s were sold or supplied to Brazil, Free France, Mexico, the U.K., and the U.S.S.R. After the war, surplus P-47s were operated by the Air Forces of Bolivia, Chile, China, Columbia, Dominican Republic, Ecuador, Honduras, Iran, Italy, Nicaragua, Peru, Portugal, Turkey, Venezuela, and Yugoslavia.

P-47D-35-RA Specifications

Wing span:	40 feet, 9.75 inches.
Length:	36 feet, 1.75 inches.
Height:	14 feet, 1.75 inches.
Wing area:	300 square feet.
Weight empty:	10,000 pounds.
Gross weight:	17,500 pounds.
Maximum take-off weight:	19,400 pounds.
Maximum take-off speed:	426 miles per hour at 30,000 feet.
Maximum initial climb:	3,120 feet per minute.
Service ceiling:	42,000 feet.
Range:	475 miles.
Maximum range:	1,800 miles at 195 mph at 10,000 feet.
Power plant:	Pratt & Whitney 2,000-hp, R-2800-63 turbocharged.
Armament:	Six or eight wing mounted .50-caliber machine guns, 2,500-lb. bomb or ten 5-inch rockets.

The P-47 Thunderbolt was the product of two Georgian immigrants, Alexander de Seversky and Alexander Kartveli, who had left their homeland to escape the Bolsheviks. The Republic P-47 Thunderbolt, also known as "Jug," was the largest single-engined fighter of its day. It was one of the main United States Army Air Force (U.S.A.A.F.) fighters of World War II. The P-47 was effective in air combat but proved especially useful in the ground attack role. The Thunderbolt also served with a number of other Allied air forces.

P-43 Lancer/XP-47B

In 1939, the Republic Aviation Company designed an AP-4 demonstrator powered by a Pratt & Whitney R-1830 radial engine with a belly-mounted turbocharger. While the resulting P-43 Lancer was in limited production, Republic had been working on an improved P-44 Rocket with a more powerful engine, as well as on a fighter designated the AP-10. The latter was a lightweight aircraft powered by the Allison V-1710 liquid-cooled V-12 engine and armed with a pair of .50-caliber machine guns. The U.S.A.A.C. backed the project and gave it the designation XP-47. As the war in Europe escalated in the spring of 1940, Republic and the U.S.A.A.C. concluded that the XP-44 and the XP-47 were inferior to the German fighters. Republic unsuccessfully attempted to improve the design, proposing the XP-47A. Alexander Kartveli subsequently came up an all-new and much larger fighter that was offered to the U.S.A.A.C. in June 1940. The Air Corps ordered a prototype in September, to be designated the XP-47B. The XP-47A, which had almost nothing in common with the new design, was abandoned. The XP-47B was of all-metal construction, except for fabric-covered tail control surfaces.

The cockpit was roomy, and the pilot's seat was comfortable, like a lounge chair, as one pilot would later put it. The pilot was provided with every convenience, including cabin air conditioning. The canopy featured doors that hinged upward. Main and auxiliary self-sealing fuel tanks were placed under the cockpit, offering a total fuel capacity of 305 U.S. gallons. Power came from a Pratt & Whitney R-2800 Double Wasp two-row eighteen-cylinder radial engine producing 2,000 hp and turning a four-bladed Curtiss Electric constant-speed propeller 146 inches in diameter. The loss of the AP-4 prototype to an engine fire ended Kartveli's experiments with tight-fitting cowlings, so the engine was placed in a broad cowling that opened at the front in a horse collar-shaped ellipse. The cowling admitted air for the engine, left and right oil coolers, and the turbo supercharger intercooler system. The engine exhaust gases were routed into a pair of waste gate-equipped pipes that ran along each side of the cockpit to drive the turbo supercharger turbine at the bottom of the fuselage about halfway between cockpit and tail.

At full power, the pipes glowed red at their forward ends and the turbine spun at 60,000 revolutions per minute. The complicated turbo supercharger system with its ductwork gave the XP-47B a deep fuselage, and the wings had to be mounted in a relatively high position. This was problematic since long landing gear were needed to provide ground clearance for the propeller. To reduce the size and weight of the long landing gear, it was fitted with an ingenious mechanism by which it telescoped out 9 inches when extended. XP-47B was a very large aircraft for its time, with an empty weight of 9,900 pounds or 65 percent more than the YP-43. Kartveli is said to have remarked: "It will be a dinosaur, but it will be dinosaur with good proportions." The armament consisted of eight .50-caliber machine guns, four in each wing. The guns were staggered to allow feeding from side-by-side ammunition boxes, each with a 350-round capacity. Although the British already possessed eight-gun fighters in the form of the Hurricane and the Spitfire, these used the smaller .303-inch guns. The XP-47B first flew on May 6, 1941 with Lowry P. Brabham at the controls. Although there were minor problems, such as some cockpit smoke that turned out to be due to an oil drip, the aircraft proved impressive in its first trials. It was eventually lost in an accident in August 1942.

P-47B/P-47C

The XP-47B gave the United States Army Air Forces (as the Air Corps became known in June 1941) cause for both optimism and apprehension. While possessing good performance and firepower, the XP-47B had its share of teething problems. Its sheer size and power made for challenging take-offs, which required long runways. There were problems with canopy jams, with the guns, with the fuel system, and with the engine installation. At high altitudes, the ignition system arced, and the loads on the control surfaces became unacceptable, causing the ailerons to lock up. The fabric-covered control surfaces also tended to rupture at high altitudes due to the air trapped in them. Republic addressed the problems, coming up with a sliding canopy that could be jettisoned in an emergency, a pressurized ignition system, and new all-metal control surfaces. While the engineers worked frantically to get their dinosaur to fly right, the U.S.A.A.F. ordered 171 P-47Bs. An engineering prototype P-47B was delivered in December 1941, with a production prototype following in March 1942, and the first production model provided in May. Republic continued to improve the design as P-47Bs were produced, and although all P-47Bs had the sliding canopy and the new General Electric turbo supercharger regulator for the R-2800-21 engine, features such as all-metal control surfaces were not standard at first. A modification unique to the P-47B was the radio mast behind the cockpit that was slanted forward to maintain the originally designed antenna wire length in spite of the new sliding canopy.

Initial deliveries of the Thunderbolt to the U.S.A.A.F. were to the 56th Fighter Group, which was also on Long Island. The 56th served as an operational evaluation unit for the new fighter. Teething problems continued. A Republic test pilot was killed in an early production P-47B when it went out of control in a dive, and crashes occurred due to failure of the tail assembly. The introduction of all-metal control surfaces and other changes corrected these problems. In spite of the problems, the U.S.A.A.F. was interested enough to order an additional 602 examples of the refined P-47C, with the first of the variant delivered in September 1942. Beginning in January 1943, Thunderbolt fighters were sent to the joint air force and civilian Millville airport in Millville, New Jersey, in order to train civilian and military pilots.

P-47C

The initial P-47Cs were very similar to the P-47B except for the strengthened all-metal control surfaces, an upgraded G.E. turbo supercharger regulator, and a short vertical radio mast. After the initial manufacture of a block of fifty-seven P-47Cs, production moved to the P-47C-1, which had an 8-inch (200-mm) fuselage extension forward of the cockpit to correct center of gravity problems, and ease engine maintenance. There were a number of other changes, such as revised exhausts for the oil coolers, and fixes to brakes, undercarriage, and electrical system. The fifty-five P-47C-1s were followed by 128 P-47C-2s, which introduced a centerline hard point for either a 500-lb. bomb or a 200-gallon (U.S.) fuel tank. The main production P-47C sub-variant was the P-47C-5, which featured a new whip antenna and the R-2800-59 engine with water-methanol injection and a war emergency power rating of 2,300 hp. The P-47B not only led to the P-47C but to a few other variants. A single reconnaissance variant designated RP-47B was built. The 171st and last P-47B was also used as a test platform under the designation XP-47E and was used to evaluate the R-2800-59 engine mentioned above, a pressurized cockpit, and eventually a new Hamilton Standard propeller. Another P-47B was later fitted with a new laminar flow wing in search of higher performance and redesignated XP-47F.

P-47 Enters Combat

P-47Cs were sent to England for combat operations in late 1942. The 56th Fighter Group was sent overseas to join the Eighth Air Force, whose 4th and 78th Fighter Groups were also equipped with the Thunderbolts. The 4th Fighter Group was built around a core of experienced American pilots, volunteers who had served with the British Royal Air Force (R.A.F.) during 1941–42 in the Eagle Squadrons. Commenting on P-47s size, British pilots joked that a Thunderbolt pilot could defend himself from a Luftwaffe fighter by running around and hiding in the fuselage. The first P-47 combat mission took place March 10, 1943 when the 4th Fighter Group took their aircraft on a fighter sweep over France. The mission was a failure due to radio malfunctions. All P-47s were refitted with British radios, and missions resumed April 8. The first P-47 air combat took place on April 15 with Major Don Blakeslee of the 4th Fighter Group scoring the Thunderbolt's first air victory. On August 17, the P-47s performed their first escort mission, protecting a B-17 force on the first leg of a raid on Schweinfurt, Germany. By the summer of 1943, the Jug was also in service with the 12th Air Force in Italy, and it was fighting against the Japanese in the Pacific with the 348th Fighter Group flying escort missions out of Brisbane, Australia.

P-47D/P-47G/XP-47K/XP-47L

Refinements of the Thunderbolt continued, leading to the definitive P-47D, of which 12,602 were built. The D model actually consisted of a series of evolving production blocks, the last of which were visibly different from the first. The first P-47Ds were actually the same as P-47Cs. Republic could not produce Thunderbolts fast enough at its Farmingdale plant on Long Island, so a new plant was built at Evansville, Indiana. The Evansville plant built a total of 110 P-47Ds, which were completely identical to P-47C-2s. Farmingdale aircraft were identified by the -RE suffix after the block number, while Evansville aircraft were given the -RA suffix. The P-47D-1 through P-47D-6, the P-47D-10, and the P-47D-11 successively incorporated changes such as the addition of more engine cooling flaps around the back of the cowl to reduce the engine overheating problems that had been seen in the field. Engines and engine subsystems saw refinement, as did the fuel, oil, and hydraulic systems. Additional armor protection was also added for the pilot. The P-47D-15 was produced in response to requests by combat units for increased range. The internal fuel capacity was increased to 375 U.S. gallons, and the bomb racks under the wings were made "wet" (equipped with fuel plumbing) to allow a drop tank to be carried under each wing, in addition to the belly tank. A variety of different drop tanks were fitted to the Thunderbolt during its career—following the early conformal 200 U.S. gallon ferry tank and the lozenge-shaped flat 200 U.S. gallon belly tank, teardrop-shaped 75 U.S. gallon and 150 U.S. gallon metal underwing drop tanks were developed. The P-47 could also carry British-designed 108 U.S. gallon and 200 U.S. gallon tanks made of plastic-impregnated paper. These tanks were cheap and were useless to the enemy if found after being dropped, though they could not store fuel for an extended period of time. With the increased fuel capacity, the P-47 was now able to perform escort missions deep into enemy territory.

The P-47D-16, P-47D-20, P-47D-22, and P-47D-23 were similar to the P-47D-15 with minor improvements in fuel system, engine subsystems, a jettisonable canopy, and bulletproof windshield. The Curtiss propeller was replaced by new and bigger propellers, with the Long Island plant moving to a Hamilton Standard propeller with a diameter of 157.875 inches, and the Evansville plant switching to a new Curtiss propeller with a diameter of 156 inches. With the bigger propellers, Thunderbolt pilots had to learn to be careful on take-offs to keep the tail down until they obtained adequate ground clearance. Failure to do so damaged both the propeller and the runway. Even with two Republic plants rolling out the P-47, the U.S. Air Force still was not getting as many Thunderbolts as they wanted, and so an arrangement was made with Curtiss to build the aircraft under license in a plant in Buffalo, New York. Most of the Curtiss Thunderbolts were intended for use in advanced flight training. The Curtiss aircraft were all designated P-47G, and a -CU suffix was used to distinguish them from other production. The first P-47G was completely identical to the P-47C, the P-47G-1 was identical to the P-47C-1, while the following P-47G-5, P-47G-10, and P-47G-15 sub-variants were comparable to the P-47D-1, P-47D-5, and P-47D-10 respectively. Two P-47G-15s were built with the cockpit extended forward to the just before the leading edge of the wing to provide twin tandem seating, and designated TP-47G. The second crew position was accommodated by substituting a much smaller main fuel tank. The Doublebolt did not go into production, but similar modifications were made in the field to older P-47s, which were then used as squadron hacks (miscellaneous utility aircraft). Curtiss built a total of 354 P-47Gs.

Bubbletop P-47s

All the P-47s to this point had a "razorback" canopy configuration, with a tall fuselage spine behind the pilot that resulted in poor visibility to the rear. The British also had this problem with their fighter aircraft and had devised the bulged "Malcolm hood" canopy for the Spitfire as an initial solution. This was fitted in the field to many North American P-51 Mustangs and to a handful of P-47Ds. However, the British then came up with a much better solution, devising an all-round vision "bubble" canopy for the Hawker Typhoon. U.S.A.A.F. officials liked the bubble canopy, and quickly adapted it to American fighters, including the P-51 and the Thunderbolt. The first P-47 with a bubble canopy was a modified P-47D-5 completed in the summer of 1943 and redesignated XP-47K. Another older P-47D was modified to provide an internal fuel capacity of 370 U.S. gallons (1,402 liters) and given the designation XP-47L. The bubble canopy and increased fuel capacity were then rolled into production together, resulting in the P-47D-25. It was followed by similar bubble-top variants, including the P-47D-26, P-47D-27, P-47D-28, and P-47D-30. Improvements added in this series included engine refinements, more internal fuel capacity, and the addition of dive recovery flaps. Cutting down the rear fuselage to accommodate the bubble canopy produced yaw instability, and the P-47D-40 introduced a dorsal fin extension in the form of a narrow triangle running from the vertical tail plane to the radio aerial. The fin fillet was retrofitted in the field to earlier P-47D bubble-top variants. The P-47D-40 also featured provisions for ten "zero length" stub launchers for 5-inch High Velocity Aerial Rockets (H.V.A.R.s), as well as the new K-14 computing gunsight. This was a license-built copy of the British Ferranti G.G.S. Mark IID computing gyroscopic sight, which allowed the pilot to dial in target wingspan and range and would then move the gunsight reticle to compensate for the required deflection.

P-47 as a Fighter-Bomber

By 1944, the Thunderbolt was in combat with the U.S.A.A.F. in all its operational theaters, except Alaska. With increases in fuel capacity as the type was refined, the range of escort missions over Europe steadily increased until the P-47 was able to accompany bombers in raids all the way into Germany. On the way back from the raids, pilots shot up ground targets of opportunity, which led to the realization that the P-47 made an excellent fighter-bomber. Even with its complicated turbo supercharger system it could absorb a lot of damage, and its eight machine guns could inflict heavy damage on lightly armored targets. The P-47 gradually became the U.S.A.A.F.'s best fighter-bomber, carrying the

500-lb. bombs, the triple-tube M-8 4.5-inch rocket launchers, and eventually H.V.A.R.s. The P-47 destroyed thousands of tanks, locomotives, and parked aircraft, and tens of thousands of trucks and other vehicles. Although the P-51 Mustang replaced the P-47 in the escort role, the Thunderbolt still ended the war with 3,752 kills claimed in over 746,000 missions of all types, at the cost of 5,222 P-47s in the war. The 56th Fighter Group was the only 8th Air Force unit still flying the P-47 in preference to the P-51 by the end of the war. The unit claimed 647 air victories and 311 ground kills, at the cost of 128 aircraft. Lieutenant Colonel Francis S. "Gabby" Gabreski scored thirty-one victories, including three ground kills, Captain Bob Johnson scored twenty-seven (with one unconfirmed probable kill leading to some giving his tally as twenty-eight), and 56th FG Commanding Officer Colonel Hubert Zemke scored 17.75 kills. In the Pacific, Colonel Neel Kearby of the 5th Air Force destroyed twenty-two Japanese planes and was awarded the Medal of Honor for an action in which he downed six enemy fighters on a single mission. He was shot down and killed over Biak in March 1944.

P-47 in Non-U.S. Service

P-47s were operated by several Allied air arms during World War II. The R.A.F. received 240 razorback P-47Ds, which they designated Thunderbolt Mk I, and 590 bubble-top P-47Ds, which they designated Thunderbolt Mk II. Except for a few evaluation aircraft, these were operated by the RAF from India for ground-attack operations, known as cab rank sorties, against the Japanese in Burma. They were armed with 500-lb. bombs, or in some cases the British 60-pounder RP-3 rocket projectiles. The Thunderbolts remained in R.A.F. service until October 1946. The Brazilian Expeditionary Force received eighty-eight P-47Ds and flew them in combat during the Italian campaign. During 1945, the 201st Fighter Squadron operated P-47Ds as part of the U.S. Fifth Air Force in the Philippines. In 791 sorties against Japanese forces, the 201st lost no pilots or planes to enemy action. The Free French Air Force received 446 P-47Ds in the last year of the war in Europe, and these aircraft would see action in the 1950s during the Algerian War of Independence. The Soviet Union also received 203 P-47Ds. The fighters were assigned to high-altitude air defense over major cities in rear areas. Unlike their Western counterparts, the Soviet Air Force made no notable use of the P-47 as a ground-attack aircraft, depending instead on their own Ilyushin Il-2.

XP-47H/XP-47J/P-47M/P-47N

Republic made several attempts to further improve the P-47D. Two XP-47Hs were built. They were major reworking of existing razorback P-47Ds to accommodate a Chrysler XI-2220-11 water-cooled inline sixteen-cylinder inverted V engine. However, such large inline engines did not prove to be especially effective. The XP-47J began as a November

1942 request to Republic for a high-performance version of the Thunderbolt using a lighter airframe and an upgraded engine with water injection and fan cooling. Kartveli designed an aircraft fitted with a tight-cowl Pratt & Whitney R-2800-57(C) with a rating of 2,800 hp, reduced armament of six .50-inch machine guns, a new and lighter wing, and many other changes. The first and only XP-47J was first flown in late November 1943. When fitted with a G.E. CH-5 turbo supercharger, the XP-47J achieved a top speed of 505 mph in level flight in August 1944, making it one of the fastest piston-engine fighters ever built. However, by that time, Republic had moved on to a new concept, the XP-72.

P-47M Thunderbolt at RIAT 2004

The P-47M was a more conservative attempt to come up with a higher-performance version of the Thunderbolt. Three P-47Ds were modified into prototype YP-47Ms by fitting the R-2800-57(C) engine and the G.E. CH-5 turbo-supercharger. The YP-47M had a top speed of 473 mph and it was put into limited production, with 130 built. However, the type suffered serious problems in the field due to the highly-tuned engine, and by the time the bugs were worked out, the war in Europe was over. The P-47N was the last Thunderbolt variant to be produced. It was designed as an escort fighter for the B-29 Superfortress bombers flying raids on the Japanese home islands. Increased internal fuel capacity and drop tanks had done much to extend the Thunderbolt's range during its evolution, and the only other way to expand the fuel capacity was to put fuel tanks into the wings. Thus, a new wing was designed with two 50-gallon (U.S.) fuel tanks. The second YP-47M with this wing flew in September 1944. The redesign proved successful in extending range to about 2,000 miles, and the squared-off wingtips improved the roll rate. The P-47N entered mass production with the upgraded R-2800-77(C) engine, with a total of 1,816 built. The very last Thunderbolt to be built, a P-47N-25, rolled off the production line in October 1945. Thousands more had been on order, but production was essentially cut off with the end of the war in August. At the end of production, cost of a Thunderbolt was $83,000 in 1945 U.S. dollars.

No. 201 Squadron P-47 Aircraft

The first P-47Ds were actually the same as P-47Cs. Republic could not produce Thunderbolts fast enough at its Farmingdale plant on Long Island, so a new plant was built at Evansville, Indiana. The Evansville plant first built a total of 110 P-47D-1-RAs, which were completely identical to P-47C-2s. Farmingdale aircraft were identified by the -RE suffix after the block number, while Evansville aircraft were given the -RA suffix. The P-47D-1 through P-47D-6, the P-47D-10, and the P-47D-11 successively incorporated changes such as the addition of more engine cooling flaps around the back of the cowl to reduce the engine overheating problems that had been seen in the field. Engines and engine subsystems saw refinement (the P-47D-10 introduced the R-2800-63, replacing the R-2800-21 seen in previous P-47s) as did the fuel, oil, and hydraulic systems. Additional armor protection was also added for the pilot.

Aircraft of the 201st

Note: Aircraft Number Legend: U.S.A.F./Serial Number/Kind/Production Block/ Factory/No. 201 Squadron Code.

42-23109-P-47D-11-RA "9": Equipment of the Lend-Lease treaty. It suffered damage on June 3, 1945 when it collided with a bulldozer on the taxiway. Lieutenant Carlos Rodríguez Corona was unhurt (pilot identified as Lieutenant David Cerón Bedolla by the F.A.M.). It was dismantled in the Philippines after the war.

42-23216-P-47D-15-RA "5": Equipment of the Lend-Lease treaty. The engine was changed on June 11, 1945. It was dismantled in the Philippines after the war.

42-23225-P-47D-15-RA "15": Equipment of the Lend-Lease treaty. It suffered damage on May 24, 1945 when the propeller hit the track while it was taxing. Lieutenant David Cerón Bedolla was unharmed. It was dismantled in the Philippines after the war. Squadron code 201 as "8" in other documents.

42-23228-P-47D-15-RA "Unknown": Equipment of the Lend-Lease treaty. It was discarded on June 1, 1945 at 11.15 a.m. when it crashed in the sea during dive-bombing practices. Lieutenant Fausto Vega Santander died in the accident. The accident site was reported half a mile southwest of Tabones Island.

42-25395-P-47D-21-RE "3": Equipment of the Lend-Lease treaty. It suffered damage on June 23, 1945, due to pilot error. It turned over when landing on the runway, hitting the front of another P-47 (42-28054). Lieutenant Manuel Farías Rodríguez broke an arm. It was dismantled in the Philippines.

42-25412-P-47D-21-RE "4": Equipment of the Lend-Lease treaty. It collided with a light pole when taking off on June 20, 1945. Lieutenant David Cerón Bedolla was unharmed. The disposition of this aircraft is unknown, but it was probably dismantled in the Philippines.

42-25629-P-47D-22-RE "Unknown": Equipment of the Lend-Lease treaty, but the history card of this device shows that it was transported to Russia under the Loan and Lease program, leaving Newark, New Jersey, on March 30, 1944. The data of the F.A.M. show this device having a change of engine on June 19, 1945.

42-27615-P-47D-23-RA "14": Equipment of the Lend-Lease treaty. It suffered damage due to anti-aircraft fire on June 20, 1945, on the left wing and the carburetor. Lieutenant José Luis Pratt Ramos was unharmed. It was dismantled in the Philippines on June 24, 1945.

42-27887-P-47D-23-RA "None": Equipment of the Lend-Lease treaty. It was discarded on May 24, 1945 when it crashed into the sea due to an engine failure. Lieutenant Mario

López Portillo was rescued. This device was not yet assigned a code from the 201st Squadron.

42-27904-P-47D-23-RA "13": Equipment of the Lend-Lease treaty. It was dismantled in the Philippines after the war.

42-27995-P-47D-23-RA "15": Equipment of the Lend-Lease treaty. It suffered damage on the Porac runway at 12 p.m. on June 18, 1945, when taking off. Lieutenant David Cerón Bedolla was unharmed. The engine was replaced. It was dismantled in the Philippines after the war.

42-28504-P-47D-28-RA "12": Equipment of the Lend-Lease treaty. It suffered damage on June 23, 1945 due to pilot error while taxiing (impacted by the device 42-25395), suffering considerable damage. Lieutenant Miguel Moreno Arreola was unharmed. The disposition of this aircraft is unknown, but it was probably dismantled after the war.

42-28505-P-47D-28-RA "None": Equipment of the Lend-Lease treaty. Left the U.S. on July 17, 1944. It was discarded due to a forced landing near Lgag, Luzon on May 21, 1945 due to engine problems. The status of Lieutenant Graco Ramirez Garrido was not reported. The device had not received a code by the 201st Squadron.

42-28523-P-47D-28-RA "6": Equipment of the Lend-Lease treaty. It left the U.S. on August 5 1944. The engine was changed on June 10, 1945. It was dismantled in the Philippines on December 31, 1945.

42-28528-P-47D-28-RA "Unknown": Equipment of the Lend-Lease treaty. It departed from the U.S. via Oakland on August 8, 1944. It was destroyed by fire on June 5, 1945 after losing power when it took off about 4 miles southeast of Porac, near Florida Blanca. This was a test flight after having received maintenance. Lieutenant José Espinosa Fuentes died in the incident.

42-28606-P-47D-28-RA "Unknown": Equipment of the Lend-Lease treaty. It was turned over in Porac on June 23, 1945 at 10.10 a.m., piloted by Lieutenant Miguel Moreno Arreola, suffering considerable damage. The historical card of this device says that it was assigned to the 9th Air Force and was discarded and dismantled on March 2, 1945.

42-29051-P-47D-28-RA "None": Equipment of the Lend-Lease treaty. It left the U.S. on November 22, 1944. It was discarded before the code of the 201st Squadron was assigned on May 22, 1945, in a forced landing due to an engine failure near Pueblo de Tarlac. Lieutenant Guillermo García Ramos was unharmed in the incident.

42-29052-P-47D-28-RA "1": Equipment of the Lend-Lease treaty. It left the U.S. on October 5, 1944. Probably flown exclusively by the commander of the 201st Squadron. It survived to be dismantled after the end of the war on April 30, 1947 in the Philippines.

42-29077-P-47D-28-RA "2": Equipment of the Lend-Lease treaty. It left the U.S. on November 22, 1944. The engine was changed on June 6, 1945. It was dismantled in the Philippines after the war.

42-75889-P-47D-16-RE "11": Equipment of the Lend-Lease treaty. The engine was changed on June 24, 1945. It was dismantled in the Philippines after the war.

42-75894-P-47D-16-RE "7": Equipment of the Lend-Lease treaty. It lost power on takeoff from Porac on June 17, 1945, crashed and caught fire. Lieutenant Carlos Garduño Núñez suffered some burns and survived.

42-25629-P-47D-21-RA "10": Loaned by the U.S.A.F. It was dismantled in the Philippines after the war.

43-33679-P-47D-30-RA "22": Equipment of the Lend-Lease treaty. It left the U.S. on April 24, 1945. It was dismantled in the Philippines on February 25, 1947.

44-33710-P-47D-30-RA "2": Equipment of the Lend-Lease treaty. It left the U.S. on April 16, 1945. It was dismantled in the Philippines on July 13, 1949.

44-33711-P-47D-30-RA "11": Equipment of the Lend-Lease treaty. It left the U.S. on April 16, 1945. The history card of this device says that it is missing from Aircraft Discrepancy Report (A.D.R.) inventory on July 25, 1945. Nothing else is known about this aircraft.

44-33713-P-47D-30-RA "3": Equipment of the Lend-Lease treaty. It left the U.S. on April 12, 1945. It was dismantled outside the country on July 13, 1949.

44-33715-P-47D-30-RA "13": Equipment of the Lend-Lease treaty. It left the U.S. on April 16, 1945. It was the device that replaced 44-33717. It was dismantled on August 12, 1945.

44-33716-P-47D-30-RA "16": Equipment of the Lend-Lease treaty. It left the U.S. on April 12, 1945. It was dismantled outside the country on July 13, 1949.

44-33717-P-47D-30-RA "4": Equipment of the Lend-Lease treaty. It left the U.S. on April 22, 1945. Apparently, it was diverted to another unit of the Allies, and replaced by the 20st Squadron by 44-33715 after a short use. It was dismantled outside the country on July 13, 1949.

44-33718-P-47D-30-RA "10": Equipment of the Lend-Lease treaty. It was dismantled outside the country on July 13, 1949.

44-33720-P-47D-30-RA "5": Equipment of the Lend-Lease treaty. Replacement to 44-33728, the code of the 201st Squadron for this device was also reported as "12" in some documents. It was dismantled outside the country on July 13, 1949.

44-33721-P-47D-30-RA "1" and "18": Equipment of the Lend-Lease treaty. F.A.M. data show that this device was assigned the code "1" at a time, but photos clearly indicate that it was wearing "18." It was dismantled outside the country on July 13, 1949.

44-33722-P-47D-30-RA "20": Equipment of the Lend-Lease treaty. It left the U.S. on April 12, 1945. It was dismantled outside the country.

44-33725-P-47D-30-RA "25": Equipment of the Lend-Lease treaty. It left the U.S. on April 16, 1945. It was dismantled on July 29, 1949.

44-33727-P-47D-30-RA "23": Equipment of the Lend-Lease treaty. It left the U.S. on April 12, 1945. It was dismantled outside the country.

44-33728-P-47D-30-RA "12": Equipment of the Lend-Lease treaty. It left the U.S. on April 20, 1945. It replaced by 44-33720. It was discarded after an accident on August 11, 1945.

44-33730-P-47D-30-RA "7": Equipment of the Lend-Lease treaty. It left the U.S. on April 20, 1945. It was dismantled outside the country on July 13, 1949

44-33732-P-47D-30-RA "8": Equipment of the Lend-Lease treaty. It left the U.S. on April 16, 1945. It was dismantled outside the country on July 13, 1949

44-33733-P-47D-30-RA "19": Equipment of the Lend-Lease treaty. It left the U.S. on April 20, 1945. It was dismantled outside the country on July 13, 1949

44-33735-P-47D-30-RA "17": Equipment of the Lend-Lease treaty. It left the U.S. on April 12, 1945. It was dismantled outside the country on July 13, 1949

44-33737-P-47D-30-RA "21": Equipment of the Lend-Lease treaty. It left the U.S. on April 12, 1945. It was dismantled outside the country on July 13, 1949

44-33738-P-47D-30-RA "9": Equipment of the Lend-Lease treaty. It left the U.S. on April 16, 1945. It was dismantled outside the country on July 13, 1949

U.S. Training Facilities Used by the 201st Fighter Squadron

(Source: U.S. Air Force Archives)

Abeline Army Airfield

Tye Army Airfield, Abeline, Texas, was built for the Army Air Corps and opened on December 18, 1942. The field briefly served as Abilene's airport. Tye Army Airfield was officially named Abilene Army Airfield and was dedicated on June 5, 1943. Air Corps' cadets learned to fly trainers and P-47 Thunderbolt fighters while stationed at the Army Airfield, a Camp Barkeley adjunct. Abilene Army Airfield was deactivated on December 31, 1945.

Boca Raton Army Airfield

Boca Raton Army Air Field was a World War II U.S.A.A.F. airfield, located 1.7 miles northwest of the 1940s borders of Boca Raton, Florida. At the beginning of World War II, Boca Raton Mayor J. C. Mitchell convinced officers of the Army Air Corps to move its technical school for radar training from Scott Field, Illinois, to Boca Raton. Radar, an acronym for radio detection and ranging, was a new top-secret technology at the time. A small airport stood just north of the present Glades Road to the west of downtown. Here the land was relatively high and dry, yet close to the ocean and shipping lanes with a good climate for flying. Boca Raton was to be home to the Boca Raton Army Air Field (B.R.A.A.F.), the Air Corps' only airborne radar training facility during the war years.

Brownsville Army Airfield

During World War II, the U.S.A.A.F. used the airport, although the Air Corps had signed a contract with Pan American Airways in 1940 for the training of aircraft mechanics at the airport. Shortly after the attack on Pearl Harbor on December 7, 1941, both Army and Navy observation aircraft began operations from the airport flying antisubmarine missions over the Gulf of Mexico.

For the first year of the United States' involvement in combat of the war, Pan American continued to operate the airport, providing training to Ferrying Command pilots and ground mechanics assigned to the 18th Transport Transition Training Detachment. With the realignment of Ferrying Command to Air Transport Command on July 1, 1942, plans were made by the Army to assume jurisdiction of the airport. On July 28, 1943, the U.S.A.A.F. 568th Army Air Force Base Unit, Air Transport Command, was assigned to the newly designated Brownsville Army Airfield in Brownsville, Texas. The mission of the 4th Fighter Operational Training Unit at the airfield was the training of pilots to ferry pursuit planes to the various theaters of war. Training was carried out by Army Air Force instructor pilots; however, Pan American Airways retained operations at the airfield flying larger twin- and four-engined transports to the airport as an overhaul facility. In May 1944, a new mission was developed to train multi-engined pilots at the base. The school began operations in June, and the pilots began to ferry large numbers of aircraft to Panama for subsequent shipment by sealift to Australia.

Camp Stoneman

The site is located in Northern California, in Contra Costa County, in the City of Pittsburg, 40 miles northeast of the city of San Francisco. The site was used as a staging area and rifle range for troop training by the U.S. Army, and was established as a Class I installation (later used as a personnel replacement and reclassification depot). The site was also used as a facility of the San Francisco Port of Embarkation, known as the West Garrison Area of Camp Stoneman.

Foster Field

Foster is a former United States Air Force base, located approximately 6 miles east-northeast of Victoria, Texas. Foster Air Force Base was established as an advanced single-engined flying school for fighter pilots 6 miles northeast of Victoria, Texas, in the spring of 1941. The airfield was activated on May 15, 1941 by the Gulf Coast Air Corps Training Center. The mission of the new airfield was the training of aviation cadets in the advanced phase of flying training. Foster was assigned to the Air Corps Advanced Flying School (Single Engine). In the advanced phase, the cadets flew advanced trainers, fighters, and fighter-bombers. Pilot wings were awarded upon graduation and were sent on to group combat training. Graduates were usually graded as flight officers (warrant officers); cadets who graduated at the top of their class were graded as second lieutenants.

Training at Foster Field for the pilots in the first five weeks included forty flight hours in the AT-6 trainer, including formation flying, day navigation, acrobatics, instruments, night flying, and simulated gunnery. During the next five weeks, the pilots trained on the AT-6 and transitioned to the P-40. Training included simulated strafing with a .30-caliber machine gun. The AT-6 was built originally to compete in the 1937 U.S. Army Air Corps as a basic combat aircraft. Experience showed that it was a mediocre combat aircraft but an excellent trainer, so it was reclassified as an Advanced Trainer.

Majors Army Field

Majors Field, located 5 miles southeast of Greenville, in Hunt County, Texas—named for Lieutenant Truett Majors, the first Hunt County native to perish in World War II—began operations on June 26, 1942, as a training center for the United States Army Air Forces. Lieutenant Majors was killed in the 1942 Battle of the Philippines in January 1942. Greenville, Texas, was chosen as a site for the U.S.A.A.F. basic flight-training center due to the efforts of the influential politician Sam Rayburn; the base was dedicated and named on January 5, 1943. In addition to training U.S. Army pilots, the airfield was the training site for the 201st Fighter Squadron of the Mexican Air Force. The training center was reassigned to 2nd Air Force on November 30, 1944 as a group-training center, primarily for the assignment of replacement personnel to combat squadrons in overseas theaters. Majors Army Air Field was inactivated on July 18, 1945 after the defeat of Germany. The city of Greenville then took ownership and then leased the site.

Matagorda Peninsula Army Airfield (Sub–base of Foster Field)

The airfield was built during 1942 by the Army Air Corps, primarily to support the Matagorda Bombing Range. In addition, it was also developed as a training school by Army Air Forces Training Command. Matagorda Army Air Field was the home of the Army Air Force Pilot School (Advanced Single Engine), and also conducted a single-engined pilot transmission school. The major military units assigned were the 62nd Single Engine Flying Training Group and 79th Bombardier Training Group.

Initially built with three runways, during the war, two additional runways were added to accommodate the large number of landings and take-offs. Aircraft assigned to the base were North American AT-6 Texans, Curtiss P-40 Warhawk, Republic P-47 Thunderbolts, and North American P-51 Mustangs. A series of curved roads on the east side of the parking ramp had dozens of buildings. After the war ended, the training school was inactivated and the facility was closed in November 1945.

Napier Field

Throughout World War II, Napier Field in Dothan, Alabama, was home to several advanced single-engined flying training squadrons (formerly known as school squadrons) equipped with the AT-6 Texan, as well as one squadron that flew the P-40 Warhawk.

Orlando Army Air Base

The United States Army Air Corps took control of the airport in 1940 for use as a training facility and renamed it the Orlando Army Air Base, Orlando, Florida. For the next six years, the airport remained under military control. In June 1941, the Army Air Corps became the U.S.A.A.F., and beginning in late 1941 through mid-1943, Orlando Army Air Base was used by I Bomber Command and later by units of the Army Air Forces Antisubmarine Command (A.A.F.A.C.) to fly antisubmarine patrols along both the east coast as well as over the Gulf of Mexico and the Florida Straits, augmenting U.S. Navy and U.S. Coast Guard aircraft in that capacity. With the lessening of the U-boat threat, Orlando A.A.B. became the home of the Army Air Forces School of Applied Tactics (A.A.F.S.A.T.) and subsequently as the Army Air Forces Tactical Center. In 1943, the A.A.F.S.A.T. began training units in night-fighter operations.

Pocatello Army Airfield

Pocatello is a World War II training base approximately 4 miles northwest of the central business district of Pocatello, a city in Bannock County, Idaho. Many of the base facilities have been razed, although four large hangars remain. The airport is also the home to the National Weather Service Pocatello Office. Pocatello Regional Airport covers an area of 3,374 acres. In 1943, the airfield was built as a Second Air Force heavy bomber (B-17, B-24) training base. The Pocatello Bombing Range No. 3 was built and used as a demolition (high explosive [H.E.]) and incendiary bombing range by the Pocatello Army Air Base. The site was also known as the Pocatello Precision Bombing Range No. 3 and the Pocatello Demolition and Incendiary Bombing Range.

Randolph Army Airfield

Randolph is a United States Air Force base located at Universal City, Texas 14.8 miles east-northeast of downtown San Antonio. In June 1941, the Air Corps became the Army Air Forces. Basic flying training at Randolph continued until March 1943, when the Army Air Forces Central Instructors School (C.I.S.) was created. For the next two years, training instructors for ground schools, instructor pilots (including civilian contract instructors) for all three phases of flying training, and officers destined for administrative duties at air training command bases were trained by the C.I.S.

Randolph produced 15,396 instructor graduates from this course before it moved to Waco Field in 1945. When the C.I.S. moved to Waco Field, it was replaced by the Army Air Forces pilot school, which specialized in transition training for B-29 bomber pilots, copilots, and engineers. Primary pilot training returned to Randolph from Good Fellow Field in December 1945. Thirty-eight pilots appeared before the Commander of Randolph Field, Texas, on August 1, 1944, for a five-week training session, which included aerial gunnery and ten hours of training in P-40.

Republic Airfield

Republic Airport was developed by Sherman Fairchild as the Fairchild Flying Field in East Farmingdale on Long Island, New York, in late 1927 because his flying field and airplane factory at Motor Avenue in South Farmingdale was inadequate to support the mass production of his Fairchild FC-2 and Fairchild 71 airplanes. Fairchild purchased property on the south side of Route 24–Conklin Street and had the airport's original layout plan prepared on November 3, 1927. Seversky Aircraft moved there in January 1935 from College Point in Queens and became Republic Aviation in 1939. Republic built more than 9,000 P-47 Thunderbolts in Farmingdale during World War II and expanded Republic Field—they erected three hangars, a control tower, and lengthened and hardened the runways.

Scott Field

Scott Field is in St. Clair County, Illinois, near Belleville and O'Fallon, 25 miles east of downtown St. Louis. With the outbreak of World War II, the Air Force General Headquarters' move to Scott was cancelled. Instead, Scott Field reverted to its former role as a training installation. On June 1, 1939, one of Scott's Balloon Groups was redesignated as a headquarters unit of the Scott Field Branch of the Army Air Corps Technical Schools. Subsequently, various technical schools moved to Scott. Its communications training era began in September 1940 with the opening of the Radio School. After September 1940, the primary wartime mission of Scott was to train skilled radio operator/maintainer.

APPENDIX IV

5th Air Force and
58th Fighter Group

(*Source: U.S. Air Force Archives*)

Fifth Air Force

The Fifth Air Force is a numbered air force of the United States Air Force Pacific Air Force (P.A.C.A.F.). It is headquartered at Yokota Air Base, Japan, and it is the U.S. Air Force's oldest continuously serving Numbered Air Force. With its origins going back over a century to 1912, the command was established on May 6, 1941 as the Philippine Department Air Force at Nichols Field, Luzon. Fifth Air Force was a U.S.A.A.F. combat air force in the Pacific Theater of World War II, engaging in combat operations primarily in the Southwest Pacific Area of Operation.

During World War II, Fifth Air Force units first engaged the Japanese during the Philippines Campaign, rearmed, it engaged the Japanese in New Guinea, the Dutch East Indies, and then as part of the liberating forces in the Philippines Campaign. In the postwar era, the Fifth Air Force was the primary U.S.A.F. occupation force in Japan. The Fifth Air Force traces its roots to the Philippines with the activation of the Air Office of the Philippine Department in March 1912, the First Company, 2nd Aero Squadron, was activated at Fort William McKinley, Luzon, on February 3, 1916. This unit was a school, operating Martin S Hydro seaplanes.

The unit operated under the Air Office until October 15, 1917, and in 1917 outside Fort Stotsenburg, Luzon, construction began on a half-mile-long dirt runway, hangars, and other support facilities to bring the local army units into the air age. A permanent Army Air Service presence in the Philippines began in December 1919 with the activation of the 3rd Aero Squadron at the facility; the unit was initially equipped with de Havilland DH-4 medium bombers. The next year it moved to the new Clark Field on October 15, 1920 where it combined with support units.

Clark Field became the Army Air Corps headquarters overseas and was the only American air base west of Hawaii. When workmen at Rockwell Field outside San Diego,

California, opened one of the crates, they found a motor with a remarkable history. Built in Detroit, it went to France, back to the United States, then to the Philippines, and with that, the 1st Observation Group at Clark was redesignated as the 4th Observation, and later the 4th Composite Group. The 4th Composite would be the mainstay of United States air power in the Philippines until 1941, and in addition to Clark Field, additional airfields at Kindley Field on Corregidor in Manila Bay and one at Camp Nichols were constructed.

58th Fighter Group

During World War II, the 58th Fighter Group operated primarily in the Southwest Pacific Theater as part of Fifth Air Force. Stationed at Clark Field in the Philippines in 1945, it consisted of the 69th, 310th, and 311th Fighter Squadrons. The unit received a Distinguished Unit Citation after strafing a Japanese naval force off Mindoro in the Philippines on December 26, 1944 to prevent destruction.

Trained for combat and moved overseas to Southwest Pacific Theater in 1943, the unit began combat operations in February 1944, providing protection for U.S. bases and escorting transports initially, then escorting bombers over New Guinea and sea convoys to Admiralty Islands. From Noemfoor, the 58th bombed and strafed Japanese airfields and installations on Ceram, Halmahera, then moved to the Philippines in November, flew fighter sweeps against enemy airfields, supported U.S. ground forces, and protected sea convoys and transport routes.

Beginning in July 1945, the 58th attacked railways, airfields, and enemy installations in Korea and Kyushu, Japan, from Okinawa. After V-J Day, the unit flew missions over Japan, before being moved without personnel or equipment to the Philippines in December to be inactivated in January 1946.

Commanders
Captain John M Sterling—January 15, 1941–unknown; Major Louis W Chick, Jr.— unknown; Colonel Gwen G. Atkinson—December 8, 1942; and Lieutenant Colonel Edward F. Roddy—March 12, 1945– unknown.

Main Bases
Selfridge Field, Michigan: January 15, 1941
Baton Rouge, Louisiana: October 5, 1941
Dale Mabry Field, Florida: March 4, 1942
Richmond A.A.B., Virginia: October 16, 1942
Philadelphia Municipal Airport, Pennsylvania: October 24, 1942
Bradley Field, Connecticut: March 3, 1943
Green Field, Rhode Island: April 28, 1943
Grenier Field, New Hampshire: September 16–October 22, 1943

Sydney, Australia: November 19, 1943
Brisbane, Australia: November 21, 1943
Dobodura, New Guinea: December 28, 1943
Saidor, New Guinea: April 3, 1944
Noemfoor: August 30, 1944
San Roque, Leyte: November 18, 1944
San Jose, Mindoro: December 30, 1944
Mangaldan, Luzon: April 5, 1945
Porac/Clark, Luzon: April 18, 1945
Okinawa: July 10, 1945
Japan: October 20, 1945
Ft. William McKinley, Luzon: December 28, 1945–January 27, 1946

Aircraft
1942–1943: Seversky P-35, Curtiss P-36 Hawk, Bell P-39 Air Cobra, Curtiss P-40 Warhawk; 1943–1945: Republic P-47 Thunderbolt

Assigned To
October 1942–March 1943: Philadelphia Fighter Wing; I Fighter Command; First Air Force.
March–April 1943: New York Fighter Wing, I Fighter Command; First Air Force.
April–October 1943: Boston Fighter Wing, I Fighter Command; First Air Force.
1943–1945: V Fighter Command; Fifth Air Force.
1944–45: 86th Fighter Wing; Fifth Air Force.

Component Squadrons Stationed with the 201st Fighter Squadron

69th Fighter Squadron
The 69th Fighter Squadron was activated in 1941 as a single-engined fighter operational and replacement training unit, initially assigned to III Fighter Command. It was reassigned to I Fighter Command in 1942. It used Bell P-39 Air Cobras and Curtiss P-40 Warhawks for training. The squadron converted to an operational squadron in 1943 and re-equipped with P-47 Thunderbolts.

Deployed to South Pacific Area in 1943, it was assigned to the Thirteenth Air Force. The squadron began combat operations in February 1944, providing protection for U.S. bases and escorting transports initially, then escorting bombers over New Guinea and sea convoys to Admiralty Islands. From Noemfoor, it bombed and strafed Japanese airfields and installations on Ceram, Halmahera, and the Kai Islands.

The squadron moved to the Philippines in November, flew fighter sweeps against enemy airfields, supported U.S. ground forces, and protected sea convoys and transport routes. Beginning in July 1945, the squadron attacked railways, airfields, and enemy installations in Korea and Kyushu, Japan, from Okinawa. After V-J Day, the squadron flew reconnaissance missions over Japan. It moved without personnel or equipment to the Philippines in December and demobilized. The aircraft was sent to depots in the Philippines and was inactivated in January 1946.

310th Fighter Squadron

The 310th Fighter Squadron was created on January 21, 1942 as the 310th Pursuit Squadron (Interceptor) and was activated on February 9 at Harding Field, Louisiana, where it flew the Bell P-39 Air Cobra and Curtiss P-40 Warhawk aircraft. During 1942 and early 1943, the squadron was both an operational and a replacement training unit initially under III Fighter Command, being reassigned to I Fighter Command in October 1942. It was also part of the air defense of the Northeast United States, being a component of several Air Defense fighter wings (Philadelphia, New York, Boston), under the First Air Force.

The squadron was converted into an operational squadron in March 1943 at Bradley Field, Connecticut, being re-equipped with Republic P-47 Thunderbolts. It was deployed to the Southwest Pacific Theater, being assigned to the Fifth Air Force in Australia in November 1943. The squadron began combat operations in February 1944, providing protection for U.S. bases and escorting transports initially, then escorting bombers over New Guinea and sea convoys to Admiralty Islands. From Noemfoor, the squadron bombed and strafed Japanese airfields and installations on Ceram, Halmahera, and the Kai Islands.

It moved to the Philippines in November, flew fighter sweeps against enemy airfields, supported U.S. ground forces, and protected sea convoys and transport routes. Beginning in June 1945, the Mexican 201st Fighter Squadron initially flew missions with the 310th Fighter Squadron, often twice a day, using borrowed U.S. aircraft. Beginning in July 1945, the squadron attacked railways, airfields, and enemy installations in Korea and Kyushu, Japan, from Okinawa. After V-J Day, it flew reconnaissance missions over Japan. The squadron moved without personnel or equipment to the Philippines in December to be inactivated in January 1946 at Fort William McKinley, Luzon.

311th Fighter Squadron

The 311th Fighter Squadron was established on January 21, 1942, as the 310th Pursuit Squadron (Interceptor) and was activated on February 9 at Harding Field, Louisiana, where it flew the P-39 and P-40 aircraft. During 1942 and early 1943, the squadron was both an operational and a replacement training unit initially under III Fighter Command, being reassigned to I Fighter Command in October 1942. It was also part of the air defense of the Northeast United States, being a component of several Air Defense fighter wings (Philadelphia, New York, Boston), under the First Air Force.

The squadron was converted into an operational squadron in March 1943 at Bradley Field, Connecticut, being re-equipped with P-47 Thunderbolts. It was deployed to the Southwest Pacific Theater, being assigned to the Fifth Air Force in Australia in November 1943. The squadron began combat operations in February 1944, providing protection for U.S. bases and escorting transports initially, then escorting bombers over New Guinea and sea convoys to Admiralty Islands. From Noemfoor, it bombed and strafed Japanese airfields and installations on Ceram, Halmahera, and the Kai Islands.

The squadron moved to the Philippines in November, flew fighter sweeps against enemy airfields, supported U.S. ground forces, and protected sea convoys and transport routes. Beginning in July 1945, it attacked railways, airfields, and enemy installations in Korea and Kyushu, Japan, from Okinawa. After V-J Day, the squadron flew reconnaissance missions over Japan. It moved without personnel or equipment to the Philippines in December to be inactivated in January 1946 at Fort William McKinley, Luzon.

Operational Data of the 201st Fighter Squadron

(Source: Final Mission Reports, 201st Mexican Fighter Squadron, June–July 1945, Mexican Air Force)

Combat Mission Recap

No.	Date	Aircraft	Mission	Target Area	Results
1	June 4	4	Bomb & strafe	Aritao	Effective
2	June 4	4	Bomb & strafe	Aritao	Effective
3	June 4	4	Bomb & strafe	Rio Santa Fe	Effective
4	June 4	4	Bomb & strafe	Rio Santa Fe	Not Observed
5	June 4	4	Bomb & strafe	Rio Santa Fe	Not Observed
6	June 5	4	Bomb	Aritao/Dupax	Not Observed
7	June 5	4	Bomb & strafe	Aritao	Effective
8	June 5	2	Direct support	Aritao	Effective
9	June 5	2	Bomb	Bayombong	Effective
10	June 5	2	Bomb & strafe	Bambang	Not Observed
11	June 6	3	Bomb & strafe	Bambang	Effective
12	June 6	2	Bomb & strafe	Bambang	Effective
13	June 6	2	Bomb & strafe	Bambang	Effective
14	June 6	2	Direct support	Bambang	Effective
15	June 6	4	Bomb	Bambang	Effective
16	June 6	3	Bomb & strafe	Bambang	Effective
17	June 6	4	Bomb	Bayombong	Not Observed
18 *	June 7	7	Bomb	Infanta	Not Completed
19	June 7	7	Bomb	Infanta	Effective
20	June 10	7	Direct support	Mariquina River	Not Observed
21	June 10	7	Direct support	Mariquina River	Not Completed
22	June 11	8	Bomb & strafe	Highway4/Lamut	Effective
23	June 11	5	Bomb & strafe	Payawan	Effective

24	June 12	7	Bomb & strafe	Mariquina River	Effective
25	June 12	7	Bomb	Bagabag/Lamut	Not Completed
26	June 13	6	Direct support	Mariquina River	Effective
27	June 13	7	Air alert	Infanta	Not Completed
28	June 14	10	Air alert	Montalban	Not Completed
29	June 15	9	Bomb & strafe	Tuguegarao	Effective
30	June 15	9	Bomb & strafe	San Andres	Not Observed
31	June 16	11	Bomb & strafe	Infanta	Effective
32	June 17	9	Bomb	Payawan	Effective
33	June 17	6	Bomb	Zolanga/Bangang	Effective
34	June 18	5	Bomb	Lenatin River	Effective
35	June 18	8	Bomb	Lenatin River	Effective
36	June 19	6	Air alert	Antipolo	Not Completed
37	June 20	8	Bomb & strafe	Montalban River	Effective
38	June 20	7	Bomb & strafe	Antipolo	Effective
39	June 21	7	Bomb & strafe	Malavite Mountain	Effective
40	June 21	7	Bomb & strafe	Alealá	Not Observed
41	June 22	8	Bomb & strafe	Agnos River	Not Observed
42	June 22	9	Bomb & strafe	Agos River	Effective
43	June 23	8	Bomb & strafe	Kanan River	Effective
44	June 23	6	Bomb	Antipolo	Effective
45	June 24	6	Bomb & strafe	Kanan River	Effective
46	June 24	6	Bomb	Infanta	Effective
47	June 25	12	Bomb & strafe	Agos River	Effective
48	June 25	9	Bomb & strafe	Infanta	Effective
49	June 26	11	Bomb	Infanta	Effective
50	June 28	10	Bomb & strafe	Limutan River	Effective
51	June 29	10	Bomb	Limutan River	Effective
52	June 30	9	Bomb	Cervantes	Not Completed
53	July 4	11	Bomb	Cervantes	Not Completed
54	July 6	8	Fighter sweep	Toko, Formosa	Effective
55	July 7	8	Fighter sweep	Toko, Formosa	Effective
56	July 8	9	Fighter sweep	Toko, Formosa	Effective
57	July 9	9	Fighter sweep	Toko, Formosa	Effective
58	Aug 8	8	Bomb	Karenko, Formosa	Not Effective
59	Aug 26	20	Convoy escort	Route to Okinawa	Effective

* Mission number 18 is the first mission lead by the 201st Squadron.

Operational Summary

Hours flown in combat zone	2,842:00
Total missions flown	96 (June 4 to July 4, 1945)
Training & transfer missions flown**	37 (July 14 to July 21, 1945)
Combat missions flown	59
Ground support missions flown	53
Offensive sorties flown	791
Defensive sorties flown	6
Total hours flown on combat missions	1,966:15
Hours flown in pre-combat	281:00
Average hours flown per pilot	87:00
1,000-lb. bombs dropped	538
500-lb. bombs dropped	500
100-lb. bombs dropped	957
Total rounds of .50-caliber used	166,922
Aircraft lost in combat	1
Aircraft damaged in combat	5
Pilots lost in combat	1
Pilots lost in accidents	1 (landing), 2 (fuel exhaustion)

** Include missions of new aircraft transfer from Biak Island, New Guinea.

Selected Biographies

(Source: Historia Oficial de la Fuerza Aérea Expedicionaria Mexicana by Lieutenant Colonel Sandoval Castarrica, originally published in Spanish in 1946)

Captain Radamés Gaxiola Andrade

Born on April 7, 1914, he made his career at the Heroic Military College and specialized as an aviator pilot. He occupies a distinguished place in the Mexican army, because with the rank of Captain 1, he held the position of Commander of the 201 Squadron. He had under his command the combat operations of this group of Mexican pilots, who participated alongside the Allies during the Second World War, on the Pacific front, in the Philippine Islands from May to October 1945.

According to Lieutenant Carlos Garduño Núñez, a subordinate of Gaxiola, he looked for his squadron to stand out in its mission, so he did not miss the opportunity offering his specialists to attack a Japanese redoubt near the coasts of Vigan, north of Subic, which gave the Americans great headaches because it was situated between high cliffs and hillsides that provided natural protection, forcing the planes to approach from one side to attack it, offering a wide advantage to the Japanese antiaircraft artillery; in fact, a plane had already been lost in an attempt to destroy that Nippon position. The only way to hit that redoubt was by a nose dive, but there were no dive bombers in the Fifth Air Force. Radamés Gaxiola knew that several of the pilots of his squadron had received training in nose dive bombing at the North Island naval in San Diego, California, with SBD Dauntless aircraft in 1944 and promptly offered their expertise in the matter. Needless to say, that the operation was successful, that Gaxiola entrusted to Lieutenant Garduño.

Gaxiola came to hold the rank of brigadier general, after having occupied the posts of Deputy Chief of the Presidential Staff, during the period of the government of Adolfo Ruiz Cortínez, and after having been Chief of the Mexican Air Force. According to Oses Cole, his last job was as a pilot at P.E.M.E.X. He died in a plane crash in 1966, near Acapulco.

Second Lieutenant Miguel Moreno Arreola

He was born in Durango, Mexico, on January 5, 1921 and died in Mexico City on December 1, 2005 following a motor-vehicle accident. He distinguished himself during World War II, flying combat missions with the 201st Squadron based in the Philippines taking missions to Japan.

While still very young, Arreola was inspired to become a pilot after personally becoming acquainted with the famous pilot Francisco Sarabia. He entered the Military Aviation School in Monterrey, graduating as an officer in June 1944. Being recognized as an outstanding pilot, he joined the 201st Squadron almost immediately and continued his training in the United States in P-47 Thunderbolt combat aircraft.

Moreno was transferred to the Philippines in March 1945 with the 201st. Moreno was assigned to a P-47 squadron and flew twenty-five combat missions over Luzon and far-reaching missions to Formosa. It was Miguel Moreno who chose the design of Disney's Pancho Pistolas as mascot of the squadron, and he also designed the monument in Manila to celebrate the lives of their comrades killed in the Philippines. On November 18, 1945 at a rally in the *Plaza de la Constitución* in Mexico City, Captain Moreno presented the Battle Flag of the Mexican Expeditionary Air Force to President Manuel Ávila Camacho.

After the war, Miguel Moreno Arreola began a thirty-five-year career in the commercial aviation industry. In 1981, he retired as captain, making his final flight in a DC-10 aircraft of *Aeronaves de Mexico* (now Aeromexico) with a total of 22,920 flight hours. He then served for many years as an executive member of the Association of Veterans of World War II. Captain Miguel Moreno Arreola also made several presentations to citizen groups and educational institutions on the 201st Squadron performance.

Lieutenant Reynaldo Pérez Gallardo

First published in English online By Lucy Guevara at the University of Texas at Austin, Oral History Project) (Reprinted with permission of the University of Texas at Austin).

As the son of a Mexican Army general and an aficionado of airplanes since childhood, Reynaldo Pérez Gallardo was a perfect candidate to join Mexico's Fighter Squadron 201, the only combat unit from that country to actively participate in World War II. This little-known squadron was made up 300 Mexican volunteers, including 38 fighter pilots such as Gallardo, who fought the Japanese in the Philippines. Gallardo was interviewed in Spanish at his North Austin home, showing scrapbooks of newspaper clippings and photographs from his 38-year military career. He has lived in Austin since 1984.

Born and raised in San Luis Potosi, (his father was governor of the state of San Luis Potosi in the 1940s) in central Mexico, Gallardo enjoyed an adventurous childhood.

His love for flying was obvious since the age of 14. Gallardo remembers those days vividly. "Instead of going to school, I would go to the aviation camp of San Luis Potosi," he said. "The airplanes of that time would get dirty from the bottom, from their body. They would get dirty with oil and I would volunteer to clean them in return that at the end of the day, they would give me a small trip, a ride around the airport in one of those airplanes," he recalled. He said that since then, he's had a desire to fly.

That passion for aviation served Gallardo well as part of the Mexican Fighter Squadron 201, which was formed by Mexican president Manuel Ávila Camacho on July 10, 1944. After training in American bases such as Majors Field in Greenville, Texas, and Pocatello Army Air Base in Pocatello, Idaho, the men were ready for their war assignment as part of the 58th fighter group of the 5th U.S. Air Force stationed in the Philippines. Also known as the "Aztec Eagles," the squadron arrived in Manila Bay on April 30, 1945. Although only in the Philippines for six months, the squadron actively participated in 59 combat missions, totaling over 1,290 hours of flight. They successfully participated in the Allied effort to bomb Luzon and Formosa in an effort to push the Japanese out of the islands. The war came to an end with the surrender of Japan on August 10, 1945. After a year of training and six months of active duty, the Aztec Eagles were able to return home. Mexico greeted them with a hero's welcome on November 18, 1945.

Gallardo feels extremely proud of being part of the Mexican Fighter Squadron 201. Although he was not truly aware of the politics behind the war, he felt it was his responsibility to answer his nation's call. "I had only been an aviation instructor at the Military Aviation School in Guadalajara for about four or five months when they called for volunteers to form a squadron and participate in war, in World War II," he said. "As it was expected, I was one of the first ones to volunteer."

Gallardo, who joined the Mexican military at the age of 16, said he was influenced greatly by his father's position in the military. After joining the Cavalry unit of the Mexican military, he also received training at the prestigious Military College of Mexico in Mexico City and at the Military Aviation School in Guadalajara, Jalisco, Mexico.

It was also during this time that Mexico began to play a more active role in the war. Initially, Mexico had supported the Axis powers during the first years of the war, by trading with the Axis. This support ended when Germany and Russia broke the Non-Aggression Pact of 1939. Germany invaded Russia in 1941 and Mexico now pledged support for the allies. It was only a day after Japan's attack on Pearl Harbor on December 7, 1941, that Mexico was once again forced to re-evaluate her European trade partners. Mexico severed its relationship with Germany and Italy on December 11, 1941 and once more expressed its full support to the Allies. The Mexican government took heavy security measures and a great effort was made to protect the railways, and Gulf of Mexico.

Mexico worked hard to ensure the safe transport of war materials sent to the United States. Mexico opposition for the Axis culminated in the deportation of Italian,

German, and Japanese diplomats. The United States and Mexico signed a series of agreements in 1941 and 1942, which would be essential for the war effort. Agreements such as the Douglas-Weichers Agreement of 1941 mandated that Mexico would sell important raw materials to the United States. The Lend Lease agreement was signed on March 28, 1942. This settlement allowed the United States to ship war supplies to Mexico. These supplies would later provide equipment for the Mexican Fighter Squadron 201. Other 1942 agreements allowed the conscription of Mexican citizens living in the United States as well as the creation of the Bracero Program on August 4, 1942. From 1943 to 1945 the Bracero Program brought over 100,000 Mexican laborers to work the fields and railways in order to alleviate America's manual labor shortage.

Mexico was finally forced to declare war on the Axis on May 22, 1942, after Germany bombed two of its oil tankers, *Portero de Llano* (Plain Keeper) and *Faja de Oro* (Golden Belt) in the Gulf of Mexico. After the first tanker, *Portero de Llano*, was attacked on May 13, 1942, German propaganda alleged that the United States was the party responsible for the aggression. Although extensive propaganda was launched in an effort incriminate the United States, Mexican officials demanded full compensation and an apology from Germany. Germany responded to this complaint by sinking another tanker, *Faja de Oro* on May 22, 1942. It was inevitable that Mexico would soon have to more actively participate in the war. The Mexican Senate and Chamber of Deputies made Mexico's entry into the war official on May 30, 1942.

With great encouragement from President Camacho, the Mexican government evaluated a plan to provide troops for the war. After realizing that Mexico lacked the resources to do this, President Camacho turned to the United States for help to prepare soldiers for combat. In an effort to have these men ready by 1943, President Camacho presented his proposal to President Roosevelt in a meeting held in Monterrey, Nuevo Leo, Mexico in April 1943. Although both nations evaluated the idea extensively and held numerous negotiations, Mexico accepted Roosevelt's proposal on March 14, 1944. President Roosevelt agreed to accept the participation of one or two Mexican air squadrons. "The intention was to form a fighter group, four squadrons," he said. "But they organized the first one and that's the one I joined to receive training in the United States."

Mexico's National Defense Secretary and family members held a modest going away ceremony for the young men in Mexico City. They left Mexico by train and arrived in Nuevo Laredo, Tamaulipas, Mexico, on July 25. 1944. They received a warm welcome from the people of Nuevo Laredo and were cheered as they marched through the town. But across the border in Laredo, Texas, the squadron received little attention. "On the North American side, we felt ignored," he said. "Few people attended, even if only out of curiosity."

From registration at Randolph Field in San Antonio, they continued to Pocatello Army Air Base in Pocatello, Idaho. The first weeks of training included instruction in armament, intelligence, and communications, among other important sections. Pilots received special training in air and combat tactics. These included fighter formation, low altitude gunnery, and night flying. Pocatello was also the training site for America's Women Air Service Pilots (WASP). The men of the squadron were astonished to see this group of skilled pilots perform air tactics on the P-47. The men also received English lessons provided by the women of the WAC, the Women Army Corps. These women also provided Spanish lessons for the American instructors in charge of the Mexican squadron. Measures were taken to accommodate the Mexican soldiers in Pocatello. Pocatello Air Base theaters featured Spanish-language movies, and the men were allowed to celebrate Mexican holidays.

The men left Pocatello for Majors Field in Greenville, Texas, on November 27, 1944. Bad weather forced officials to seek a warmer place to complete training. Majors Field in Greenville, Texas, a 45-minute drive northeast of Dallas, was designated as the new training site. The Mexican Fighter Squadron 201, many accompanied by their wives, faced strong biases from the people of Greenville. Greenville, a town that had described itself as "The Blackest Land and the Whitest People" demonstrated their dislike for the squadron's presence by not renting apartments to squadron wives. Sentiments towards the men changed after Captain Miller, the officer in charge of the squadron's training, clarified that these men came from good families.

In Greenville, the men received combat aviation instruction: 120 hours that focused on formation flying combat tactics, and gunnery. The training included both low and high altitude practice runs on the P-47 fighter airplane.

Youth and an impulsive personality brought an abrupt change in Gallardo's assignment. Because he disobeyed orders and buzzed (flew low) over the city, Gallardo was restricted from flying and given a temporary assignment as the officer in charge of the squadron's mechanics. "This was helpful to me because I was able to learn a lot," he said. "I was in charge of the ground services. I felt very sad, but I knew that I would one day fly again and I did."

The men left to the Philippines on March 27, 1945. "We traveled mainly during the night, they took many precautions during the day because of the submarine threat that was present in the coast of California," he said. "We spent something like 30 days at sea."

He recalled feelings of distrust towards the Mexican fighter pilots, from the men of the 58th Fighter group. But, he said, these sentiments ended after the men of the squadron began to successfully complete missions. "I remember one, which in my opinion was of great importance," he said. "The American Air Force had decided to destroy the bridge over the Marikina River. This would stop the progress of Japanese forces across the island. So we went try to destroy it. As it was expected, the Japanese put a great effort into defending it. May be it was luck, or maybe fate that gave me the opportunity to drop a bomb over it."

The men of the squadron participated in numerous missions, slowly gaining the confidence of the American pilots. Gallardo remembered an incident. "The North Americans used to call us the 'White Noses' because our mechanics had painted the nose of our airplanes white. We became very popular. On one occasion, I was in the hospital getting treated for little things that happen to us over there when a wounded soldier that was next to me noticed that I wasn't North American. He was very injured, but got up and came to the bed where I was lying. He asked me, 'Do you fly a white nose?' and I said 'yes.' He embraced me and said, 'You can't imagine how much we love you, because you have helped us so much.'" Gallardo distinctly remembers the end of the war.

"We were watching a movie when it was abruptly suspended by an officer. With great emotion the officer told us that the most modern bomb in existence had been dropped on the Japanese Empire for the second time today and they [the Japanese] are asking to be allowed to surrender. We couldn't believe it," he recalled. Although the men were advised to proceed with caution, they knew that they would soon return home. Before returning to Mexico, the men of the Mexican Fighter Squadron 201 built a monument in honor of the seven members of their group killed.

November 18, 1945 marked the return of the men and a great celebration in Mexico. They paraded down Madero Avenue and met with President Camacho at the Zocalo, Mexico's national palace.

"Mexico City, all of Mexico City, which is very big, was standing along the streets," he said. "They were excited and anxious to see us. They were proud and happy to see us return. We felt very proud." Twenty men of the Mexican Fighter Squadron 201 received U.S. Air Medals as well as the Philippine Presidential Unit Citation from the president of the Philippines in 1952. Other medals awarded were the Mexican Medal of Valor and World War II Victory Medals. Gallardo received the U.S. Air Medal as well as the Mexican Medal of Merit and one for his service in the Far East. Monuments honoring "*El Escuadron 201*" can be found throughout Mexico and its members are still honored and respected today.

Gallardo returned to Mexico feeling a strong sense of responsibility to share his experience and knowledge with others. After the war, he was responsible of choosing and training new aviators.

Gallardo married his wife Angelina in 1969; the couple had two children. He was an aviator for the government of Michoacán, Mexico, during this time. He served as director of the security department of the Mexican Social Security offices and as a Civil Aeronautics Inspector in 1975.

After a long military and civil service career in Mexico, Gallardo decided to move to the United States, making Austin, Texas, his home in 1984. He owns a business and also divides his spare time between his family and hobbies such as sailing. He lives a peaceful life and is extremely proud of his accomplishments. Gallardo had advice for young people, based, he said either on his training or what his parents taught him.

"Maybe because of fate we are Mexican. However, because we are, we should feel responsible for what we are. A soldier behaves well because that's what he was taught. A Mexican should behave well because he is Mexican. I want for Mexicans to be proud of their name, of their nationality, and want them to try to better themselves," he said. "In order for a county to progress, an individual must progress first."

First Lieutenant Amador Sámano Piña

One of the few Mexican pilots to leave a written account of his wartime experiences was the former First Lieutenant Amador Samano Pina. He was born in July 1919 in Metepec, Mexico. In 1936, Sámano Piña joined the Mexican Army as a cadet in the *Heroico Colegio Militar* (Mexico's equivalent to West Point). Then he graduated as an infantry second lieutenant on January 1, 1939. After serving in an infantry battalion, he requested his transfer to the *Escuela Militar de Aviacion* (Military Aviation School) on January 1, 1940, which was granted. On July 2, 1943, he survived a crash in a Vultee BT-13 basic trainer. His instructor Lieutenant Miguel Uribe Carballeda was killed during the accident, but Sámano Piña recovered to complete his training and receive his wings on September 1, 1943.

After his graduation, he was assigned to the 3rd Aerial Squadron at Tampico, Veracruz, flying North American AT-6 Texan advanced trainers on antisubmarine patrols over the Gulf of Mexico. During this deployment, it was reported that Sámano Piña survived another accident. He was later attached to a government agency. On February 3, 1944, he was assigned to the 201st Fighter Squadron, as an armament officer, and later selected to go with this unit as part of the Aeronautical Training Group for training in the United States, which later became, on January 1, 1945, the *Fuerza Aerea Expedicionaria Mexicana*.

While in the Philippines, Lieutenant Sámano Piña was part of C Flight, known as *Gavilanes* (Sparrow Hawks), under the command of Lieutenant Hector Espinoza Galvan (K.I.F.A. on July 16, 1945). During his tour, Sámano Piña was credited with twenty combat missions, about seventy hours of combat time, and thirty-three hours' flying time in the theater of operations.

For his service in the M.E.A.F., Sámano Piña was promoted to the rank of captain. He left the service for a short time after his return to Mexico and went to fly for the *Compania Mexicana de Aviacion* (known today as Mexicana), but returned to active duty in 1947.

From 1950 to 1958, Sámano Piña commanded the 201st, and during that period, he was promoted to lieutenant colonel. He retired from the air force, with the rank of brigadier general, in June 1966. He was killed at his house in Cuernavaca, Morelia, on February 3, 1987, during an attempted robbery.

Awards Received by the Members of the 201st Fighter Squadron

(Source: U.S. Air Force Personnel Center)

Air Medal

Background

The Air Medal, established by Executive Order 9158, May 11, 1942, was amended by Executive Order Number 9242, September 11, 1942.

Criteria

The Air Medal is awarded to U.S. and civilian personnel for single acts of heroism or meritorious achievements while participating in aerial flight and foreign military personnel in actual combat in support of operations. Required achievement is less than that required for the Distinguished Flying Cross, but must be accomplished with distinction above and beyond that expected of professional airmen. It is not awarded for peace time sustained operational activities and flights.

Medal Description

The medal is a bronze compass rose of sixteen points with a *fleur-de-lis* design on the top point. On the obverse, in the center, is an American eagle, swooping downward (attacking) and clutching a lightning bolt in each talon. The reverse has a raised disk on the compass rose, left blank for the recipient's name and rank.

Ribbon Description

The ribbon has a broad stripe of ultramarine blue in the center flanked on either side by a wide stripe of golden orange, and with a narrow stripe of ultramarine blue at the edge, the original colors of the Army Air Corps.

American Campaign Medal

Background
The American Campaign Medal was authorized November 6, 1942 by Executive Order Number 9265 that was signed by President Franklin D. Roosevelt. The medal was issued to commemorate the service performed by personnel of the Navy, Marine Corps, and Coast Guard who served during the periods and in the areas designated below.

Criteria
This medal is awarded for service within the American Theater between December 7, 1941 and March 2, 1946, under any of the following conditions: permanent assignment outside the continental United States (C.O.N.U.S.); permanent assignment as aircrew members of airplanes making frequent flights over ocean waters for a period of thirty consecutive days or sixty non-consecutive days; outside the C.O.N.U.S. in a passenger status or TDY for thirty consecutive days or sixty non-consecutive days; in active combat against the enemy, if personnel were awarded a combat decoration or furnished a certificate by the unit's commander stating that they actually participated in combat; or served within the C.O.N.U.S. for an aggregate period of one year

Medal Description
The medal is 1.25 inches in diameter, bearing in front an offshore scene depicting a cruiser, an airplane, and a sinking submarine underneath the inscription "American Campaign."

Ribbon Description
The ribbon is predominantly medium blue, striped white, black, red, and white from right to left and left to right within each edge. In the center are three stripes of red, white, and blue. The blue stripe is worn to the wearer's right.

Army Good Conduct Medal

Background
The Army Good Conduct Medal was authorized by Executive Order Number 8809, on June 28, 1941, and is awarded to enlisted members who have honorably completed three continuous years of active military service subsequent to August 26, 1940, and who are recommended by their commanding officers for exemplary behavior, efficiency, and fidelity. Persons awarded this medal must have had character and efficiency ratings of excellent or higher throughout the qualifying period, including time spent in attendance at service schools, and there must have been no convictions by court martial.

Criteria

During wartime, the Army Good Conduct Medal may be awarded on completion of one year of continuous service rather than three. Executive Order 9323, March 31, 1943, lowered this time limit for service during World War II, and it was amended by Executive Order Number 10444 on April 10, 1953, applying the one-year ruling to the Korean Conflict (1950–1954) and to any future period in which the United States is at war, including the war in Vietnam (1964–1973).

Medal Description

The medal, designed by Joseph Kiselewski, has on the obverse an eagle with wings displayed and inverted, standing on closed book and a Roman sword. Encircling it is the inscription "Efficiency, Honor, Fidelity." The reverse has a five-pointed star, slightly above center, with a scroll beneath for the recipient's name. Above the star are the words "For Good" and below the scroll the word "Conduct." A wreath, formed of a laurel branch on the left and an oak branch on the right, surrounds the whole design.

Ribbon Description

Only one Good Conduct Medal may be awarded to any individual. Additional awards of the medal are indicated by a bar, with loops or knots indicating additional awards. Clasps are in bronze (one to five awards), silver (five to nine awards), and gold (ten or more awards). An individual who is awarded a Good Conduct Medal while serving in another branch of service and is then awarded an Army Good Conduct Medal would wear both medals and ribbon bars.

Asiatic-Pacific Campaign Medal

Background

The Asiatic-Pacific Campaign Medal was authorized on November 6, 1942 by Executive Order Number 9265 that signed by President Franklin D. Roosevelt. The medal was issued to commemorate the service performed by personnel of the Navy, Marine Corps, and Coast Guard who served during the periods and in the areas designated below.

Criteria

This medal is awarded for service in the Asiatic-Pacific Theater between December 7, 1941 and March 2, 1946 under any of the following conditions: permanent assignment; passenger status or on temporary duty for thirty consecutive days or sixty non-consecutive days; in active combat against the enemy, if personnel were awarded a combat decoration or furnished a certificate by the unit's commander stating that they participated in combat; or personnel who were assigned or attached members of units during the period for which campaign participation credit or assault landing credit was accorded to the unit are awarded the bronze service star and arrowhead, respectively, to denote their participation in the action.

Medal Description
The medal is 1.25 inches in diameter, depicting in front a tropical landing beneath the words Asiatic-Pacific Campaign.

Ribbon Description
The ribbon is basically yellow, with yellow, red, and white stripes near each edge. In the center are three equal stripes of blue, white, and red. The blue stripe is worn to the wearer's right.

Legion of Merit

Background
The Legion of Merit, the first United States decoration created specifically for citizens of other nations, was established by an Act of Congress of July 20, 1942, and amended by an executive order on March 15, 1955.

Criteria
It is conferred on officers and enlisted men of the armed forces of the United States and on nationals of other countries who have distinguished themselves by exceptionally meritorious conduct in the performance of outstanding services since September 8, 1939, the date of the president's proclamation of the state of emergency that led to World War II. The Legion of Merit may be awarded for combat or noncombat services; in the case of American military personnel, if the award is for combat service it is shown by the wearing of a combat V device.

Medal Description
The Legion of Merit is also the first award to have different degrees. If a holder of the Legion of Merit in one degree is subsequently given another such award, it is never in a degree lower than the original one. The degrees of chief commander and commander are conferred on members of foreign governments only and are awarded for services comparable to those for which the Distinguished Service Medal is given to members of the United States armed forces.

Philippine Liberation Medal

Background
The Philippine Liberation Ribbon is awarded for participation in the Philippines' liberation from October 17, 1944 to September 3, 1945.

Criteria

Members are eligible for this medal if they participated in the initial landing operations on Leyte or adjoining islands from October 17, 1944 to October 20, 1944. Personnel are considered as having participated in such operations if they landed on Leyte or adjoining islands, were on ships in Philippine waters, or were crew members of airplanes that flew over Philippine territory during the period. Members are also eligible if they participated in any engagement against the enemy during the campaign on Leyte and adjoining islands. Personnel are considered as having participated in such operations if they were members of or present with units actually under enemy fire or air attack, or were crewmembers in an airplane under enemy aerial or ground fire.

Medal Description

Persons who meet more than one of the conditions above are authorized to wear a bronze service star on the ribbon for each additional condition under which they may qualify.

Ribbon Description

It is a red ribbon with equal blue and white stripes in the center. The blue stripe is worn to the wearer's right.

Philippine Presidential Unit Citation

Background

This emblem was awarded to members of the armed forces of the United States for services culminating in the liberation of the Philippine Islands during World War II. The conditions were the same as would be required for award of the Presidential Unit Citation of the United States. The award is made in the name of the President of the Republic of the Philippines. The ribbon is slightly larger for the Army and worn on the right breast; for the other services, the ribbon is the standard size.

Criteria

The citation was first awarded to units of the armed forces of the United States in recognition of participation in the war against the Japanese Empire during the periods December 7, 1941 and May 10, 1942, inclusive, and October 17, 1944 to July 4, 1945, inclusive.

Ribbon Description

The ribbon has three wide stripes of equal width. Starting from the left, a wide stripe of blue, a wide stripe of white and a wide stripe of red. The ribbon is enclosed in a rectangular 1/16-inch gold frame with laurel leaves.

Medalla Por Servicio en el Lejano Oriente (Mexican Service in the Far East Medal)

This was a special medal that was the only decoration ever awarded for foreign combat by Mexican military personnel.

APPENDIX VIII

201st Fighter Squadron Personnel Losses

(*Source: Historia Oficial de la Fuerza Aérea Expedicionaria Mexicana by Lieutenant Colonel Sandoval Castarrica, originally published in Spanish in 1946*)

Second Lieutenant Crisóforo Salido Grijalva

Killed in a flight accident, Texas, USA, January 23, 1945. On January 23, several pilots were assigned to mission No. 58, a training mission, which consisted of aerial gunnery. Second Lieutenant Crisóforo Salido Grijalva in the company of Lieutenant Rodriguez Corona was preparing to take-off from the runway at Majors Field. Salido Grijalva requested permission to start the take-off and received the order to start the taxi to the beginning of the runway 12–30, without noticing the second lieutenant started the take-off in the taxi track, which had a length of 980 feet. He tried to get airborne but never achieved it, despite the desperate warning from his companions in the air. When Salido Grijalva tried to brake, it was too late, and his plane crashed into the mud at the end of the track and flipped over.

Lieutenant Javier Martínez Valle

Killed in a flight accident, Texas, USA, March 13, 1945. On March 10, 1945, the pilots of the 201st Squadron practiced shooting on a moving target. This consisted of a plane towing the target while the pilots fired at it. For some reason, the P-47 of Lieutenant Javier Martínez Valle hit the cable that was towing the target, which damaged the aircraft causing the Lieutenant to lose control and fall to the ground with the subsequent fatality. His plane fell on Padre Island, which was a muddy terrain, so it was very difficult to recover the body.

Second Lieutenant Fausto Vega Santander

Killed in a flight accident, Philippines, June 1, 1945. In 1943, he took the pilot and specialization course in miniature aircraft in San Antonio Texas. He was awarded the "Service in the Far East" medal for his dedication, honor, and patriotism against the Axis powers. He had the sad honor of being the first Mexican military man who died in the Pacific Theater, on June 1, 1945, in a plane crash, when in a formation of eight planes, under the command of Lieutenant José Espinosa Fuentes. He was conducting a bombing training mission against an islet, located about a mile and a half southeast of the small Tabones Islands, off the west coast of Luzon Island, Philippines. He lost control of his aircraft and was killed in the crash. The U.S. Air Force Search Service confirmed that the P-47 aircraft had sunk into the sea without the pilot appearing.

Lieutenant José Espinoza Fuentes

Killed in a flight accident, June 5, 1945. On December 16, 1943, he became entitled to the rank of lieutenant flying pilot for having successfully completed the training course and learning at Naval Air Station Corpus Christi, Texas. He was awarded the medal of "Service in the Far East," for self-denial, honor, and patriotism against the Axis powers. Fuentes volunteered to test-fly one of the P-47s that had been handed down by the 358th Fighter Group. The aircraft engine lost power after take-off. Standard procedure was to crash-land straight off the end of the runway. However, the area was covered with tents and full of soldiers, so Fuentes turned his aircraft right, struck the Pampanga sugar mill, and died in the resulting fire. He was buried the same day in the Number 2 American Cemetery in Manila, the Philippine Islands. Later, his remains were transferred to Mexico and deposited in the "Fallen Eagles" lot, in the Panteón of Dolores in Mexico City. Years later, his remains were moved to the monumental gallery dedicated to the F.A.E.M.

Second Lieutenant Hugo Gonzalez y Gonzalez

Killed in a flight accident, USA, July 9, 1945 (Replacement Group pilot). No additional information available.

Lieutenant Héctor Espinosa Galván

Killed in a flight accident New Guinea, July 16, 1945. Thirteen pilots left their base to the Biak, New Guinea, on an aircraft transport mission. Twelve returned to Porac on the 19th. Not so Lieutenant Espinosa Galván. According to an official report by American

Army Lieutenant G. T. Roberts, Espinosa Galván died at 4.45 p.m. on July 16, as a result of a crash in the vicinity of Biak, New Guinea, where the unit commanded by Lieutenant Roberts was heading. From the reference information, it is clear that the formation left Zamboango, Mindanao, on the same day to Biak, losing the route for about an hour. This loss caused greater fuel consumption than calculated. At six hours of flight, Lieutenant Espinosa Galván reported to his leader to be short of gasoline, so this led to the formation to conduct an emergency landing on the island of Noemfoor. The lieutenant never landed in Noemfoor for causes that the leader does not know. When the formation was about 30 miles from Biak, Lieutenant Espinosa informed Lieutenant Roberts that he had finished his fuel and that he was descending to make a landing, seeing Espinosa's plane collide with the waters, disappearing into the sea without the pilot appearing on the surface. It is known that the search started with the departure of a C-47 aircraft in order to make the rescue, but this work continued without any result. Subsequent reports confirm that Lieutenant P. A. Héctor Espinosa Galván disappeared in the waters of the sea without returning to the surface.

Captain Pablo L. Rivas Martínez

Missing off New Guinea, July 19, 1945. Officially declared dead in 1947. Captain Rivas Martínez was lost on the July 19, 1945 when he flew *en route* from Biak, New Guinea, to Morotai Island, an enemy region. According to reports of Second Lieutenant Guillermo Garcia Ramos, who flew with him as a wingman, he lost sight of the captain when trying to cross an area of atmospheric disturbance. The Rescue Service of the Far East Air Force reported days later that the search undertaken had been negative. The case spawned a legal and moral problem at the same time. The penalty that this loss caused increased when considering the situation in which the family would remain. Unfortunately, Mexican military legislation did not foresee such cases, and for her there is no perceptible benefit or compensation for family members more than when the military man dies.

Second Lieutenant Mario López Portillo

Killed in a flight accident, Philippines, July 21, 1945. On July 21, 1945, during the missions of transporting new P-47 aircraft for the 201st Squadron, he lost his life in the line of duty, along with an American flight leader, when his plane crashed into a mountain in the Bataan area 6 miles southwest of Laman, between Balanea and Mariveles when leaving Leyte towards the Porac Air Base. The site of the tragedy was located on July 27 and on August 3 an expedition organized by Colonel Cárdenas, rescued the remains of Second Lieutenant López Portillo. It was interned in the Number 2 American Cemetery in Manila, the Philippine Islands. Later his remains were transferred to the Panteón of

Dolores in the lot of the "Fallen Eagles." Years later, his remains were transferred to the monumental gallery dedicated to the F.A.E.M.

Lieutenant Roberto Gomez Moreno

Killed in a flight accident, U.S.A., September 26, 1945 (Replacement Group pilot). No additional information available.

Radio Operator Sergeant Francisco Rodriguez Castaneda

Died in Santa Fe, New Mexico Military Hospital due to illness contracted in the Philippines, November 2, 1945. No additional information available.

APPENDIX IX

The Bracero Program

(Source: Roy Rosenzweig Center for History and New Media, George Mason University)

The Bracero (manual laborer) Program, which brought millions of Mexican guest workers to the United States, ended more than four decades ago. Current debates about immigration policy—including discussions about a new guest worker program—have put the program back in the news and made it all the more important to understand this chapter of American history. Yet while top U.S. and Mexican officials re-examine the Bracero Program as a possible model, most Americans know very little about the program, the nation's largest experiment with guest workers. Indeed, until very recently, this important story has been inadequately documented and studied, even by scholars.

The Bracero Program grew out of a series of bi-lateral agreements between Mexico and the United States that allowed millions of Mexican men to come to the United States to work on short-term, primarily agricultural, labor contracts. From 1942 to 1964, 4.6 million contracts were signed, with many individuals returning several times on different contracts, making it the largest U.S. contract labor program. An examination of the images, stories, documents, and artifacts of the Bracero Program contributes to our understanding of the lives of migrant workers in Mexico and the United States, as well as our knowledge of, immigration, citizenship, nationalism, agriculture, labor practices, race relations, gender, sexuality, the family, visual culture, and the Cold War era.

The Bracero Program was created by executive order in 1942 because many growers argued that World War II would bring labor shortages to low-paying agricultural jobs. On August 4, 1942, the United States concluded a temporary intergovernmental agreement for the use of Mexican agricultural labor on United States farms (officially referred to as the Mexican Farm Labor Program), and the influx of legal temporary Mexican workers began. But the program lasted much longer than anticipated. In 1951, after nearly a decade in existence, concerns about production and the U.S. entry into the Korean conflict led Congress to formalize the Bracero Program with Public Law 78.

The Bracero Program was controversial in its time. Mexican nationals, desperate for work, were willing to take arduous jobs at wages scorned by most Americans. Farm workers already living in the United States worried that braceros would compete for jobs and lower wages. In theory, the Bracero Program had safeguards to protect both Mexican and domestic workers for example, guaranteed payment of at least the prevailing area wage received by native workers; employment for three-fourths of the contract period; adequate, sanitary, and free housing; decent meals at reasonable prices; occupational insurance at employer's expense; and free transportation back to Mexico at the end of the contract. Employers were supposed to hire braceros only in areas of certified domestic labor shortage and were not to use them as strikebreakers. In practice, they ignored many of these rules and Mexican and native workers suffered while growers benefited from plentiful, cheap, labor. Between the 1940s and mid-1950s, farm wages dropped sharply as a percentage of manufacturing wages, a result in part of the use of braceros and undocumented laborers who lacked full rights in American society.

Endnotes

Chapter 1

1. "Los Orígenes," (Fuerza Aérea Mexicana), Mexican Secretary of National Defense. www. gob.mx/sedena/documentos/los-origenes-fuerza-aerea-mexicana. (accessed on August 5, 2018).
2. "Evolución," (Fuerza Aérea Mexicana), Mexican Secretary of National Defense. www.gob. mx/sedena/documentos/evolucion-fuerza-aerea-mexicana. (accessed on August 5, 2018).
3. "Material aéreo histórico de la F.A.M.," Mexican Secretary of National Defense. www.gob. mx/sedena/documentos/material-aereo-historico-de-la-f-a-m. (accessed on August 5, 2018).
4. "Biografías," Mexican Secretary of National Defense. www.gob.mx/sedena/ documentos/ biografias. (accessed on August 5, 2018).

Chapter 2

1. Hamilton, N. L., "Mexico: The Limits of State Autonomy." *Latin American Perspectives* 2, no. 2 (1975): 81–108, www.jstor.org/stable/2633191, p. 88. (accessed on August 1, 2018).
2. *Ibid.*, p. 91.
3. *Ibid.*, p. 93.
4. *Ibid.*, p. 98.
5. *Ibid.*, p. 99.
6. *Ibid.*, p. 100.
7. *Ibid.*, p. 103.
8. *Ibid.*, p. 104.
9. "Mexican Support for the United States," *New York Times, April 22, 1943*, p. 5.
10. "George C. Marshall to President Franklin Roosevelt, September 18, 1943," *Roosevelt Papers, Special Collections*, (New York: Franklin D. Roosevelt Library), p. 3.

11. *Ibid.*
12. Harrison, "United States– Mexican Military Collaboration, during World War II." Ph. D dissertation, (Washington D. C.: Georgetown University, 1976), pp. 225–226.
13. *Ibid.*, pp. 222–224.
14. Wood, W. "A Re-Examination of Mexican Support for the United States during World War II," Ph.D. thesis, (Columbia: University of Missouri, 1989), p. 314.
15. *Ibid.*, p. 6.
16. "Messersmith to Duggan, February 17, 1944," Index 1580, MP, (Washington D.C: Department of State).
17. *Ibid.*
18. Hams, A. R., Brigadier General, U.S., Military *Attaché*, Mexico City to Major General Guy V. Henry, Joint Mexican–United States Defense Commission, February 9, 1944, Index 1575, MP, (Washington, D.C.: U.S. Department of Defense).
19. "Messersmith to Duggan, February 17, 1944."
20. "Harris to Chief, Military Intelligence Service, February 14, 1944," Index 1579, MP. (Washington, D. C. War Department).
21. *Ibid.*
22. "Messersmith to Duggan, February 19, 1944," Index 1582, MP, (Washington, D. C.: U.S. Department of State).
23. "Messersmith to Roosevelt, March 15, 1944," Index 1587, MP, (Washington, D. C.: U.S. Department of State).
24. Castarrica, E. R., *Historia Ofical de la Fuerza Aérea Expedidonaria Mexicans* (Mexico: Secretaria de la Defensa National, 1946), pp. 28–29.
25. "Messersmith to Duggan, March 9, 1944," Index 1584, MP, (Washington, D. C.: U.S. Department of State).
26. Henry G. V., Major General, March 17, 1944, RG 59, 812, (Washington, D.C. U.S. Department of State).
27. *Ibid.*
28. "Messersmith to Duggan, March 9, 1944"
29. "Messersmith to Hull, March 15, 1944," RG 59, 812.20V460, (Washington, D.C.: U.S. Department of State).
30. Henry.
31. *Ibid.*
32. *Ibid.*
33. *Ibid.*
34. Messersmith, G., "Military Collaboration by Mexico during the war–Squadron 201." Index 2031, MP, (Washington, D.C.: U.S. Department of State), p. 13,
35. "Messersmith to Duggan, April 17, 1944," RG 59, file 812.20V459–1/2, (Washington, D.C.: U.S. Department of State).
36. "Hall to Messersmith, April 16, 1944," RG 59, file 812.20V474, (Washington, D.C.: U.S. Department of State).
37. Cárdenas, A., General, *Mis Dos Misiones*, (Mexico: Talleres Graficos de la Nacion, 1949), p. 21.
38. *Ibid.*
39. "Messersmith to Duggan, April 17, 1944," RG 59, file 812.20V459–1/2, (Washington, D.C.: U.S. Department of State).
40. "Hall to Messersmith, April 16, 1944."
41. Cárdenas, p. 33.
42. *Ibid.*, p. 39.
43. *Ibid.*, p. 35.

44. *Ibid.*, p. 37.
45. *Ibid.*, p. 44.
46. Vega, J., *The Mexican Expeditionary Air Force in World War II: The Organization, Training, and Operations of the 201st Squadron*, Research Department, (Montgomery: Air Command and Staff College, 1997), p. 13.
47. Camacho, M., "Good Neighbors–Good Friends, Mexico, the Bridge Between Latin and Saxon Cultures," Broadcast from Monterrey, Mexico, April 20, 1943 (*Vital Speeches of the Day*, Vol. IX, pp. 420-421).

Chapter 3

1. Mathewson, L., Lieutenant Colonel, "Memorandum to Commanding General, Army Air Forces," *Subject: Progress Report of the Joint Mexican–United States Defense Commission, 24 April 1942.* (Washington, D. C.)
2. Cline, H. F., *The United States and Mexico*, (New York: Athenaeum University Press, 1968), p. 277.
3. *Ibid.*
4. Castarrica, E. R., *Historia Ofical de la Fuerza Aérea Expedidonaria Mexicans* (Mexico: Secretaria de la Defensa National, 1946), pp. 147–168.
5. Castarrica, pp. 37–41.
6. *Ibid.*, pp. 151–154.
7. "History of the 201st Mexican Fighter Squadron, 1 February–18 March 1945," *Majors Field, 72nd Fighter Wing, Second Air Force*, (Maxwell Air Force Base: Air Force Historical Research Agency), p. 28.
8. Castarrica, pp. 161–166.
9. Castarrica, p. 23.
10. Vega, J., *The Mexican Expeditionary Air Force in World War II: The Organization, Training, and Operations of the 201st Squadron*, Research Department. (Montgomery: Air Command and Staff College, 1997), p. 6.

Chapter 4

1. "History of the 201st Mexican Fighter Squadron," Air Force History Support Office, Microfilm roll A0768, Frame 1676. 2, *Majors Field Flight Report, February 20, 1945, 2nd Section*, (Washington D.C.: Department of the Air Force).
2. Hagedom, D., *Republic P-47 Thunderbolt: The Final Chapter, Latin American Air Forces Service*, (St. Paul: Phalanx Publishing Co., Ltd., 1991), p. 12.
3. *Ibid.*
4. "Alas de Mexico," *Gaxiola Andrade memoirs, 201st*, Air Force History Support Office, Microfilm roll A0768, frame 1749, (Washington D.C.: Department of the Air Force), pp. 55, 75, 103.
5. "History of the 201st Mexican Fighter Squadron," Air Force History Support Office, Microfilm roll A0768, (Washington D.C.: Department of the Air Force).
6. *Ibid.*
7. *Ibid.*
8. *Ibid.*
9. *Ibid.*
10. *Ibid.*

11. *Ibid.*
12. *Ibid.*
13. *Ibid.*
14. *Ibid.*
15. *Ibid*
16. *Ibid*
17. *Ibid.*
18. Cárdenas, A., General, *Mis Dos Misiones*, (Mexico: Talleres Graficos de la Nacion, 1949), p. 56.
19. *Ibid.*
20. *Ibid.*
21. *Ibid.*
22. *Ibid.*
23. *Ibid.*
24. *Ibid.*
25. *Ibid.*
26. Cárdenas, pp. 21–23.
27. Cárdenas, p. 6.
28. Cárdenas, pp. 24– 25.
29. *Ibid.*, p. 26.
30. *Ibid.*
31. *Ibid.*

Chapter 5

1. Castarrica, Enrique Sandoval, *Historia oficial de la Fuerza Aérea Expedicionaria Mexicana* (Mexico: Secretaría de la Defensa Nacional, 1946), pp. 553-563.
2. Castarrica, pp. 553-555.
3. *Ibid.*, pp. 554-555.
4. *Ibid.* p. 555.
5. *Ibid.*, pp. 556-557.
6. *Ibid.*, pp. 558-560.
7. *Ibid.* p. 560.
8. *Ibid.* p. 561.
9. *Ibid.*, pp. 562-563.
10. *Ibid.*, pp. 228-230.

Chapter 6

1. Servín, M. P., *The Mexican-Americans: An Awakened Minority*, (Beverly Hills: Glencoe Press, 1974), p. 24.
2. Oppenheimer, R. "Acculturation or Assimilation: Mexican Immigrants in Kansas, 1900 to World War II," *The Western Historical Quarterly*, Vol. 16, no. 4 (1985), p. 429.
3. Servín, pp. 12-13, 55.
4. Oppenheimer, p. 436.
5. *Ibid.*, p. 444.
6. *Ibid.*

7. Roediger, D. R., *How Race Survived US History: From Settlement and Slavery to the Obama Phenomenon,* (New York: Verso, 2008), p. 165.

8. Takaki, R. T. *Double Victory: A Multicultural History of America in World War II,* (Boston: Little, Brown and Co., 2000), p. 92.

9. García, A., *Mexican Americans: The New Americans,* (Westport: Greenwood Publishing Group, 2002), p. 166.

10. Griswold del Castillo, R., *World War II and Mexican American Civil Rights,* (Austin: University of Texas Press, 2008), p. 70.

11. *Ibid.*

12. *Ibid.,* p. 1.

13. Takaki, pp. 96-98.

14. Gamboa, E., *Mexican Labor and World War II: Braceros in the Pacific Northwest, 1942-1947,* (Austin: University of Texas Press, 1990), p. 88.

15. García, p. 167.

16. *Ibid.,* p. 36.

17. *Ibid.*

18. Griswold del Castillo, p. 4.

19. Guglielmo, T. A., "Fighting for Caucasian Rights in World War II Texas," *Journal of American History 92, no. 4 (2006),* p. 1215.

20. *Ibid.*

21. *Ibid.*

22. Merton, R., "Discrimination and the American creed," Robert MacIver (ed), *Discrimination and National Welfare,* (New York: Harper, 1949).

23. *Ibid.*

24. Steele, R., "The Federal Government Discovers Mexican Americans," in Griswold del Castillo, ed., *World War II and Mexican American Civil Rights,* (Austin: University of Texas Press, 2008), p. 19.

25. *Ibid.*

26. "Medal of Honor Recipients-World War II (Recipients G–L)," *United States Army Centre of Military History,* history.army.mil/html/moh/wwII-g-l.html (accessed on August 5, 2018).

27. *Ibid.*

28. Francis, C. E., *The Tuskegee Airmen: The Men who Changed a Nation,* (Philadelphia: Branden Publishing, 1997), p. 370.

29. Hillstrom, K., *The Zoot Suit Riots: Defining Moments* (Detroit: Omnigraphics, Inc., 2012), p. 55.

30. *Ibid.*

31. Merton, R., "Discrimination and the American creed, in Robert MacIver" (ed), *Discrimination and National Welfare,* (New York: Harper, 1949).

32. *Ibid.*

33. Hillstron, pp. 67-74.

34. *Ibid.*

35. Merton, p. 100.

36. Hillstron, p. 105.

37. Castarrica, E. R., *Historia Ofical de la Fuerza Aérea Expedidonaria Mexicans* (Mexico: Secretaria de la Defensa National, 1946), p. 33.

38. *Ibid.*

39. *Ibid.*

40. *Ibid.*

41. "Panchito," *Fandom Comics Community, Disney Comics Wiki.* disneycomics.wikia.com/
wiki/Panchito. (accessed on August 1, 2018).

Chapter 7

1. "History of the 201st Mexican Fighter Squadron," *Air Force History Support Office, August
5, 1944–February 1, 1945, 4th Section*, (Washington D. C.: Department of the Air Force).
2. *Ibid.*
3. Castarrica, E. R., *Historia Ofical de la Fuerza Aérea Expedidonaria Mexicans* (Mexico:
Secretaria de la Defensa National, 1946), p, 37.
4. "History of the 201st Mexican Fighter Squadron," *Air Force History Support Office, August
5, 1944–February 1, 1945, 9th Section*, (Washington D. C.: Department of the Air Force).
5. Castarrica, p. 85.
6. "History of the 201st Mexican Fighter Squadron," *Air Force History Support Office,
February 1–18 March 18, 1945, 23rd and 26th Section*, (Washington D. C.: Department of
the Air Force).
7. "History of the 201st Mexican Fighter Squadron," *Air Force History Support Office, August
5, 1944–February 1, 1945, 11th Section*, (Washington D. C.: Department of the Air Force).
8. *Ibid.*
9. Castarrica, p. 110.
10. *Ibid.*, p. 111.
11. "History of the 201st Mexican Fighter Squadron," Air Force History Support Office,
Majors Field Flight Report, February 20, 1945, 2nd Section, (Washington D. C.:
Department of the Air Force), p. 43.
12. Castarrica, pp. 212, 226.
13. Bledsoe, M., *Thunderbolt: Memoirs of a World War II Fighter Pilot*, (Washington D. C.:
Van Nostrand Reinhold, 1982), p. 331.
14. Castarrica, p. 230.
15. *Ibid.*
16. Maurer, M., *Air Force Combat Units of World War II: Statistical report of V Fighter
Command*, (Montgomery: Office of Air Force History, 1983), enclosure #41.
17. Maurer, M., *Air Force Combat Units of World War II: Training and Indoctrination of 201st
Mexican Squadron*, (Montgomery: Office of Air Force History, 1983), enclosure #40.
18. Castarrica, p. 173.

Chapter 8

1. Diary of Héctor Espinosa Galvan in Cárdenas, A., General, *Mis Dos Misiones*, (Mexico:
Talleres Graficos de la Nacion, 1949), pp. 77-78.
2. *Ibid.*
3. *Ibid.*
4. *Ibid.*
5. *Ibid.*, p. 79.
6. *Ibid.*, pp. 79-80.
7. *Ibid.*
8. *Ibid.*, p. 81.
9. *Ibid.*
10. *Ibid.*, p. 82.
11. *Ibid.*

12. *Ibid.*, pp. 84-85.
13. Cervantes M. *Memoirs, Fuerza Aérea Mexicana*, National Defense Secretariat, p. 22.
14. *Ibid.*
15. *Ibid.*
16. Diary of Héctor Espinosa, pp. 77-78.
17. *Daily News, S.S. Fairisle*, April 4, 1945. (Washington D.C.: U.S. Navy Archives).
18. Cervantes M. *Memoirs*, p.22.
19. *Ibid.*
20. *Ibid.*
21. Diary of Héctor Espinosa, p. 88.
22. *Ibid.*, p. 83.
23. *Ibid.*, pp 83– 84.
24. Cervantes, M., *Memoirs*, p. 26.
25. *Ibid.*, p. 85.
26. *Ibid.*, p. 23.
27. *Ibid.*, p. 24.
28. *Ibid.*, p. 86.
29. *Ibid.*, pp. 85-86.
30. *Ibid.*, p. 87.
31. *Ibid.*, p. 88.
32. Morison, S., History of United States Naval Operations in World War II: The Liberation of the Philippines: Luzon, Mindanao, the Visayas, 1944–1945, (New York: Book Sales, 2001), pp. 206-207.
33. Diary of Héctor Espinosa Galvan, p. 27.
34. Kenney, G. C., *A Personal History of the Pacific War,* (New York: Duell, Sloan and Pearce, 1949), p. 544.
35. Kenney, pp. 111-116.
36. Diary of Héctor Espinosa Galvan, p. 51.
37. *Ibid.*
38. *Ibid.*
39. *Ibid.*
40. "201st Mexican Fighter Squadron," document no. K110.40201-1. *Air Force History Support Office,* (Washington, D.C.: Department of the Air Force).

Chapter 9

1. Morton, L., *Fall of the Philippines: The War in the Pacific*, (New York: St. John's Publications, 2016), p. 22.
2. *Ibid.*
3. *Ibid.*, p. 43.
4. Castarrica, E. R., *Historia Ofical de la Fuerza Aérea Expedidonaria Mexicans* (Mexico: Secretaria de la Defensa National, 1946), p, 239.
5. *Ibid.*, p. 247.
6. *Ibid.*
7. *Ibid.*
8. *Ibid.*
9. *Ibid.*
10. *Ibid.*

11. *Ibid.*
12. Diary of Héctor Espinosa Galvan in Cárdenas, A., General, *Mis Dos Misiones*, (Mexico: Talleres Graficos de la Nacion, 1949), p. 67.
13. Castarrica, 251.
14. *Ibid.*
15. Maurer, M., *Air Force Combat Units of World War II: Statistical report of V Fighter Command*, (Montgomery: Office of Air Force History, 1983), p. 100.
16. *Ibid.*
17. *Ibid.*
18. *Ibid.*
19. Castarrica, p. 260.
20. Maurer, p. 109.
21. Diary of Héctor Espinosa Galvan, p. 69.
22. Castarrica, p. 262.
23. Maurer, p. 119.
24. *Ibid.*, p. 123.
25. Castarrica, p. 269.
26. *Ibid.*

Chapter 10

1. Beebe, R. E., Brigadier General, "History of the 58th," Microfilm roll B0155, Air Force History Support Office, frames 613-614; *The Luzon Plan, dated April 11, 1945*, from RG18, Box 1201, entry 7, (Washington D.C.: Department of the Air Force).
2. Cervantes M. *Memoirs*, Fuerza Aérea Mexicana, National Defense Secretariat, p. 28.
3. *Ibid.*
4. Castarrica, E. R., *Historia Ofical de la Fuerza Aérea Expedidonaria Mexicans* (Mexico: Secretaria de la Defensa National, 1946), p. 271.
5. Beebe.
6. Cervantes, p. 29.
7. Beebe.
8. Castarrica, 176.
9. Cervantes, p. 35.
10. Castarrica, 180.
11. Kupferer, A., *No Glamor. No Glory: The Story of the 58th Fighter Group of World War II*, (Morgantown: Taylor Publishing Co., 1989), p. 258.
12. Diary of Héctor Espinosa Galvan, p. 80.
13. Kupferer, p. 258.
14. Cervantes, p. 30.
15. Castarrica, 188.
16. Kupferer, p. 258
17. Cárdenas, A., General, *Mis Dos Misiones*, (Mexico: Talleres Graficos de la Nacion, 1949), pp. 96-97.
18. Kupferer, p. 267.
19. Castarrica, p. 191.

Chapter 11

1. Castarrica, E. R., *Historia oficial de la Fuerza Aérea Expedicionaria Mexicana* (Mexico: Secretaría de la Defensa Nacional, 1946), p. 16.
2. *Ibid.*
3. Andrade, Dale, *Luzon*, CMH Pub 72-28, "The Campaigns of World War II." (Washington: U.S. Army Center of Military History, 1996), p. 3.
4. *Ibid.*, p.4.
5. *Ibid.*, p. 6.
6. *Ibid.*
7. *Ibid.*, p. 8.
8. *Ibid.*, p. 9.
9. *Ibid.*, p. 11.
10. *Ibid.*
11. *Ibid.*, p. 12.
12. *Ibid.*, p. 14.
13. *Ibid.*
14. *Ibid.*, p. 16.
15. *Ibid.*, p. 18.
16. *Ibid.*
17. *Ibid.*, p. 20.
18. *Ibid.*, p. 21.
19. *Ibid.*
20. *Ibid.*
21. *Ibid.*
22. *Ibid.*, p. 24.
23. *Ibid.*
24. *Ibid.*, p. 26.
25. *Ibid.*
26. *Ibid.*, p. 28.
27. *Ibid.*
28. *Ibid.*
29. Castarrica, p. 266
30. United States Army in World War II, Special Studies, *Chronology 1941–1945*. Compiled by Mary H. Williams, (Washington, D.C.: Office of the Chief of Military History, Department of the Army, 1960), p. 306.
31. *Ibid.*
32. *Ibid.*
33. *Ibid.*, p. 307.
34. *Ibid.*
35. *Ibid.*, p. 308.
36. *Ibid.*
37. *Ibid.*, p. 309.
38. *Ibid.*
39. *Ibid.*, p. 310.
40. *Ibid.*, p. 311.
41. *Ibid.*
42. *Ibid.*, p. 312.
43. *Ibid.*
44. *Ibid.*, p. 313.

45. *Ibid.*
46. *Ibid.*, p. 314.
47. *Ibid.*, p. 267.
48. *Ibid.*, p. 267.
49. *Ibid.*, p. 267-268.
50. *Ibid.*, p. 269.
51. *Ibid.*, pp. 269-270.
52. *Ibid.*, p. 271.
53. *Ibid.*, pp. 272-273.
54. *Ibid.*, pp. 273-274.
55. *Ibid.*, pp. 274-275.
56. *Ibid.*, p. 275.
57. *Ibid.*, pp. 277-278.
58. *Ibid.*, pp. 278-280.
59. *Ibid.*, pp. 280-283.
60. *Ibid.*, pp. 283-285.
61. *Ibid.*, pp. 285-287.
62. *Ibid.*, pp. 287-288.
63. *Ibid.*, pp. 292-293.
64. *Ibid.*, pp. 297-298.
65. *Ibid.*, pp. 293-295.
66. *Ibid.*, pp. 297-298.
67. *Ibid.*, pp. 298-299.
68. *Ibid.*, pp. 299-301.
69. *Ibid.*, pp. 304-305.
70. *Ibid.*, pp. 302-304.
71. *Ibid.*, pp. 304-305.
72. *Ibid.*, pp. 305-306.
73. *Ibid.*, pp. 308-309.
74. *Ibid.*, pp. 309-311.
75. *Ibid.*, pp. 311-312.
76. *Ibid.*, pp. 312-313.
77. *Ibid.*, pp. 313-314
78. *Ibid.*, pp. 314-315.
79. *Ibid.*, pp. 315-316.
80. *Ibid.*, pp. 316-318.
81. *Ibid.*, pp. 325-326.
82. *Ibid.*, p. 325
83. *Ibid.*, p. 333.
84. Andrade, p. 29

Chapter 12

1. Castarrica, E. R., *Historia oficial de la Fuerza Aérea Expedicionaria Mexicana* (Mexico: Secretaría de la Defensa Nacional, 1946), p. 338.
2. *Ibid.*, p. 338
3. *Ibid.*
4. *Ibid.*
5. *Ibid.*, p. 339.

6. *Ibid.*
7. *Ibid.*, p. 342.
8. *Ibid.*
9. *Ibid* pp. 342-343.
10. *Ibid.*, p. 344.
11. *Ibid.*
12. V Fighter Command, A-2 Daily Intelligence Summary, 8–9 July 1945, Reports # 189, 190.
13. Kenney, General George C., Commander Far East Air Forces. Letter to Commanding General, Army Air Forces (Thru: Commander-in-Chief, A.F.P.A.C.). Subject: Transmittal of Report of Lieutenant Colonel A. W. Kellond, June 24, 1945, dated September 9, 1945.
14. Cárdenas, A., General, *Mis Dos Misiones*, (Mexico: Talleres Graficos de la Nacion, 1949), p. 112.
15. Kenney, George C. *General Kenney reports: A personal History of the Pacific War.* Washington, D.C.: Office of Air Force History, United States Air Force, 1987.
16. Castarrica, p. 351.
17. *Ibid.*

Chapter 13

1. Cervantes M. *Memoirs*, Fuerza Aérea Mexicana, National Defense Secretariat, p. 38.
2. Manchester, W., *American Caesar: Douglas MacArthur, 1880–1964* (Boston: Little, Brown and Company, 1978), p. 453.
3. Castarrica, E. R., *Historia oficial de la Fuerza Aérea Expedicionaria Mexicana* (Mexico: Secretaría de la Defensa Nacional, 1946), pp. 338-339.
4. Cárdenas, A., General, *Mis Dos Misiones*, (Mexico: Talleres Graficos de la Nacion, 1949), p. 120.
5. Kenney, George C. *General Kenney reports: A personal History of the Pacific War.* Washington, D.C.: Office of Air Force History, United States Air Force, 1987.
6. *Ibid.*
7. Castarrica, p. 501.
8. *Ibid.*
9. Castarrica, p. 512.
10. Air Force Historical Research Agency, Maxwell Air Force Base, Alabama, document 145.96-97. 11.
12. Cárdenas, p. 505.
13. *Ibid.*, pp, 145-146.
14. *Ibid.*
15. *Ibid.*, pp. 146-147.
16. *Ibid.*
17. *Ibid.*, pp. 147-148
18. *Ibid.*, pp. 148-149.
19. *Ibid.*, pp. 149-150.
20. *Ibid.*, pp. 151.
21. *Ibid.*, pp. 151-154.
22. *Ibid.*, p. 154-155.
23. *Ibid.*, p. 157.
24. *Ibid.*
25. Castarrica, p. 508.
26. *Ibid.*

27. *Ibid.*

28. *Ibid.*

29. "Thousands from Laredo Welcome Mexican Fighters," *The Laredo Times*, November 19, 1945, p. 1.

30. Cárdenas, pp. 509-510.

Bibliography

"201st Mexican Fighter Squadron," document no. K110.40201-1. *Air Force History Support Office,* (Washington, D. C.: Department of the Air Force)

"Alas de Mexico," *Gaxiola Andrade Memoirs, 201st,* Air Force History Support Office, Microfilm roll A0768, frame 1749, (Washington D.C.: Department of the Air Force)

Andrade, Dale, *Luzon,* CMH Pub 72-28, "The Campaigns of World War II." (Washington: U.S. Army Center of Military History, 1996)

Beebe, R. E., Brigadier General, "History of the 58th," Microfilm roll B0155, Air Force History Support Office, frames 613– 614; *The Luzon Plan, dated April 11, 1945,* from RG18, Box 1201, entry 7, (Washington D. C.: Department of the Air Force)

Bledsoe, M., *Thunderbolt: Memoirs of a World War II Fighter Pilot,* (Washington D. C.: Van Nostrand Reinhold, 1982)

Camacho, M., "Good Neighbors–Good Friends, Mexico, the Bridge Between Latin and Saxon Cultures," Broadcast from Monterrey, Mexico, April 20, 1943 (*Vital Speeches of the Day,* Vol. IX, pp. 420-421)

Cárdenas, A., General, *Mis Dos Misiones,* (Mexico: Talleres Graficos de la Nacion, 1949)

Castarrica, E. R., *Historia Ofical de la Fuerza Aérea Expedidonaria Mexicans* (Mexico: Secretaria de la Defensa National, 1946)

"Daily News," S.S. *Fairisle,* April 4, 1945. (Washington D.C.: U.S. Navy Archives)

Diary of Héctor Espinosa Galvan in Cárdenas, A., General, *Mis Dos Misiones,* (Mexico: Talleres Graficos de la Nacion, 1949)

Francis, C. E., *The Tuskegee Airmen: The Men who Changed a Nation,* (Philadelphia: Branden Publishing, 1997)

Gamboa, E., *Mexican Labor and World War II: Braceros in the Pacific Northwest, 1942–1947* (Austin: University of Texas Press, 1990)

García, A., *Mexican Americans: The New Americans* (Westport: Greenwood Publishing Group, 2002)

"George C. Marshall to President Franklin Roosevelt, September 18, 1943," *Roosevelt Papers, Special Collections,* (New York: Franklin D. Roosevelt Library)

Griswold del Castillo, R., *World War II and Mexican American Civil Rights* (Austin: University of Texas Press, 2008)

Guglielmo, T. A., "Fighting for Caucasian Rights in World War II Texas," *Journal of American History 92, no. 4 (2006)*

Hagedom, D., *Republic P-47 Thunderbolt: The Final Chapter, Latin American Air Forces Service* (St. Paul: Phalanx Publishing Co., Ltd., 1991)

"Hall to Messersmith, April 16, 1944," RG 59, file 812.20V474 (Washington, D.C.: U.S. Department of State)

Hamilton, N. L., "Mexico: The Limits of State Autonomy." *Latin American Perspectives* 2, no. 2 (1975): 81-108, www.jstor.org/stable/2633191

"Harris to Chief, Military Intelligence Service, February 14, 1944," Index 1579, MP. (Washington, D.C. War Department)

Hams, A. R., Brigadier General, U.S., Military *Attaché*, Mexico City to Major General Guy V. Henry, Joint Mexican-United States Defense Commission, February 9, 1944, Index 1575, MP (Washington, D.C.: U.S. Department of Defense)

Harrison, "United States-Mexican Military Collaboration, during World War II." Ph. D dissertation (Washington D.C.: Georgetown University, 1976)

Henry G. V., Major General, March 17, 1944, RG 59, 812 (Washington, D.C. U.S. Department of State)

Hillstron, K., *The Zoot Suit Riots: Defining Moments* (Detroit: Omnigraphics, Inc., 2012)

"History of the 201st Mexican Fighter Squadron, 1 February–18 March 1945, "*Majors Field, 72nd Fighter Wing, Second Air Force*, (Maxwell Air Force Base: Air Force Historical Research Agency)

"History of the 201st Mexican Fighter Squadron," Air Force History Support Office, Microfilm roll A0768, Frame 1676. 2, *Majors Field Flight Report, February 20, 1945, 2nd Section* (Washington D.C.: Department of the Air Force)

"History of the 201st Mexican Fighter Squadron," *Air Force History Support Office, August 5, 1944–February 1, 1945, 4th Section* (Washington D.C.: Department of the Air Force)

"History of the 201st Mexican Fighter Squadron," *Air Force History Support Office, August 5, 1944–February 1, 1945, 9th Section* (Washington D.C.: Department of the Air Force)

"History of the 201st Mexican Fighter Squadron," Air Force History Support Office, *Majors Field Flight Report, February 20, 1945, 2nd Section* (Washington D.C.: Department of the Air Force)

Kupferer, A., *No Glamor. No Glory: The Story of the 58th Fighter Group of World War II* (Morgantown: Taylor Publishing Co., 1989)

Mathewson, L., Lieutenant Colonel, "Memorandum to Commanding General, Army Air Forces," *Subject: Progress Report of the Joint Mexican-United States Defense Commission, 24 April 1942* (Washington, D.C.)

Maurer, M., *Air Force Combat Units of World War II: Statistical report of V Fighter Command*, (Montgomery: Office of Air Force History, 1983)

"Medal of Honor Recipients-World War II (Recipients G–L)," *United States Army Centre of Military History*, history.army.mil/html/moh/wwII-g-l.html

Merton, R., "Discrimination and the American creed," Robert MacIver (ed.), *Discrimination and National Welfare* (New York: Harper, 1949)

"Messersmith to Duggan, February 17, 1944," Index 1580, MP (Washington D.C: Department of State)

"Messersmith to Duggan, February 19, 1944," Index 1582, MP (Washington, D.C.: U.S. Department of State)

"Messersmith to Duggan, March 9, 1944," Index 1584, MP (Washington, D.C.: U.S. Department of State)

"Messersmith to Duggan, April 17, 1944," RG 59, file 812.20V459-1/2 (Washington, D.C.: U.S. Department of State)

"Messersmith to Hull, March 15, 1944," RG 59, 812.20V460 (Washington, D.C.: U.S. Department of State)

"Messersmith to Roosevelt, March 15, 1944," Index 1587, MP (Washington, D.C.: U.S. Department of State)

Messersmith, G., "Military Collaboration by Mexico during the war—Squadron 201." Index 2031, MP (Washington, D.C.: U.S. Department of State)

Mexican Secretary of National Defense, Blvd. Manuel Ávila Camacho, Esq. Av. Industria Militar. S/N, Lomas de Sotelo, Mexico City, CP 11200

"Mexican Support for the United States," *New York Times, April 22, 1943*

Morison, S., History of United States Naval Operations in World War II: The Liberation of the Philippines: Luzon, Mindanao, the Visayas, 1944–1945 (New York: Book Sales, 2001)

Oppenheimer, R. "Acculturation or Assimilation: Mexican Immigrants in Kansas, 1900 to World War II," *The Western Historical Quarterly, Vol. 16, no. 4* (1985)

"Panchito," *Fandom Comics Community, Disney Comics Wiki*. disneycomics. wikia.com/wiki/ Panchito.

Roediger, D. R., *How Race Survived US History: From Settlement and Slavery to the Obama Phenomenon* (New York: Verso, 2008)

Servín, M. P., *The Mexican-Americans: An Awakened Minority* (Beverly Hills: Glencoe Press, 1974)

Steele, R., "The Federal Government Discovers Mexican Americans," in Griswold del Castillo, ed., *World War II and Mexican American Civil Rights* (Austin: University of Texas Press, 2008)

Takaki, R. T. *Double Victory: A Multicultural History of America in World War II*, (Boston: Little, Brown and Co., 2000)

"Thousands from Laredo Welcome Mexican Fighters," *The Laredo Times*, November 19, 1945

V Fighter Command, A-2 Daily Intelligence Summary, 8–9 July 1945, Reports # 189, 190. Kenney, General George C., Commander Far East Air Forces. Letter to Commanding General, Army Air Forces (Thru: Commander-in-Chief, A.F.P.A.C.). Subject: Transmittal of Report of Lieutenant Colonel A. W. Kellond, June 24, 1945, dated September 9, 1945.

Vega, J., *The Mexican Expeditionary Air Force in World War II: The Organization, Training, and Operations of the 201st Squadron*, Research Department, (Montgomery: Air Command and Staff College, 1997)

Wood, W. "A Re-Examination of Mexican Support for the United States during World War II," Ph.D. thesis (Columbia: University of Missouri, 1989)